THE

PHILOSOPHY OF THE UPANISHADS

AND

ANCIENT INDIAN METAPHYSICS

THE

PHILOSOPHY OF THE UPANISHADS

AND

ANCIENT INDIAN METAPHYSICS.

AS EXHIBITED IN A SERIES OF ARTICLES CONTRIBUTED TO THE CALCUTTA REVIEW.

BY

ARCHIBALD EDWARD GOUGH

GYAN

Published by

Gyan Publishing House
5, Ansari Road
Daryaganj, New Delhi-110002
Phone: 011-47034999, 9811692060
E-mail: books@gyanbooks.com

Distribution Network
gyanbooks.com
India, USA, Canada, UK, Australia

ISBN: 978-93-6280-347-4 (PB)
First Published, 1882

2nd Impression 2024

Printed at: Gyan Press, Delhi.

THE PHILOSOPHY OF THE UPANISHADS AND ANCIENT INDIAN METAPHYSICS
Author: ARCHIBALD EDWARD GOUGH

THE

PHILOSOPHY OF THE UPANISHADS

AND

ANCIENT INDIAN METAPHYSICS.

THE

PHILOSOPHY OF THE UPANISHADS

AND

ANCIENT INDIAN METAPHYSICS.

AS EXHIBITED IN A SERIES OF ARTICLES CONTRIBUTED TO THE CALCUTTA REVIEW.

BY

ARCHIBALD EDWARD GOUGH, M.A.

LINCOLN COLLEGE, OXFORD,

PRINCIPAL OF THE CALCUTTA MADRASA.

LONDON:

TRÜBNER & CO., LUDGATE HILL.

1882.

PREFACE.

I HOPE that this book may be more or less useful to two classes of readers.

Those interested in the general history of philosophy will find in it an account of a very early attempt, on the part of thinkers of a rude age and race, to form a cosmological theory. The real movement of philosophic thought begins, it is true, not in India, but in Ionia; but some degree of interest may still be expected to attach to the procedure of the ancient Indian cosmologists. The Upanishads are so many "songs before sunrise,"—spontaneous effusions of awakening reflection, half poetical, half metaphysical, that precede the conscious and methodical labour of the long succession of thinkers to construct a thoroughly intelligible conception of the sum of things. For the general reader, then, these pages may supply in detail, and in the terms of the Sanskṛit texts themselves, a treatment of the topics slightly sketched in the third chapter of Archer Butler's first series of "Lectures on the History of Ancient Philosophy." The Upanishads exhibit the pantheistic view of things in a naïvely poetical expression, and at the same time in its coarsest form.[1]

To readers specially interested in Indian matters an introduction to the Upanishads is indispensable, and these pages will help to supply a want hitherto unsupplied. The Upanishads are an index to the intellectual peculiarities of the Indian character. The thoughts they express are the ideas that prevail throughout all subsequent Indian literature, much of which will be fully comprehensible to those only who carry with them a knowledge of these ideas to its perusal. A study of the Upanishads is the starting-point in any intelligent study of Indian philosophy. As regards religion, the philosophy of the Upanishads is the groundwork of the various forms of Hinduism, and the Upanishads have been justly characterised by Goldstücker as "the basis of the enlightened faith of India."

The Upanishads are treatises of various length, partly poetical, partly theosophical, which close the canon of Vedic revelation. The term Upanishad imports mystic teaching, and the synonymous term Vedānta means a final instalment of the Veda. The Upanishads are also called Vedāntas, and the Aupanishadī Mīmānsā or philosophy of the Upanishads, in its developed form, is known as the Vedāntic system. Śruti, the Vedic revelation, consists of two parts, of a lower and a higher grade,—the Karmakāṇḍa, or portion treating of sacrifices, immemorial usages, and theogony;

[1] "Wollen wir den sogenannten Pantheismus in seiner poetischen, erhabensten, oder wenn man will, krassesten Gestalt nehmen, so hat man sich dafür in den morgenländischen Dichtern umzusehen, und die breitesten Darstellungen finden sich in den Indischen."—HEGEL.

and the Jñānakāṇḍa, or portion treating of the release of the soul from metempsychosis, by means of a recognition of its real nature as one with the characterless and impersonal Self. This impersonal Self, Brahman, as distinguished from the personal soul, the living, conscious, and migrating spirit, the Jīva or Jīvātman or Vijñānātman, is also styled the Paramātman or highest Self. The mystic teaching in which the Vedic revelation culminates is relative to the nature of this highest and impersonal Self. The Karmakāṇḍa, or ritual portion of the Veda, is contained in the Mantras or hymns of the Ṛishis, the spontaneous effusions of primitive Indian nature-worship, and the Brāhmaṇas or liturgic and legendary compilations of the specialised sacrificial functionaries. Theosophic teaching is present, in combination with liturgic and mythologic elements, in the Āraṇyakas, a portion of the Vedic aggregate intimately allied to the Brāhmaṇas. This teaching is further segregated and explicitly set forth in the Upanishads, and forms the Jñānakāṇḍa or theosophic portion of the Vedic revelation. As compared with the religion of sacrifices and ancestral rites, this teaching forms a higher religion, a more perfect way, for the recluses of the forest,—a religion which will be seen to be largely metaphysical. Treatises bearing the name of Upanishads are numerous. Those in highest esteem have always been the Chhāndogya, Bṛihadāraṇyaka, Īśa, Kena, Kaṭha, Praśna, Muṇḍaka, Māṇḍūkya, Aitareya, Taittirīya, Śvetāśvatara, Maitrāyaṇīya, and Kaushītakībrāhmaṇa Upanishads. The date of the Upanishads, like that of most of the ancient works of Sanskṛit literature, is altogether uncertain. Any date that may have been assigned is purely conjectural; and all that we can affirm in this regard is, that in relation to that literature they are of primitive antiquity, and the earliest documents of Indian religious metaphysics.

The greatest of the expositors of the philosophy of the Upanishads is Śankara or Śankarāchārya. A great part of the matter of this volume is extracted from the various writings ascribed to him. He is said to have been a native of Kerala or Malabar, and to have flourished in the eighth century of the Christian era. He is generally represented as having spent the greater part of his life as an itinerant philosophic disputant and religious controversialist. The Buddhists in his time were flourishing and widely predominant in India under the patronage of powerful Rajas, and we may presume that the great Vedāntic doctor was thoroughly intimate with the tenets of Buddhist philosophy and religion. His exposition of some of these in his commentary on the aphorisms of the Vedānta is admirably perspicuous. The teaching of Śankara himself is the natural and legitimate interpretation of the doctrines of the Upanishads. It is known as Advaitavāda, the theory of universal unity, abstract identity, or absolute idealism. The Advaitavādins or Indian idealists are therefore often styled the Śānkaras or followers of Śankara. They represent Indian orthodoxy in its purest form. The commentaries on the Upanishads ascribed to Sankara are elucidated in the glosses of Ānandajṅānagiri, a writer to whom reference will be found from time to time in the following pages. The most illustrious of the successors of Śankara, and, next to Śankara, the greatest of the Indian schoolmen, is Mādhava or Mādhavāchārya, known also by the surname of Sāyaṇa. He will also be referred to in this book. His great work is his series of grammatical and exegetic commentaries on the Vedas. In philosophical discussion his language is remarkably quaint and striking. An opponent arguing in a circle is a man trying to stand on his own shoulders, and in refuting another he finds himself breaking a bubble with a thunderbolt.[1] Mādhavāchārya flourished in the fourteenth century.

This book is based upon a series of articles I contributed some years ago to the *Calcutta Review.* The first of these, intitled "Ancient Indian Metaphysics," was published in the number for October 1876. This was followed by five articles on the "Philosophy of the Upanishads," the first of these appearing in January 1878, and the last in April 1880. I beg to record my best thanks to Mr. Thomas Smith, the proprietor of the *Review*, for his kind permission to me to utilise the materials of these articles in preparing the present work. The materials I have reproduced are for the most part the translations. These, already containing the most important texts of the Upanishads, were indispensable for any new presentation of primitive Indian metaphysics. They have in every case been rewritten, new matter has been added, and everything old is transformed and transposed, so that this book is not to be regarded as a reprint, but as a new work. My translations will be found to include the whole of the Muṇḍaka, Kaṭha, Śvetāśvatara, and Māṇḍūkya Upanishads, the greater part of the Taittirīya and Bṛihadāraṇyaka, and portions of the Chhāndogya and Kena, together with extracts from the works of the Indian schoolmen. The matter of the book has been taken in

[1] Cf. "Who breaks a butterfly upon a wheel?"—POPE.

every case at first hand from original Sanskṛit sources. Wherever the work is expository, I have studiously avoided interpolation, the purpose being to present the primitive Indian philosophy precisely as it is, in the terms of the philosophers themselves, and to leave the reader to form his own judgment about it. The Sanskṛit philologist has to work in a hard and unproductive soil, and this judgment may not perhaps be very favourable. At any rate, I make no claim. There is nothing that a writer on ancient thought, and particularly on ancient Oriental thought, has to be more upon his guard against, than the *vitium subreptionis*, the permission to his own preconceptions to insinuate themselves among the data he has to deal with. In every expository paragraph, therefore, every statement, every figure, and every simile is extracted from a Sanskṛit authority. Most of these are to be found in any Sanskṛit treatiṣe on the Vedānta. They may all be found in the following works, which, with others, have furnished the matter of this book,—the various Upanishads themselves, Śankara's commentaries on the Upanishads, Ānandajñānagiri's glosses on these commentaries, Śankara's commentary on the Śārīrakasūtra or aphorisms of the Vedānta philosophy, Govindānanda's gloss on this commentary, the Vedāntasāra, the Vidvanmanorañjinī, the Subodhinī, the Upadeśasahasrī, the Padayojanikā or commentary on the Upadeśasahasrī, the Vivekachūḍāmaṇi, the Ātmabodha, the Sarvadarśanasangraha, the Sānkhyatattvakaumudī, and the Sānkhyapravachanabhāshya.

As this book is the outcome of a personal study of the Sanskṛit originals, I may be permitted to point out the conclusions in regard to early Indian philosophy, which, thus far, I have arrived at for myself. These are :—

First, That the earliest succession of cosmological conceptions in India was this—

(1.) Brahmavāda and Māyāvāda, the theory of the Self and the self-feigning world-fiction, afterwards developed into the Vedāntic system :

(2.) Śūnyavāda and Vijñānavāda, the theory of the aboriginal vacuum or blank, and of the sensational and fluxional nature of the world, presented in Buddhism :

(3.) Purushabahutvavāda and Pradhānavāda, the theory of a plurality of Selves, and of the reality and independent existence of the world, presented in the doctrine of the Sānkhyas or "enumerative" philosophers.

Secondly, That Māyā is part and parcel of the primitive Indian cosmological conception, as exhibited in the Upanishads themselves, and not, as Colebrooke imagined, and has led his successors to imagine, a later graft upon the old Vedāntic philosophy.

Thirdly, That as regards the alleged affinity between the Indian and the Neo-platonic philosophy, it is possible that a phrase or two, a simile here and there, of the Indian sophists, may have found their way into the Alexandrian schools, and influenced the work of Ammonius, Plotinus, and their successors ; but that the Neo-platonic philosophy, as a whole, has its virtual pre-existence in the earlier constructions of Hellenic thought, and naturally develops itself out of them.

As regards this third conclusion, the general reader will be able to form his own opinion. I think he will pronounce that India had little intellectual wealth for exportation to the Alexandrian emporium.

A. E. G.

MARSHAM HALL,
NORWICH,
July 21, 1882.

CONTENTS.

CHAPTER I.

THE ANTECEDENTS OF INDIAN METAPHYSICS—METEMPSYCHOSIS.

CHAPTER II.

THE QUEST OF THE REAL—BRAHMAN AND MAYA, THE SELF AND THE WORLD-FICTION.

CHAPTER III.

THE RELEASE FROM METEMPSYCHOSIS.

CHAPTER IV.

THE MUNDAKA UPANISHAD.

CHAPTER V.

THE KATHA UPANISHAD.

CHAPTER VI.

THE BRIHADARANYAKA UPANISHAD.

CHAPTER VII.

THE SENSATIONAL NIHILISM OF THE BUDDHISTS—THE COSMOLOGY OF THE SANKHYAS.

CHAPTER VIII.

THE SVETASVATARA UPANISHAD.

CHAPTER IX.

THE PRIMITIVE ANTIQUITY OF THE DOCTRINE OF MAYA.

THE

PHILOSOPHY OF THE UPANISHADS.

CHAPTER I.

THE ANTECEDENTS OF INDIAN METAPHYSICS—METEMPSYCHOSIS.

"The one spirit's plastic stress
Sweeps through the dull dense world, compelling there
All new successions to the forms they wear;
Torturing the unwilling dross that checks its flight
To its own likeness, as each mass may bear;
And bursting in its beauty and its might,
From trees and beasts and men into the heavens' light."
—SHELLEY.

"Alors j'ai essayé de traverser la scène mobile du monde pour pénétrer jusqu'au fond immuable, au principe inépuisable de la vie universelle. Là, je l'avoue, j'ai eu un moment d'éblouissement et d'ivresse; j'ai cru voir Dieu. L'être en soi, l'être infini, absolu, universel, que peut-on contempler de plus sublime, de plus vaste, de plus profond? C'est le dieu Pan, évoqué pour la confusion des idoles de l'imagination et de la conscience humaines. Mais ce Dieu vivant, que d'imperfections, que de misères il étale, si je regarde dans le monde, son acte incessant! Et si je veux le voir en soi et dans son fond, je ne trouve plus que l'être en puissance, sans lumière, sans couleur, sans forme, sans essence déterminée, abîme ténébreux où l'Orient croyait contempler la suprême vérité, et où l'admirable philosophie grecque ne trouvait que chaos et non-être. Mon illusion n'a pas tenu contre l'évidence, contre la foi du genre humain. Dieu ne pouvait être où n'est pas le beau, le pur, le parfait."—VACHEROT.

CHAP. I.

The scope of the work.

IT is the purpose of the following pages to present the earliest types of Indian thought in the terms of the thinkers themselves, and in relation to the popular

CHAP. I.

medium in which they had their life. The reader will be conducted along the first and only important stages of the history of Indian philosophy. The data are such that this history can only be worked out by looking at the form of the several cosmical conceptions, and finding out how they rise one out of another in the process of conflict and supersession. The earliest Indian notion of the totality of things is given in the Upanishads. These, the earliest records of Indian speculation, propound the miseries of metempsychosis, and the path of release from these miseries by recognition of the sole reality of the Self, and the unreality of the world and of all the forms of life that people it. They retain the popular religious imagery, and prescribe the purification of the mind, the renunciation of the world, the practice of rigid and insensible postures of the body, and prolonged meditative abstraction to reach the unity of characterless thought, as the several stages towards the recognition of the one and only Self, and ecstatic vision of, and re-union with it. This is the safe starting-point from which to follow the logical movement. The further progress of the history of Indian philosophy will rest on probabilities. Certainty as regards the chronological succession is beyond the reach of the Orientalist, and he has to be content with approximations to it. When everything is done, and the history of Indian philosophy has been fairly traced, the work will always remain little more than a preliminary and outlying portion of the general history of the human mind. The work will be an exhibition of the thoughts of thinkers of a lower race, of a people of stationary culture, whose intellectual growth stands almost apart from the general movement of human intelligence.

Indian philosophy the work of a lower race, of mixed Negrito, Tatar, and Aryan blood.

A writer on the history of Indian philosophy has to deal with the mental produce of an unprogressive portion of mankind. Negroid aborigines, Tatar hordes, and successive Aryan swarms have severally contributed their blood to mould the Brāhman theosophist. Like every other thinker, he is limited by the type of nervous mechanism he has inherited, by the ancestral conditions of his life, and by the material and spiritual present which environs him. It is under these limitations that he is to make himself what he is. As regards the limitations of race and hereditary nature, the greatest confusion has been introduced into the popular study of Indian matters by the term Aryan. This word has been fertile in every variety of fallacy, theoretical and practical. Before the work of thought begins in India the invading Aryan tribes have become Indo-Arians or Hindus. They have been assimilated to and absorbed into the earlier and ruder populations of modified Negrito and Tatar type, whom they at first fought against as the dark-skinned Dasyus, and made to till the soil and drudge for them as Śūdras.

As Professor Huxley says, "The old Sanskrit literature proves that the Aryan population of India came in from the north-west at least three thousand years ago. In the Veda these people portray themselves in characters that might have fitted the Gauls, the Germans, or the Goths. Unfortunately there is no evidence whether they were fair-haired or not. India was already peopled by a dark-complexioned people, most like the Australian aborigines, and speaking a group of languages called Dravidian." These races were Negroid indigenes recruited with Tatar blood. "They were fenced in," he proceeds, "on the north by the barrier of the Himālayas; but the Aryans poured in from the plains of Central Asia over the Himālayas into the great river basins of the Indus and the Ganges, where they have been in the main absorbed into the pre-existing population, leaving as evidence of their immigration an extensive modification of the physical characters of the population, a language, and a literature."

CHAP. I.

The Aryan infusion scanty.

Following Dr. Latham and Mr. Norris, Dr. Carpenter points out that it is only by an error that the ordinary Hindu population are supposed to be the descendants of this invading branch of the Aryan stock. "The influence," he says, "of the Aryan invasion upon the language and population of Northern India was very much akin to that of the Norman invasion upon those of England." This analogy, it must be remarked, is superficial, and fails in a most important point. The Norman invaders were not of a higher stock than the English, the Saxons, and the Anglo-Danes; the Aryan immigrants into India underwent a progressive deterioration through climatic influences and intermixture with low and melanous races akin to the Bhils, the Kols, and Sonthals of the present day. "The number of individuals of the invading race was so small in proportion to that of the indigenous population as to be speedily merged in it, not, however, without contributing to an elevation of its physical characters; a large number of new words having been in like manner introduced, without any essential change in the type of the original languages," the various dialects of Northern India. "And thus the only distinct traces of the Aryan stock are to be found in the Brahmanical caste, which preserves, though with great corruption, the original Brahmanical religion, and keeps up the Sanskṛit as its classical language. It is certain, however, that this race is far from being of pure descent, having intermingled to a considerable extent with the ordinary Hindu population."

Low thoughts in high words the difficulty of the Orientalist.

In treating of Indian philosophy, a writer has to deal with thoughts of a lower order than the thoughts of the everyday life of Europe. Looking at the language he inherits and the general medium of intelligence in which he lives, the thoughts of the European are rich with the substance of Hebrew, Greek, and Christian culture. It is to be noted also that such rudiments of philosophic thought as are to be found in the Indian

CHAP. I.

cosmologies are embedded in masses of religious imagery of a rude and inartistic kind. We are treading the rock-cut temples of Ellora, not the Parthenon. The great difficulty lies in this, that a low order of ideas has to be expressed in a high order of terms, and that the English words suggest a wealth of analysis and association altogether foreign to the thoughts that are to be reproduced. Translation from a lower to a higher language is a process of elevation. However vigilant he may be, a writer on Indian philosophy will find it hard to say neither too much nor too little,—to present the facts as he finds them without prejudice and without predilection. It is all but impossible to place oneself in the position of the ancient Indian sages,—to see things as they saw them, and to name them in the names they gave them. The effort is nothing less than an endeavour to revert to a ruder type of mental structure, to put aside our hereditary culture, and to become for the time barbarians.

Stationary and progressive order contrasted.

It will be well to bear in mind the characters of an unprogressive as contrasted with the characters of a progressive, variety of the human race. These are tendencies engrained in the nervous system, and transmitted from generation to generation. They are hereditary, inborn habitudes, and no one can foresee how far they will give way before foreign influences, or be modified by them. The contrast between the lower and the higher human varieties, between the stationary and the advancing social orders, is instructively set out by the historian Grote. "The acquisition of habits of regular industry, so foreign to the natural temper of man, was brought about in Egypt and Assyria, in China and Hindustan, before it had acquired any footing in Europe; but it was purchased either by prostrate obedience to a despotic rule, or by imprisonment within the chain of a consecrated institution of caste. Even during the Homeric period of Greece these countries had attained a certain civilisation in mass, without the acquisition of any high mental qualities or the development of any individual genius. The religious and political sanction determined for every one his mode of life, his creed, his duties, and his place in society, without leaving any scope for the will or reason of the agent himself." Grote in the next place speaks of the Semitic races, the Jews, Phœnicians, Carthaginians, of their individual impulse and energy, as also of their strenuous ferocity of character, and then contrasts all these races with the "flexible, many-sided, and self-organising Greek, not only capable of opening, both for himself and for the human race, the highest walks of intellect and the full creative agency of art, but also gentler by far in his private sympathies and dealings than his contemporaries on the Euphrates, the Jordan, or the Nile." And elsewhere he points out that in no city of historical Greece did there prevail either human sacrifices or deliberate mutilation, such as cutting off the nose, ears, hands, feet, and so forth, or castration, or selling of children into slavery, or polygamy, or the feeling of unlimited obedience towards one man; all of these being customs which might be pointed out as existing among the contemporary Carthaginians, Egyptians, Persians, Thracians, and other peoples.

Indian thought is a tropical philosophy of inertion.

The Orientalist will have to look in the face this fact of the inferiority of the hereditary type of Indian character. His work may be hard and unproductive, but at least it is necessary to a full and complete survey of the products of the human mind. He has much to do and little to claim as regards the value of his labours, and he will not demur to the judgment of Archer Butler: "It presents a fearful contrast to observe the refinement to which speculation appears to have been carried in the philosophy of India, and the grossness of the contemporary idolatry, paralleled in scarcely any nation of the earth, as well as the degraded condition of the mass of the people, destitute of active energy, and for the most part without a shadow of moral principle to animate the dull routine of a burthensome and scrupulous superstition. The aim of human wisdom is the liberation of the soul from the evils attending the mortal state. This object is attempted by one modification or other of that intense abstraction which, separating the soul from the bonds of flesh, is supposed capable of liberating it in this life from the unworthy restrictions of earthly existence, and of introducing it in the next to the full enjoyment of undisturbed repose, or even to the glories of a total absorption into the divine essence itself. In all this we may detect the secret but continual influences of a climate which, indisposing the organisation for active exertion, naturally cherished those theories which represent the true felicity of man to consist in inward contemplation and complete quiescence."

The social antecedents of Brahmanism and Buddhism.

A few words must be said about the social state that preceded the rise of Indian philosophy. In using the word philosophy, it is to be taken loosely, as designating a large amount of pictorial conception covering an inner nucleus of rudimentary ideas. We are dealing with religion as well as with metaphysics. In India religion and metaphysics have grown up in one promiscuous growth, and have never had a separate life. They cannot be disengaged from each other, and we can seldom point to such and such an item in any structure as philosophical, and such and such another item as religious. A few words only can be given to an explanation of the social order that preceded the rise of the Brahmanical and Buddhist forms of thought and faith, and the reader must refer for further information, if he needs it, to the writings of Professor Max Müller and Dr. John Muir. Let us, then, station ourselves in the communities in which the Rishis lived, the seers that saw and fashioned the Vedic hymns. The Indian tribes have already reached a settled state of order and prosperity. They are gathered together in farms, in huts of sun-dried mud, and houses of stone, in hamlets and in fenced towns, under village chiefs and Rajas. The outward aspects of their life are not unlike those of the rural India of to-day. The same villages, the same thatched huts of the peasantry, with mud-walled yards for cattle, and the same square courts and stuccoed garden-houses of the village chiefs and princelets. There is the same silence, broken only by the creaking pulleys of the village well and the occasional bark of village curs, the same green mantle on the stagnant wayside pools, the same square tank; the sunlight glinting as to-day through the delicate foliage of the tamarind, the glossy leaves of the peepul, and the feathery tufts of the bamboo. There is the same overpowering glare upon the surface of the earth, and there are the same liquid depths of overarching blue overhead, but the horizon is fringed with jungle, and the levels are grassy and less arid than to-day, for the forests are dense and widely spread, and the rainfall is more abundant. In such surroundings, for the most part tranquil and dreamlike, but at times terrific with shocks of tropical storm and rain, the Indians of the Vedic age till their rice and barley, irrigate their fields with watercourses, watch the increase of their flocks and herds, and make a hard or easy livelihood as blacksmiths, wheelwrights, boat-builders, weavers, leeches, soldiers, poets, priests. They live upon the produce of their cattle and of their fields, drink wine and moon-plant juice, and exercise their leisure in sacrificial feasts and in games and spectacles.

Personification of elemental forces.

The powers of nature present themselves to them as so many personal agents. Every striking and unexpected change in the things around them is an extra-human volitional activity. They see God in clouds and hear him in the wind. They impute their whole self to all they see around them, anthropomorphising all nature. The environment is a divine community, in the midst of which the human communities have their life. To use the words of Archer Butler, "Man's early tendencies are constantly leading to a wide and vague application of his whole nature, to see himself in everything, to recognise his will, and even his sensations, in the inanimate universe. This blind analogy is almost the first hypothesis of childhood. The child translates the external world by himself. He perceives, for example, successions under the law of causality, but he adds to this causality his own consciousness of voluntary effort. He perceives objects under the law of extension, but he has little conception of an extension which should overpass his own power of traversing it. The child personifies the stone that hurts him; the childhood of superstition, whose genius is multiplicity, personifies the laws of nature as gods; the childhood of philosophy, whose genius is unity, makes the world itself a living, breathing animal, whose body nature is, and God the soul."

Thus it is that to the communities in which the Ṛishis dwell a multitude of personalities manifest themselves, in rain, in fire, in wind, in storms, and in the sun. They stand above and round about the people, in ever-varying aspects, powerful to befriend or to injure them.

Sky and Earth are the father and mother of gods and men. Aditi, the illimitable expanse, is the mother of chiefs and heroes. Mitra, presiding over the day, wakes men and bids them bestir themselves betimes, and stands watching all things with unwinking eye. Varuṇa, ruling the night, prepares a cool place of rest for all that move, fashions a pathway for the sun, sends his spies abroad in both the worlds, knows every wink of men's eyes, cherishes truth and hates a lie, seizes the evil-doer with his noose, and is prayed to to have mercy

CHAP. I.

on the sinful. Youthful, lustrous, and beautiful, the Aśvins go out in their golden car before the dawn, with health and wealth for man. Ushas, the Dawn, the daughter of the sky, untouched with age, but bringing age to men, dispels the darkness, drives away the lurking enemy, visits every house, wakes the sleepers, sends the labourers afield, and makes the birds to fly aloft. Agni, the fire-god, of manifold birth, the offspring of the fire-drills, fed with sacrificial butter, bears the oblation aloft to the gods, brings the gods to the sacrifice, and is generally internunciary between gods and men. Sūrya, the sun-god, proceeds through the sky in his chariot with seven mares, seeing all things, looking down upon the good and evil works of men. Indra, ruling the firmament, overthrows Vṛitra, the enemy that obscures the brightness of the sky, splits up the clouds with his thunderbolt, sends down the rain upon the earth, restores the sun to the heavens, protects the Aryan colour, and destroys the dark and degraded Dasyus, godless, prayerless, uninformed of sacrificial rites. Parjanya, the thunderer, scatters showers from his waterskin, and fills the earth and sky with fatness. "The winds blow, the lightnings play, plants spring up, the sky fructifies, the glebe teems for the good of all, as Parjanya visits the earth with moisture." The Maruts, the personified dust-storms, armed with lightnings, clothed with rain, make darkness in the day, water the earth, and mitigate the heat. Soma, the mountain milk-weed, invigorates the gods, exhilarates mankind, clothes the naked, heals the sick, gives eyes to the blind. With Yama, the regent of the dead, the departed dwell in happiness with the forefathers of their tribes.

The spiritual instinct languid. Absence of moral aspiration.

These and many others are the luminous beings that stand around them, and require to be flattered with hymns, to be fed with butter, to be refreshed with soma-juice, that they may become friendly and fatherly, and may send rain, food, cattle, children, and length of days to their worshippers. As yet these worshippers feel themselves at one with the things around them; roused to work or fight in the glare and heat of the long bright day, by the freshness of the dawn and the harsh notes of tropical birds; resting as best they may in the starlit night, seldom silent, for the most part resonant with monotonous croakings from the marsh, shrill with the crickets on grass and plant and tree, and not without peril from the violence of prowling savages from the adjacent jungle. There is little of moral or spiritual significance in this propitiation of the forces of nature. A sinner is for the most part nothing else than a man that fails to pay praise, and prayer, and sacrifice to the deities, often only the dark-skinned savage that infests the Indo-Arian village. The good man is he that flatters, feeds, and wins the favour of the gods. CHAP. I.

δῶρα θεοὺς πείθει, δῶρ' αἰδοίους βασιλῆας.

The gods eat the oblations, giving in return the good things of life, rain to the arid fields, food, cattle, chariots, wealth, children, health, a hundred years of life. Life is as yet no burden to them; there is nothing of the blank despair that came in later with the tenet of metempsychosis and the misery of every form of sentient life. Pleasures are looked for in this world; land is to be had for the conquest; their harvests are enough for the wants of all; their flocks and herds are many; and pleasures are looked for again in the after-life in the body in the kingdom of Yama. As among other undeveloped races, the sacrifices are offered as propitiatory presents, as compensations for liturgic errors, and as the necessary subsistence of the gods that enables them to watch over the well-being of mankind. This is the persuasion that prevailed into later times, and thus it appears in the Bhagavadgītā: "Prajāpati of old

CHAP. I.

created beings with their rites of sacrifice, and said, Hereby shall you propagate yourselves: this shall be to you the cow of plenty. Sustain with this the gods, and let the gods sustain you: supporting each other in turn, you shall attain the highest happiness. Fed with sacrifice, the gods shall give you the food that you desire. He that gives them nothing and eats the food they give, is a thief indeed. The good who eat the leavings of the sacrifice are loosed from their guilt, but they that cook for themselves alone, and not for the gods, eat sin. Living things are made of food; the food proceeds from rain; the rain proceeds from sacrifice."

The Vedic worship becomes mechanical.

This worship of the personified powers of nature with a view to material benefits gradually hardened into a series of rites to be performed by the priesthood. Each sacrifice came to operate in a blind and mechanic way towards the production of a specified result. The sequence of the fruit upon the performance of the function presented itself as part of the fixed succession of events. Minute rules were framed for every step of the sacrificial procedures, and explanations invented to give to every implement and every act its several symbolic import. Expiatory formulas were provided to make up for inadvertences and omissions which might otherwise frustrate the purposes of the initiated votary and the priestly experts he employed. In this process lies the transition from the religion of the Mantras, the hymns, the spontaneous effusions of the primitive seers or Ṛishis, to the religion of the Brāhmaṇas, the petrified ceremonial and formal symbolism of the liturgists. This later form of Vedic religion received the name of the Karmakāṇḍa, or ritual department of the Vedas. In the course of time it came to be held that the sacrifices performed without knowledge of their theologic import produced their desired effect—some material good, the birth of children, the prolongation of life, a series of successes in tribal feuds, and the like; leading the worshipper at the highest by the lunar path to a sojourn in the paradise of the deities, to be followed by a return to a fresh embodiment. Performed with proper insight into their theologic significance, they raised the votary after death along the solar path into the mansion of the supreme divinity, the sphere of Brahmā, there to reside till the close of the passing æon.

First beginnings of cosmologic speculation in the Vedic hymns.

But in the midst of this life of the primitive Hindu in communion with the gods of nature, there are discernible the first stirrings of reflection. Questions begin to be asked in the hymns of the Rishis in regard to the origin of earth and sky. Sometimes they said they were made by the gods, or by one or other of the gods, working after the fashion of a human artificer. At other times they said the gods begot them. One of the Rishis asks about the earth and sky, "Which of these was first, and which was later? You wise, which of you knows?" Another asks, "What was the forest, what the tree, they cut the sky and earth out of, that abide and wear not out, while the days and many dawns have worn away?"[1] In one hymn earth and sky are the work of Viśvakarman. In another it is Hiraṇyagarbha, the Golden Germ, that arose in the beginning, the lord of things that are, that establishes the sky and the earth, that is the giver of life and breath. In another it is Varuṇa, either alone or associated with Mitra, who fixes the heavens, measures out the earth, and dwells as ruler in all the worlds. Agni is sometimes the son of Earth and Sky; at other times he is said to have stretched out the earth and sky, to have inlaid the sky with stars, and to have made all that flies, or walks, or stands, or moves. In other

[1] Ṛigveda x. 31, 7. The question is answered in the Taittirīya-brāhmaṇa ii. 8, 9: Brahman—the Self that permeates and vitalises all things and all forms of life—was the forest, Self the tree from which they cut out the earth and sky. See Muir's Sanskrit Texts, vol. v. p. 32.

CHAP. I.

places it is Indra that has begotten the sun, the sky, the dawn; that has set up lights in the sky, that upholds the two worlds, the waters, the plains, the hills, and the sky.

> "What poet now, what sage of old,
> The greatness of that god hath told,
> Who from his body vast gave birth
> To father sky and mother earth?
> Who hung the heavens in empty space,
> And gave the earth a stable base,
> Who framed and lighted up the sun,
> And made a path for him to run."[1]

Elsewhere it is Soma, the deified moon-plant, that generates the earth and sky, that puts light into the sun, and stretches out the atmosphere. In another hymn Aditi, the endless visible expanse, is all that is: "Aditi is sky, Aditi is air, Aditi is mother, father, son. Aditi is all the gods, and is the five tribes of men. Aditi is whatever has been born, Aditi is whatever shall be born." The five tribes of men are the Brāhmans, Kshatriyas, and Vaiśyas, the priestly, military, and agricultural orders, more or less of Aryan extraction, the Śūdras, or indigenous serfs and slaves grafted into the Hindu communities, and the Nishādas, or tribes of unreclaimed barbarians outside the Hindu pale.

In Rigveda x. 72, 2 we read: "Brahmaṇaspati has forged these births of the gods, as a blacksmith fans his flame: in the primal age of the gods entity came forth out of nonentity."

The Purushasūkta.

In the Purushasūkta, Rigveda x. 90, the world is made,—the Rik, the Sāman, and the Yajush, the three Vedic aggregates, the Brāhman, Rājanya, Vaiśya, and Śūdra, the four orders of people in the Hindu pale, are produced,—out of Purusha, the highest deity, the personality that permeates all living things, offered up by the gods, the Sādhyas and the Rishis, as a sacrificial

[1] Muir's Metrical Translations from Sanskṛit Writers, p. 173.

victim. Here the idea of the emanation of the world from a divine spirit internal to all embodied sentiencies is presented in a form gross, obscure, and almost unintelligible to the modern mind. "Purusha has a thousand heads, a thousand eyes, a thousand feet. He compasses the earth on every side, and stands ten fingers' breadth beyond. Purusha is all this; he is that which has been, and that which is to be: the lord also of immortality, and the lord of that which grows up with food. Such is his greatness, and Purusha is more than this: one quarter of him is all existing things, three-quarters that which is immortal in the sky." It will be hereafter necessary to return to this hymn, as it contains a portion of the mythologic imagery of the subsequent Vedic philosophy of the Upanishads, and to exhibit its natural interpretation in accordance with that philosophy by Sāyaṇa, or, as he is otherwise known, the schoolman Mādhavāchārya.

The Nāsadīyasūkta.

Meanwhile, to proceed to another hymn. The effusions of awakening reflection reach their highest energy in the celebrated Nāsadīyasūkta, Rigveda x. 129. It is in this hymn that is first suggested the primitive type of Indian thought, the thesis of all the Upanishads, viz., the emanation of the world and of all the forms of life that successively people it, out of the sole reality, the Self that permeates and vitalises all things, through the agency of the unreality that overspreads it, the self-feigned fiction, the cosmical illusion, Māyā. "It was not entity, nor was it nonentity," says the Rishi. The cosmical illusion neither is nor is not; it is a self-feigned fiction, a spurious semblance of being, for it is Self alone that is. And yet it is not merely nothing, for then the world of experience would not be here and everywhere, for living souls to pass through. "No air was then, no sky above." In the state of things in which the various spheres of experience and the sentient lives that inherit them have not yet reappeared from their last disappearance into the fontal, spiritual essence, in the infinite series of æons, there is as yet nothing thinkable, nothing nameable. "What shrouded all? where? in the receptacle of what? Was it water, the unfathomable abyss?" Water, be it noted, became in the later philosophy of the Brāhmans one of the many names of the inexplicable principle of unreality, the world-fiction. "Death was not then, nor immortality." These are things that have no meaning in the sole life of the undifferenced Self. "There was no distinction of day or night. That One breathed without afflation, self-determined: other than, and beyond it, there was naught." This one, the all, is the sole reality, the aboriginal essence, the undifferenced Self, the Brahman or Ātman of the later Hindu quietist. "Darkness there was, wrapped up in darkness. All this was undifferenced water. That one that was void, covered with nothingness, developed itself by the power of self-torture. Desire first rose in it, the primal germ: this sages seeking with the intellect have found in the heart to be the tie of entity to nonentity." The Self in its earliest connection with the cosmical illusion becomes the creative spirit, the Īśvara of the philosophy of the Upanishads. The creative spirit is said in the Taittirīya Upanishad to perform self-torture, to coerce itself, as the scholiasts say, to rigorous contemplation, to a prevision of the world that is to be, and this prevision is its desire to project the spheres, and to part itself illusively into all the innumerable forms of life that are to pass through them. "The ray stretched out across these, was it above or was it below? There were generating forces, there were mighty powers; a self-determined being on this side, an energy beyond. Who indeed knows? who can say out of what it issued, whence this creation? The gods are on this side of its evolution: who then knows out of what it came into existence? This creation, whether any made it, or any made it not? He that is the overseer in the highest heaven, he indeed knows, or haply he knows not."

The hymns of reflection lead up to the philosophy of the Upanishads.

Thus there is in the Vedic hymns a second line of movement, and this leads us to the primitive type of Indian philosophy as it develops itself in the Upanishads. The hymns made in generation after generation by the Rishis, fashioned by them as a car is fashioned by a wheelwright, or fabricated or generated by the gods, were transmitted by memory from age to age, till they became of inscrutable origin and authority, of no mere personal authorship, but timeless revelations coming forth afresh in each successive æon. The period of the hymns or Mantras was followed, as has been seen, by the period of the ritual and legendary compilations known as the Brāhmaṇas. Of these Brāhmaṇas, particular portions, to be repeated only by the recluses of the forest, were styled Āraṇyakas, and to the Āraṇyakas were attached the treatises setting forth as a hidden wisdom the fictitious nature of the religion of rites as part and parcel of the series of mere semblances, the world-phantasmagory, and the sole reality of the all-pervading and all-animating Self, or Brahman. This hidden wisdom, the philosophy of the Upanishads, in contradistinction from the Karmakāṇḍa or ritual portion, received the name of Jñānakāṇḍa, or gnostic portion, of the Śruti, or everlasting revelation. There were now virtually two religions, the Karmamārga, or path of rites, for the people of the villages, living as if life with its pleasures and pains were real, and the Jñānamārga, or path of knowledge, for the sages that had quitted the world and sought the quiet of the jungle, renouncing the false ends and empty fictions of common life, and intent upon reunion with the sole reality, the Self that is one in all things living.

Climatic, ethnological, and religious degeneration in the Hindu pale.

After this brief notice of the period that preceded the rise of philosophy in India, it will be necessary, in the second place, to point out certain modifications of

CHAP. I.

the primitive forms of faith, which followed the climatic degeneration of the Indo-Arian tribes, and the degradation of the race through intermixture with and assimilation to the melanous indigenes.

The worship of S'iva, the typical Yogin.

The worship of Śiva or Mahādeva is towards the close of this period introduced from the mountains of the north, the new deity being identified with the Rudra of the Vedic poets, the howling god of tempests, the father of the Maruts. In Hindu mythology Śiva often appears as the divine pattern of the fasting devotee, intent upon the attainment of ecstatic and magical powers through savage self-torture and self-induced vacuity, apathy, and trance. In this character he is the lord of Yogins, the great typical ascetic, living in the solitude of forest and mountain, sitting motionless, with matted hair and body smeared with ashes, with breath suppressed, with vision withdrawn from all outward things, with every thought and feeling crushed within him. The practice of self-torture is alien to the cheerful spirit of the Vedic worshipper, aspiring to health and wealth and length of days, and an after-life in the realms of Yama amidst the fore-

Self-torture, thaumaturgy, and ecstasy, Yoga.

fathers of mankind. It was from the semi-savage races, with which they were coalescing, and which they were elevating, that they now adopted the practice of fixing the body and the limbs in statue-like repose, and inducing cataleptic rigidity and insensibility, as a higher state than the normal state of human life,—the practice known as Yoga,—union, ecstasy, the melting away of the consciousness into a state of characterless indetermination. The process seems to be accompanied with intervals of morbid nervous and cerebral exaltation, in which the self-torturer loses all distinction between perception and imagination, and appears to himself and others to be invested with superhuman powers. He becomes enabled to raise up the forefathers of the tribes before him by a mere act of will, to animate a plurality of bodies at the same time, to control the elements, to walk through the air, to enter into the earth with the same ease as into water, to remain unhurt in fire, dry in water, and so forth. "Among the lower races, and high above their level, morbid ecstasy, brought on by meditation, fasting, narcotics, excitement, or disease, is a state common and held in honour among the very classes specially concerned with mythic idealism."[1] "Throughout the lower civilisation men believe, with the most vivid and intense belief, in the objective reality of the human spectres which they see in sickness or exhaustion, under the influence of mental excitement or of narcotic drugs. One main reason of the practices of fasting, penance, narcotising, and other means of bringing on morbid exaltation, is that the patients may obtain the sight of spectral beings, from whom they look to gain spiritual knowledge, and even worldly power."[2]

Revival of widow-burning.

To the close of this period also, and through intermixture with the ruder indigenes, may probably be referred the revival of the ancient rite of burning the widow upon the funeral pile together with the corpse of the husband. The actual incremation formed no part of the ancient Vedic ritual, which directs that the widow be placed upon the pile by the side of the deceased husband, and then led down again by the brother-in-law, by an adopted son, or by an old servant, and bidden to return to the living world. The bow, or the sacrificial implements of the deceased, are to be burnt together with the corpse. The fact that the widow thus ascended the pile is taken by Mr. Tylor to indicate the actual practice of the immolation of widows before the Vedic age, a practice that outlived the precept for its suppression, and came to a public revival under later influences. With climatic degeneration, and with degradation through absorption of semi-savage

[1] Tylor's Primitive Culture, vol. i. p. 277. [2] Ibid., 402.

CHAP. I. blood, probably came the relapse into the primitive Aryan rite of widow-sacrifice. Funeral human sacrifice was a general rite of the Aryan nations while yet in a rude and barbarous condition. "The episodes of the Trojan captives laid with the horses and hounds on the funeral pile of Patroklos, and of Evadne throwing herself into the funeral pile of her husband, and Pausanias' narrative of the suicide of the three Messenian widows, are among its Greek representatives. In Scandinavian myth Baldr is burnt with his dwarf foot-page, his horse, and saddle: Brynhild lies on the pile by her beloved Sigurd, and men and maids follow after them on the hell-way. Old mentions of Slavonic heathendom describe the burning of the dead with clothing and weapons, horses and hounds, and, above all, with wives."[1]

Polyandry.

Other marks of degradation are the polyandry of Draupadī, the fierce blood-thirst of Bhīma, and other savage incidents in the Mahābhārata. Polyandry is one of the usages of the ruder races the Indo-Arians encroached upon, and received as serfs, as subjects, and as neighbours, prevailing in Tibet, in the Himalayan and sub-Himalayan regions under Tibetan influence, in the valley of Kashmir, and in the far south of the peninsula among the Tudas of the Nīlgiri hills, the Coorgs of Mysore, and the Nayars of Malabar.

Beliefs in the migration of the soul, and the misery of every form of life.

But of all the marks of this degradation of national type, the most noteworthy is the growing belief in metempsychosis, and the assertion of the misery of every form of sentient life,—a belief and assertion with which later Indian literature is replete to saturation. It is this expectation of a renewal of a life of misery in body after body, in age after age, and æon after æon, and the feverish yearning after some means of extrication from this black prospect, that is, as will be seen, the first motive to Indian speculation. The sum and substance, it may almost be said, of Indian philosophy, is from

[1] Primitive Culture, vol. i. p. 419.

first to last the misery of metempsychosis, and the mode of extrication from it. Of this fact the student of Indian philosophy should never for a moment lose sight, or he will lose his way in what will then seem to him a pathless jungle of abstractions.

The doctrine of transmigration formed no part of the faith of the earlier Vedic worshipper. The ancient poets had looked forward to a second life in the body, among the fathers of their tribes, and in the realms of Yama. As to punishments in a future state they are silent. In the later period of Vedic religion,[1] the period of petrified forms already referred to, a passage of the Śatapathabrāhmaṇa relates how Bhṛigu, the son of Varuṇa, visiting the four uttermost parts of the world, saw men cut into pieces and eaten by others. The eaters being asked the meaning of this by Bhṛigu, said that they were revenging upon their victims the wrongs they had suffered at their hands in the former world. This marks the first beginning of the expectation of penal retribution in a future state of being. The doctrine of metempsychosis, a belief widely spread among the lower races of men, coming slowly and surely to lay hold of the Hindu mind, this penal retribution came to be expected in a series of embodiments in vegetal, animal, human, and extra-human shapes. Each living soul was to pass from body to body, from grade to grade, from sphere to sphere of life, in obedience to a retributive operation by which suffering followed evil-doing with the blind and fatal movement of a natural law. As the life has been, such will the next embodiment be in the series of lives, the present and the future with their pains and transitory pleasures being the outcome of what the soul has done in its anterior embodiments. The series of lives has had no beginning, and shall have no end, save to the perfected sage finally resolved into the fontal essence of the uni-

[1] See Muir's Sanskṛit Texts, vol. v. p. 322.

CHAP. I.

verse. A life of such and such experiences follows from works of such and such a nature, good works sending the soul upwards in the scale of embodiments into a life human, superhuman, or divine, and evil works sending the soul downwards into bestial, insect, vegetal, penal, embodiments in this world, or in a nether world of torture. In this world, above, below, there is no place of rest; paradises and purgatories are but stages in the endless journey. In every state there is nothing to expect but vanity, vexation, and misery. *Omnis creatura ingemiscit.* There is nothing to look for but grief and pain, broken at best with pleasures themselves fleeting, empty, and unsatisfying: nothing to look for but sickness, decay, the loss of loved ones, death, and the fatal recurrence of fresh birth, through an endless succession of embodiments. Each present suffering, intolerable as it is, is the precursor to another and another, through lives without end. The very merit that wins a sojourn in a paradise or the rank of a divinity must sooner or later be exhausted, for the bankrupt soul to descend to a lower sphere. The pleasures of the paradise themselves are tainted with the fear of their expiry, and with the inequalities of the inmates of the paradise.

No true help from the gods. Pain in paradise.

> "The happier state
> In heaven, which follows dignity, might draw
> Envy from each inferior."

The soul floats helpless along the stream of lives, like a gourd on the surface of a river. A stream of lives, wave upon wave—

> "Labitur et labetur in omne volubilis ævum."

There is now no longer for the Hindu the cheering prospect of an after-life with his fathers, but the dreary vista lies before him of death after death, to be born that he may suffer and may die, to be born again that he may suffer and may die again, and this to endless ages,—to die and go he knows not whither, perhaps into an ephemeral insect life, perhaps into penal fire, perhaps into a higher life, but every life alike transitory, and with another death beyond it. A fitting concomitant to the practice of savage self-torture is this belief of metempsychosis, with its attendant horror and despair. "The rich, their children round them, are filled with anguish at the hour of death, and like theirs is the sorrow of those in a paradise upon the expiry of their merits. At the hour of death great is the anguish of a thriving prince, and like his is the sorrow of those in a paradise upon the expiry of their merits. In the paradise itself they are dependent, and cannot help themselves. The sorrow of the celestial sojourners at the loss of their merits, is like the sorrow of the rich at the loss of their riches. In the performance of rites there is pain, in the fruition of the recompense of those rites there is pain, upon the expiry of the recompense there is the direful pain of fresh birth into the world. For what shall the living soul pass into on its return from paradise? shall it pass into a high, a middle, or a low embodiment, or shall it be born into a place of punishment?"[1] The series of lives of misery is without beginning no less than without end, and no one knows what he has done in the far past and laid up for the future. Birth from works and fresh works from new birth, as plant from seed and seed from plant, and who shall assign the priority to either? In the never-ceasing onward flow of things there is no longer anything more than a seeming perpetuity for the gods themselves, and many thousand Indras are said to have passed away as æon has followed æon. The Hindu looks to the flow of lives through which he has passed, to the flow of lives through which he has to pass, till he can find no fixity or stability in any kind of world. All things are passing, and passing away; and what remains? anything or nothing? Here we have, as will

The intolerable prospect of life after life and death after death.

[1] Âtmapurâṇa xvi. 91–95.

CHAP. I. be shortly seen, the first point of transition to the metaphysical era. Something must be found that shall be fixed and changeless in the midst of all this change; some place of rest must be provided to limit this vista of restless misery and migration.

In the Upanishads the tenet of transmigration is already conspicuous. Thus in the Chhāndogya we read: "Whatever these creatures are in this world, lion, or wolf, or boar, or worm, or moth, or gnat, or mosquito, that they become again and again." And again: "Those whose life has been good will quickly attain a new embodiment—embodiment as a Brāhman, a Kshatriya, or a Vaiśya. Those whose life has been evil will quickly pass into an evil embodiment—embodiment as a dog, or a hog, or a Chaṇḍāla." In the post-Vedic literature the nature of the retributive embodiments is treated of in minute and fanciful detail. Thus, in the twelfth book of the laws of the Mānavas, it is said: "The greatest sinners, after passing through terrible regions of torture for long periods of years, pass into the following embodiments: The slayer of a Brāhman enters into the body of a dog, a boar, an ass, a camel, a bull, a goat, a sheep, a stag, a bird, a Chaṇḍāla, or a Pukkaśa, according to the proportion of his guilt; a Brāhman that drinks strong drinks shall enter into the body of a worm, an insect, a moth, of a fly that feeds on ordure, or of a noxious animal. A thievish Brāhman shall pass thousands of times into the bodies of spiders, snakes, chameleons, crocodiles, and of malignant vampires."[1] And then follows a long series of other penal states of life, proportioned to the guilt of the agents that are to pass through them.

The belief in metempsychosis prevalent among the lower races of mankind.

Mr. Tylor[2] has shown how widely the belief has prevailed among semi-savage tribes, of the passage of the human soul into the trunks of trees and the bodies

[1] Mānavadharmaśāstra xii. 54, sqq.
[2] Primitive Culture, vol. ii. pp. 6, sqq.

of animals. The Sonthals are said to believe the souls of the good to enter into fruit-bearing trees. The Powhattans believed the souls of their chiefs to pass into particular wood-birds, which they therefore spared. The Tlascalans of Mexico thought that the souls of their nobles migrated after death into beautiful singing-birds, and the spirits of plebeians into beetles, weasels, and other insignificant creatures. The Zulus of South Africa are said to believe the passage of the dead into snakes, or into wasps and lizards. The Dayaks of Borneo imagine themselves to find the souls of the dead, damp and bloodlike, in the trunks of trees. The belief in the passage of the soul into trees, and animals, and fresh human bodies having no place in Vedic literature prior to the Upanishads, it is reasonable to suppose the Hindus to have taken it from the indigenes, in the course of their absorption of indigenous blood.

Current in Egypt. Adopted in Greece by Empedocles, the Pythagoreans, and Plato.

It is well known that metempsychosis was one of the beliefs of the ancient Egyptians in regard to the destination of the soul. The tenet connects itself with a belief in the fore- as well as the after-life of the sentient and thinking principle. From the Egyptians it is adopted at intervals into the Greek philosophy. It first appears in the teaching of Pythagoras. Empedocles fancies that the blood he has shed in an earlier form of life is crying out against him in this, and that he is to be a fugitive and a wanderer upon the earth for thirty thousand years. Exiled from the presence of the gods, divine though it be, his soul is to pass through a succession of penal embodiments, until it regains its purity. It is to enter into the shapes of plants and trees, of fishes and birds, and other animals, some of these shapes being higher than others, as the laurel among trees, the lion among the beasts. From the Pythagoreans the doctrine is taken up by Plato, as in unison with his belief of the pre-existence and

CHAP. I.

Philosophy the release from metempsychosis in the Phædon.

post-existence of the soul, and as explanatory of the inequalities of human fortune. Thus in the Phædon:—

"Are we to suppose, says Socrates, that the soul, an invisible thing, in going to a place like itself, invisible, pure, and noble, the true Hades, into the presence of the good and wise God, whither, if God will, my soul is also soon to go,—that the soul, I say, if this be her nature and origin, is blown away and perishes immediately on quitting the body, as the many say? It is far otherwise, my dear Simmias and Cebes. The truth is much more this, that if the soul is pure at its departure, it drags after it nothing bodily, in that it has never, of its own will, had connection with the body in its life, but has always shunned it, and gathered itself unto itself; for this avoidance of the body has been its constant practice. And this is nothing else than that it philosophises truly, and practises how to die with ease. And is not philosophy the practice of death?

"Certainly.

"That soul, I say, itself invisible, departs to a world invisible like itself—to the divine, and immortal, and rational. Arriving there, its lot is to be happy, released from human error and unwisdom, fears, and wild passions, and all other human ills, and it dwells for all future time, as they say of the initiated, in the society of the gods. Shall we say this, Cebes, or say otherwise?

"It is so, said Cebes, beyond a doubt.

"But do you think the soul will depart in perfect purity if it is polluted and impure at the time it quits the body, as having always been the companion and servant of the body, in love with and fascinated by it, and by the bodily desires and pleasures, until it comes to think that nothing is true but that which has a bodily shape, which a man may touch, and see, and eat, and drink, and gratify his sensuality upon; and if, at the same time, it has been accustomed to hate, and fear, and shun the intelligible world, which is dark and invisible to the bodily eye, and can be attained only by philosophy?

"It cannot possibly, he replied.

"It is engrossed by the corporeal, which the continual companionship with the body, and constant attention to it, have made natural to it.

"Very true.

"And this, my friend, may be conceived to be that ponderous, heavy, earthy element of sight, by which such a soul is weighted and dragged down again into the visible world, because it is afraid of the invisible and of the world below, and prowls about tombs and sepulchres, in the neighbourhood of which certain shadowy apparitions of souls have been seen, souls which have not departed clean and pure, but still hold by the things of sight, and are therefore seen themselves.

"That is likely enough, Socrates.

"Indeed it is likely, Cebes; and these must be the souls, not of the good, but of the evil, who are necessitated to haunt such places in expiation of their former evil way of life; and they continue to wander until the desire of the bodily element which still cleaves to them is gratified, and they are imprisoned in another body. And they are then most likely tied to the same natures which they have made habitual to themselves in their former life.

"What natures do you mean, Socrates?

"I mean to say that men who have followed after gluttony, and wantonness, and drunkenness, and have had no thought of avoiding them, would put on the shape of asses and animals of that sort. What do you think?

"What you say is exceedingly probable.

"And those who have preferred the portion of injustice, and tyranny, and violence will put on the shape of wolves, or hawks and kites; or where else should we say that they would go?

"No doubt, said Cebes, they pass into shapes such as those.

"And it is pretty plain, he said, into what bodies each of the rest would go, according to the similitude of the lives that they have led.

"That is plain enough, he said.

"Even among them some are happier than others; and the happiest in themselves and in the place they migrate to, are those who have practised the social and civil virtues that men call temperance and justice, which are acquired by habit and exercise, without philosophy and reflection.

"Why are they the happiest?

"Because they will be likely to pass into some gentle social nature like their own, such as that of bees or ants, or even back again into the form of man, and moderate men would spring from them.

"That is possible.

"But none but he who is a philosopher or lover of learning, and altogether clean and pure at departing, is permitted to reach the gods."

In this place Plato approaches more nearly than in any other passage in his Dialogues to the Oriental tenets of the migration of the soul from body to body, and the sole efficiency of supersensible thinking in disengaging the soul from these successive lives of sense. For Socrates, in the Phædon, it is philosophy alone that can purify the soul, detach it from the body, and lift it up into communion with the eternal and unchanging archetypes. But the Platonic abstraction is a contemplation of the eternal ideas, the patterns after which the visible world was moulded, the universal verities discernible through the things of sense; not a Hindu meditation on formless being, on the characterless Self, nor a Buddhist meditation on the vacuity into which all things are resolvable; and the Platonic after-life of the free intelligence is a positive exercise of intellection, neither a Hindu absorption into the fontal essence, nor a Buddhist extinction into the aboriginal nothingness of things.

Asiatic and European pessimism.

The thesis of universal misery is a natural sequel of the doctrine of the migration of the soul. In his Dialogues concerning Natural Religion, Hume has painted for us the miseries of life in dark colours, but these are not nearly dark enough for the Hindu. For him, the miseries of his present life, hunger, thirst, and faintness, weariness, care, sickness, bereavement, dying pangs, are to repeat themselves in life after life, and death after death, in endless iteration. The morbid reverie of the hypochondriac is gaiety by the side of this Indian pessimism, and this pessimism is the ever-present thought, the very motive power of Indian speculation.

Hume's picture of the miseries of life.

"The whole earth, believe me, Philo, is cursed and polluted. A perpetual war is kindled amongst all living creatures. Necessity, hunger, want, stimulate the strong and courageous; fear, anxiety, terror, agitate the weak and infirm. The first entrance into life gives anguish to the new-born infant and to its wretched parent: weakness, impotence, distress, attend each stage of that life; and it is at last finished in agony and horror.

"Observe too, says Philo, the curious artifices of nature in order to embitter the life of every living being. The stronger prey upon the weaker, and keep them in perpetual terror and anxiety. The weaker, too, in their turn, often prey upon the stronger, and vex and molest them without relaxation. Consider that innumerable race of insects, which either are bred on the body of each animal, or, flying about, infix their stings in him. These insects have others still less than themselves which torment them. And thus, on each hand, before and behind, above and below, every animal is surrounded with enemies, which incessantly seek his misery and destruction.

"Man alone, said Demea, seems to be an exception to this rule. For, by combination in society, he can easily master lions, tigers, and bears, whose greater strength and agility naturally enable them to prey upon him.

"On the contrary, it is here chiefly, cried Philo, that the uniform and equal maxims of nature are most apparent. Man, it is true, can by combination surmount all his *real* enemies, and become master of the whole animal creation; but does he not immediately raise up to himself *imaginary* enemies, the demons of his fancy, who haunt him with superstitious terrors and blast every enjoyment of life? His pleasure, as he imagines, becomes in their eyes a crime; his food and repose give them umbrage and offence; his very sleep and dreams furnish new materials to anxious fear; and even death, his refuge from every other ill, presents only the dread of endless and innumerable woes. Nor does the wolf molest more the timid flock, than superstition does the anxious breast of wretched mortals.

"Besides, consider, Demea, this very society by which we surmount those wild beasts, our natural enemies, what new enemies does it not raise to us? what woe and misery does it not occasion? Man is the greatest enemy of man. Oppression, injustice, contempt, contumely, violence, sedition, war, calumny, treachery, fraud; by these they mutually torment each other, and they would soon dissolve that society which they had formed, were it not for the dread of still greater ills which must attend their separation.

"But though these external insults, said Demea, from animals, from men, from all the elements which assault us, form a frightful catalogue of woes, they are nothing in comparison of those which arise within ourselves, from the distempered condition of our mind and body. How many lie under the lingering torment of diseases? Hear the pathetic enumeration of the great poet—

> 'Intestine stone and ulcer, colic pangs,
> Demoniac frenzy, moping melancholy,
> And moonstruck madness, pining atrophy,
> Marasmus, and wide-wasting pestilence.
> Dire was the tossing, deep the groans: Despair
> Tended the sick, busiest from couch to couch.
> And over them triumphant Death his dart
> Shook, but delayed to strike, though oft invoked
> With vows, as their chief good and final hope.'

"The disorders of the mind, continued Demea, though more secret, are not perhaps less dismal and vexatious. Remorse, shame, anguish, rage, disappointment, anxiety, fear, dejection, despair; who has ever passed through life without cruel inroads from these tormentors? How many have scarcely ever felt any better sensations? Labour and poverty, so abhorred by every one, are the certain lot of the far greater number; and those few privileged persons who enjoy ease and opulence, never reach contentment or true felicity. All the goods of life united would not make a very happy man, but all the ills united would make a wretch indeed; and any one of them almost (and who can be free from every one?), nay, often the absence of one good (and who can possess all?) is sufficient to render life ineligible.

"Were a stranger to drop on a sudden into this world, I would show him, as a specimen of its ills, a hospital full of diseases, a prison crowded with malefactors and debtors, a field of battle strewed with carcases, a fleet foundering in the ocean, a nation languishing under tyranny, famine, or pestilence. To turn the gay side of life to him, and give him a notion of its pleasures, whither should I conduct him? To a ball, to an opera, to court? He might justly think that I was only showing him a diversity of distress and sorrow."

CHAP. I.

The similar picture of the Indian schoolmen.

The Indian schoolmen produce a very similar list[1] of human ills. The miseries that await the soul in its migration from body to body, are threefold in their nature. Death itself is no release from suffering, and the prospect is unending. There are first the personal afflictions that attach to the body and the mind, pains of the body arising from disordered temperament, and pains of the mind proceeding from lust, anger, avarice, fear, envy, stupefaction, despondency, and severance from all the soul would fain cling to. The whole head is sick and the whole heart faint. These are the ills that, in the words of Hume, "arise within ourselves, from the distempered condition of the mind and body." Next, there is the series of miseries that spring from the environment, injuries at the hands of men, and evils from beasts and birds and snakes and other creeping things, and hurts from plants and trees and stocks and stones. These, in the list of Hume, are the "external insults from animals, from men, from all the elements." Thirdly, there is the train of ills proceeding from supernatural agency, the terrors of evil beings and demoniacal possession. These are the "imaginary enemies, the demons of man's fancy, that haunt him with superstitious terrors."

To recapitulate: the period in which Indian philosophy had its rise, is the period in which the original worship of the forces of nature has given place to the mechanical repetition of prescriptive usages and sacred formulas. Side by side with the decay of living faith in the personified elemental powers there has gone on a degeneration of the Indo-Arian tribes, partly from climatic influences, partly from intermixture with the rude indigenes. This degradation of the national type marks itself in the worship of the terrific Śiva,

[1] The list is given as in the Sānkhyatattvakaumudī. The three series of miseries are in Sanskṛit *ādhyātmika*, *ādhibhautika*, and *ādhidaivika*.

and in the practice of savage self-torture, and the production of morbid cerebral conditions; in the revival of the primitive Aryan rite of widow-immolation; in the polyandry and Kshatriya savageries pictured in the Mahābhārata; and finally, and above all, in the ever-active belief in the migration of the soul, and in the misery of every form of sentient life.

CHAPTER II.

THE QUEST OF THE REAL—BRAHMAN AND MAYA, THE SELF AND THE WORLD-FICTION.

"A presence that disturbs him with the joy
Of elevated thoughts; a sense sublime
Of something far more deeply interfused,
Whose dwelling is the light of setting suns,
And the round ocean, and the living air,
And the blue sky, and in the mind of man;
A motion and a spirit that impels
All thinking things, all objects of all thought,
And rolls through all things."—WORDSWORTH.

"Nature itself plainly intimates to us that there is some such absolutely perfect Being, incomprehensible to our finite understandings, by certain passions which it hath implanted in us, that otherwise would want an object to display themselves upon; namely, those of devout veneration, adoration, and admiration, together with a kind of ecstasy and pleasing horror."—CUDWORTH.

CHAP. II.

Fixity amidst the flux of things.

LOOKING behind them and before them, the Indian sages, meditating in the solitude of the jungle, find that the series of lives through which each sentient thing is passing is flowing forward without a pause, like a river. Is the river to lose itself at last in the sea? The sum of all the several series of lives, and of all the spheres through which the living soul proceeds, is also in perpetual flow. The sum of migrating forms of life, and of the spheres through which they migrate, is the ever-moving world. Everything in it is coming into being and passing out of being, but never is. The sum of lives and of the spheres of living things is not real, for it comes and goes, rises and passes away, without ceasing, and that alone is real that neither passes into being nor passes out of being, but simply is. To be is to last, to perdure. What is there that lasts? CHAP. II.

Repose and peace amidst the miseries of life.

Every one of the countless modes of life that perpetually replace each other is a new form of misery, or at best of fleeting pleasure tainted with pain, and nothing else is to be looked for in all the varieties of untried being. In every stream of lives there is the varied anguish of birth, of care, hunger, weariness, bereavement, sickness, decay, and death, through embodiment after embodiment, and through æon after æon. Evil thoughts, evil words, and evil deeds push the doer downward in the scale of sentiencies, and into temporary places of torment. Good thoughts, good words, and good deeds push the doer upwards into higher embodiments, and into temporary paradises. It is the same wearisome journey above and below, miseries and tainted pleasures that make way for new miseries, and no end to it all. Good no less than evil activity is an imperfection, for it only prolongs the stream of lives. Action is the root of evil. Is there nothing that rests inert and impassive, untouched with all these miseries of metempsychosis?

Unity amidst the plurality of experience.

Again, the scenes through which the sage finds himself to be migrating are manifold and varied, and present themselves in a duality of experience,—the subject on the one side, the object on the other. The more he checks the senses and strives to gaze upon the inner light, when he sits rigid and insensate seeking ecstasy, —the more this plurality tends to fade away, the more this duality tends to melt into a unity, a one and only being. A thrill of awe runs through the Indian sage as he finds that this pure and characterless being, this light within the heart, in the light of which all things shine, is the very Self within him, freed from the flow of experiences for a while by a rigorous effort of abstraction. A perfect inertion, a perfect abstraction, have enabled him to reach the last residue of all abstrac-

CHAP. II.

tion, the fontal essence, the inner light, the light beyond the darkness of the fleeting forms of conscious life.

These are found at intervals in sleep without a dream.

Times there are, moreover, when he wakes from sleep unbroken with a dream, and is aware that he has slept at ease, untouched for a space with the miseries of metempsychosis. Dreamless sleep, like ecstasy itself, is a transient union with the one and only being that perdures, and does not pass away as all things else are passing, that is inert and untouched with the miseries of migration, that is beyond the duality of subject and object, and beyond the plurality of the things of experience. Dreamless sleep is, like ecstasy, an unalloyed beatitude; it is a state in which all differences are merged, and for the sleeper the world has melted away. His very personality has passed back into the impersonality of the true Self; and if only this state could be prolonged for ever, it would be a final refuge from the miseries of life.

They are found permanently in union with the characterless Self,

Thus, then, that which only is, while all things else come and go, pass, and pass away; that which is untouched with the hunger, thirst, and pain, and sorrow that wait upon all forms of life; that which is one while all things else are many; that which stands above and beyond the duality of all modes of consciousness, is the Self, the one Self within all sentiencies, the spiritual principle that permeates and vitalises all things, and gives life and light to all things living, from a tuft of grass up to the highest deity. There is one thing that *is*, and only one—the light within, the light in which these pleasures and pains, these fleeting scenes and semblances, come and go, pass into and pass out of being. This primordial light, this light of lights, beyond the darkness of the self-feigned world-fiction, this fontal unity of undifferenced being, is pure being, pure thought, pure bliss. It is thought in which there is neither thinker nor thing; bliss without self-gratulation, bliss in which there is nothing that rejoices and nothing rejoiced at; the unspeakable blessedness of exemption from vicissitude and misery. "All things live upon portions of its joy." "Who could breathe, who could live, if there were not this bliss within the ether in the heart?" It is not an empty abstraction; that the Indian mystic in his hour of ecstasy knows well. It is positive and self-affirming; for, says Śankarāchārya, the last residuum of all abstraction is not nonentity but entity. It is the object[1] of the notion "I," and is present to every soul. It is above and beyond[2] all modes of conscious thought. "Words turn back from it, with the mind, not reaching it." It can only be spoken of as "not this, not that," spoken of in negatives, and by unsaying what is said. "It is thought," says the Kena Upanishad, "by him that thinks it not; he that thinks it knows it not; it is unknown to them that know it, known to them that know it not." It is at once necessitated to thought and withheld from positive conception: *cognoscendo ignoratur et ignorando cognoscitur.*

which is the object of the notion "I."

Such is the Brahman, the ultimate spiritual reality of primitive Indian philosophy, out of which, in its everlasting union with its counterfeit, Māyā, the self-feigning world-fiction, proceeds the phantasmagory of metempsychosis. Avidyā, Māyā, Śakti, the illusion, the fiction, the power that resides within the Self as the future tree resides within the seed,[3]—it is out of this, overspreading the one and only Self, that all things living, from a tuft of grass to the highest deity, with all the spheres through which they migrate, have emanated to form a world of semblances. They are all alike figments of this inexplicable world-fiction, the cosmical illusion.[4] Personal souls and their environments are fleeting and phantasmagorical, the dreams of

Brahman, the impersonal Self.

[1] *Ahampratyayavishaya, ahampadapratyayalakshitārtha.*

[2] *Sarvabuddhipratyayātīta.*

[3] *Vaṭakaṇikāyāṃ vaṭa iva*, Śankara.

[4] *Viśvamāyā, viśvajananī śaktiḥ.*

CHAP. II.

the spirit of the world;[1] and being such, they may be left behind, if by any means the sage can wake to their unreality, and find his true being in the original essence, the one Self, the only light of life. If only he knows it, he is already this Self, this Brahman, ever pure, intelligent, and free.[2] Pure as untouched by the world-fiction, passionless, inert; intelligent as self-luminous, giving light to all the movements of the minds of living things; free as unembodied, exempt from the miseries of metempsychosis.

Etymology of the word Brahman.

The original idea of the term Brahman is indicated in its etymology. It is a derivative of the root *bṛih*, to grow, to increase. Thus the scholiast Ānandagiri, with reference to a passage in which Brahman is identified with one of its manifestations, the breath of life, says, "Brahman is from *bṛih*, to grow, and every one knows how the body grows by respiration and other functions." And in another place, in his gloss on Śankara's commentary on the Taittirīyaka Upanishad, "The term Brahman comes from *bṛih*, to grow, to expand, and is expressive of growth and greatness. This Brahman is a vastness unlimited in space, in time, and in content, for there is nothing known as a limit to it, and the term applies to a thing of transcendent greatness." Perhaps the earliest sense of the term was the plastic power at work in the process of things, viewed as an energy of thought or spirit, a power present everywhere unseen, that manifests itself most fully in vegetable, animal, and human life. The cause of all changes in the order of metempsychosis, it is itself unchangeable. It has nothing before it or after it, nothing within it or without it.[3] It transcends space and time, and every kind of object.[4] It is the uncaused cause of all, but in its real nature, and putting the world-fiction and its figments

Brahman infinite.

[1] *Jagadātman, i.e.,* Brahman manifesting itself in Īśvara.

[2] *Nityaśuddhabuddhamukta.*

[3] *Tad etad brahmāpūrvam anaparam anantaram avāhyam.*

[4] *Deśakālavishayātivartin.*

out of view, it is, in the phrase of Śankara's commentary on the Śvetāśvatara Upanishad, "neither cause nor not cause, nor both cause and not cause."

Brahman incogitable and ineffable.

"It is," in the words of the Kena Upanishad, "other than the known and above the unknown." To quote the scholium of Ānandagiri, that which is other than the knowing subject is either known or unknown, and thus the text, by denying in regard to Brahman both the known and the unknown, identifies Brahman with the Self of the knowing subject.

"The eye reaches it not, speech reaches it not, thought reaches it not: we know not, we understand not, how one should teach it: it is other than the known, above the unknown. Thus have we heard of the ancients, who proclaimed it to us.

"That which is not uttered by the voice, that by which the voice is uttered: know thou that that only is the Self, and not that which men meditate upon as such.

"That which is not thought by the thought, that by which the thought is thought: know thou that that only is the Self, and not that which men meditate upon as such."

"Thought," says Śankara in his exposition of this text, "is the internal organ, mind, intelligence. Thought is the inward sense or faculty that co-operates with all the several organs of sense and motion. Thus the text, 'Desire, volition, doubt, faith, patience and impatience, and shame, and thought, and fear,—all this is that inner sense.' The inner sense presents itself only in the form of desire, volition, and the other modifications, and therefore a man cannot recognise with his inward sense the intelligential light that gives light to those modifications. This pure light actuates the inner sense by irradiation; and as this pure light or Self transcends all objects of outer and inner sense, the inward sense is incompetent to approach it. The inward sense can only operate when enlightened by the intelligential

Brahman the light that irradiates the mental modes.

CHAP. II.

light within, and therefore it is that the expositors of Brahman speak of the mind and its modifications as permeated and objectivised by the Self within." In plain words, when we are told that it is the Self that thinks the thought, we are to understand, in the language of the Indian mystics, that it is the Self that gives the light to the mental modes in which they shine—that is, it is the Self that causes the otherwise unconscious modes to become the conscious modes of mind. To return to the text of the Kena Upanishad.

"That which one sees not with the eye, that by which the eyes see: know thou that that only is the Self, and not that which men meditate upon as such.

"That which one hears not with the ear, that by which the ear is heard: know thou that that only is the Self, and not that which men meditate upon as such.

"That which one breathes not with the breath, that by which the breath is breathed: know thou that that only is the Self, and not that which men meditate upon as such."

Similarly in the Bṛihadāraṇyaka Upanishad:—

"This same imperishable is that which sees unseen, hears unheard, thinks unthought, and knows unknown. There is no other than this that sees, no other than this that hears, no other than this that thinks, no other than this that knows. Over this imperishable the expanse is woven woof and warp.[1]

"As in dreamless sleep the soul sees, but sees not this or that, so the Self in seeing sees not; for there is no intermission in the sight of the Self that sees; its vision is one that passes not away; and there is nothing second to that, other than that, apart from that, that it should see."

Brahman is pure thought, eternal, and objectless.

What is meant here is that the thought or intelligence with which the Self is one, is something beyond

[1] The expanse is here a synonym for Māyā, the self-feigning world-fiction.

the relation of subject and object;[1] it is, in the words of Rāmatīrtha's commentary on the Upadeśasahasrī, an eternal objectless cognition.[2] The Self is said to be omniscient, but the reader must not be misled; this only means that it is self-luminous, that it gives light to all things, and to all the modifications of the minds of sentient beings. Withdraw the light of the Self, the Indian sages say, and the whole process of things will lapse into blindness, darkness, nothingness. The omniscience of the Self is its irradiation of all things.[3] To cite Ānandagiri,[4] "It is not literally, but by a figure that the Self is said to be all-knowing. The cognitions of the everyday thinker in the sensible world presuppose faculties and organs; the knowledge that is the essence of the idea or Self does not presuppose faculties and organs, for in that case it could not exist, as it does exist, in the state of dreamless sleep, in which the functions of the faculties and organs have ceased."

Brahman not to be confused with the personal absolute, or Christian Deity.

It will be well here to point out once for all that we are to tread warily among these epithets of Brahman. If we are to use the language of European philosophy, we must pronounce the Brahman of the Upanishads to be *unconscious*, for consciousness begins where duality begins. The ideal or spiritual reality of Brahman is not convertible with conscious spirit. On the contrary, the spiritual reality that, according to the poets of the Upanishads, underlies all things, has *per se* no cognition of objects; it transcends the relation of subject and object; it lies beyond duality. It is true that these poets speak of it as existence, intelligence, beatitude. But we must be cautious. Brahman is not intelligence in our sense of the word. The intelligence, the thought, that is the Self and which the Self is, is described as eternal knowledge, without objects, the imparting of light to the cognitions of migrating sentiencies. This

[1] *Jñātṛijñeyabhāvātirikta.*

[2] *Nityaṃ nirvishayaṃ jñānam.*

[3] *Sarvāvabhāsakatva.*

[4] *Sarvajñam brahmopacharyate.*

CHAP. II.

thought is characterless and eternal; their cognitions are charactered, and come and go. Brahman is beatitude. But we must again be cautious. Brahman is not beatitude in the ordinary sense of the word. It is a bliss beyond the distinction of subject and object, a bliss the poets of the Upanishads liken to dreamless sleep. Brahman *per se* is neither God nor conscious God; and on this it is necessary to insist, to exclude the baseless analogies to Christian theology that have sometimes been imagined by writers, Indian and European. Be it then repeated that the Indian philosophers everywhere affirm that Brahman *is* knowledge, not that Brahman *has* knowledge; that this knowledge is without an object known, and that omniscience is predicable of Brahman only by a metaphor. If we were to misinterpret such knowledge by the word "consciousness," we should still have to say that Brahma *is* consciousness, not that Brahman *has* consciousness or is a conscious spirit.

To return to the text of the Bṛihadāraṇyaka.

Brahman the pure light of characterless knowledge.

"As in dreamless sleep the soul hears, but hears not this or that, so the Self in hearing hears not; for there is no intermission in the hearing of the Self that hears; its audition is one that passes not away; and there is nothing second to that, other than that, apart from that, that it should hear.

"As in dreamless sleep the soul thinks, but thinks not this or that, so in thinking the Self thinks not; for there is no intermission in the thought of the Self that thinks; its thought is one that passes not away; and there is nothing second to that, other than that, apart from that, that it should think.

"As in dreamless sleep the soul knows, but knows not this or that, so in knowing the Self knows not; for there is no intermission in the knowledge of the Self that knows, for its knowledge is one that passes not away; and there is nothing second to that, other than that, apart from that, that it should know."

When overspread with the self-feigning world-fiction, the Self is that out of which all things and all forms of life proceed. It is, in the words of the Muṇḍaka Upanishad, that on knowing which all things are known; in the words of the Chhāndogya, that by instruction in which the unthought becomes thought, and the unknown known. As the Indian scholiasts say: If we know Brahman we know all things: if we know what clay is, we know what all the variety of pots and pans are, that the potter fashions out of clay; if we know what gold is, we know what all the varieties of earrings, bracelets, and other trinkets are, that the goldsmith fashions out of gold. Thus, to quote the Chhāndogya Upanishad:—

Brahman that which being known, all things are known,—the ἀρχή.

"Śvetaketu was the grandson of Aruṇa. His father Āruṇi said to him: Śvetaketu, thou must enter on thy sacred studentship. None of our family, my dear son, is unstudied, a Brahman only in lineage. Śvetaketu therefore at the age of twelve repaired to a spiritual preceptor, and at the age of four-and-twenty came home after going through all the Vedas, conceited, pedantic, and opinionated. His father said to him: Śvetaketu, tell me, my son, since thou art so conceited, pedantic, and opinionated, hast thou asked for that instruction by which the unheard becomes heard, the unthought thought, the unknown known?

"Holy sir, how is that instruction given?

"His father said: My son, as everything made of clay is known by a single lump of clay, being nothing more than a modification of speech, a change, a name, while the clay is the only truth:

"As everything made of gold is known by a single lump of gold, being nothing more than a modification of speech, a change, a name, while the gold is the only truth:

"As everything made of steel is known by a single pair of nail-scissors, being nothing more than a modi-

CHAP. II. fication of speech, a change, a name, while the steel is the only truth:

"Such, my son, is that instruction."

Brahman is, as has been already seen, said to be "existent, thought, bliss." In the Taittirīya Upanishad the Self is said to be "truth, knowledge, infinity." Śankarāchārya's remarks on this passage of the Taittirīya will serve also to illustrate the foregoing extract from the Chhāndogya. "Self," he says, "is truth; Self is knowledge; Self is infinity. A thing is true if it is neither more nor less than it is taken to be. It is false if it is more or less than that. Hence every form of derived or emanatory existence is fictitious, nothing more than a modification of speech, a change, a name, and the clay is the only truth. That which *is* being found to be the only truth, the words 'the Self is truth' negative all modification of the Self. It follows that Brahman is the cause or fontal essence. It operates as such, because it is the reality. Lest it should be supposed that Brahman being that of which all things are made, it must be unspiritual, like the potter's clay, the text proceeds to say that the Self is knowledge. The term knowledge is abstract, standing as an epithet of Brahman together with truth and infinity. If knowledge meant here a subject knowing, the epithet would be incompatible with the other two. If Brahman were a knowing subject, it would be modified in its cognitions, and how then could it be the truth? A thing is infinite when it cannot be limited at any point. If the Self were a knowing subject, it would be limited by the *cognita* and the cognitions. Another text says: That is the infinite in which nothing else is known, and that is the finite in which one knows something else. As predicated of the Self along with truth and infinity, knowledge is thus an abstract term. The words 'Self is knowledge' are intended at once to deny agency and action, and to deny that the Self or Brahman is an unspiritual thing such as the potter's clay in the familiar example. The same words 'Self is knowledge' might be imagined to imply the finitude of Self, forasmuch as all the cognitions of everyday life are limited or finite. The epithet 'infinite' is added to exclude this idea of finitude. The term infinite is negative, refusing the presence of limits; the epithets truth and knowledge are positive, giving a sense of their own. The knowledge of Brahman is nothing else than the essence of the Self itself, like the light of the sun, or the heat of fire. It is the eternal essence of the Self, and does not depend on conditions foreign to itself, as our experiences do."

Brahman the principle of reality. The co-eternal principle of unreality, Māyā, the world-fiction.

These remarks must suffice for the present in regard to Brahman. The several elements of the cosmical conception of the poets of the Upanishads are so closely interfused, that it is not possible with any ingenuity altogether to separate them for convenience of exposition. So far as may be, however, these elements must be exhibited in successive order, proceeding from Brahman to Māyā; from Māyā to the union, from before all time, between Brahman and Māyā; from this union to the resultant procession of migrating souls and of the spheres of their migration, and the hierarchic emanations Īśvara, Hiraṇyagarbha, and Virāj, severally representing the sums of living things in the three several states of dreamless sleep, of dreaming sleep, and of waking consciousness; and finally reverting to the "fourth," so called in contradistinction to the three states or modes of life, that is, to the original unity of characterless being or Brahman. Brahman *per se* is the principle of reality, the one and only being; Self alone is, and all else only seems to be. This principle of reality, however, has been from everlasting associated with an inexplicable principle of unreality; and it is from the fictitious union of these principles, the one real, the other only a self-feigned fiction, that the spheres and

CHAP. II. the migrating forms of life, the external and internal world, proceed.

Māyā the illusion in every individual soul.

Māyā may be regarded both in parts and in the whole. Viewed in parts, it is the particular illusion that veils from each form of life its own true nature as the one and only Self. Under its influence every kind of sentient being is said to identify itself, not with the Self that is one and the same in all, but with its counterfeit presentment,[1] the invisible body that accompanies it through its migrations, and the visible bodies that it animates successively. Thus every living thing is a fictitiously detached portion, an illusive emanation of Brahman. Māyā overspreads Brahman as a cloud overspreads the sun, veiling from it its proper nature, and projecting the world of semblances, the phantasmagory of metempsychosis. For every form of life, from the lowest to the highest, from a mere tuft of grass up to the highest deity, its own proper nature is veiled, and a bodily counterfeit presented in lieu of it, by the primeval illusion or self-feigning fiction, Avidyā or Māyā. Hence all individual existences, and the long miseries of metempsychosis, in the procession of the æons without beginning and without end; for the world is from everlasting, and every genesis of things is only a palingenesia. The procession of the æons is often likened to a succession of dreams. The world is often said to be the mind-projected figment of migrating souls.[2] It is, says Śankarāchārya, only an emanation of the internal sense of sentient beings, and this is proved by the fact that the world is resolved back into their inner sense in their intervals of dreamless sleep.[3] As emanating from such illusion, the world of me-

[1] Technically styled its *upādhi*. The totality of Māyā is the *upādhi* of Īśvara. Portions of Māyā are the several upādhis of the jīvas or migrating souls.

[2] *Sarvam hy antaḥkaraṇavikāram eva jagat, manasy eva sushupte pralayadarśanāt.* Elsewhere the phrase *manovijhṛimbhitam.*

[3] *Prapanchasya māyayā vidyamānatvam, na tu vastutvam.*

tempsychosis has an existence, but this existence is unreal.

Māyā the illusion in all souls, the unreal emanatory principle of the world, coeternal with Brahman.

Māyā, viewed as a whole, is the cosmical illusion, the self-feigning world-fiction, that is without beginning.[1] It is said to be "neither entity nor nonentity, nor both in one, inexplicable by entity and by nonentity, fictitious, and without beginning." It is not a mere nothing, but a *nescio quid.* It is an illusion projected by illusion, an unreal unreality, the three primitive elements of pleasure, pain, and indolence[2] in coequality, overspreading the one and only Self from everlasting. It is the sum of the illusions of all individual souls, as a forest is an aggregate of trees. It is the power, cognitive and active, of Īśvara, the *artifex opifexque mundi deus,* the Archimagus, or Demiurgus, who is the first emanation of Brahman. It is his power of illusory creation, the power out of which proceed all migrating souls and all that they experience in their migrations. Brahman, or Self *per se,* is changeless, but in union with Māyā becomes[3] fictitiously the basis of this baseless world, and underlies the world-fiction out of which the ever-changing figment-worlds proceed in æon after æon. From the reflection upon Māyā, the world-fiction, of Brahman, the one and only Self, proceeds the first and highest of all emanations, Īśvara, the cosmic soul, the Demiurgus. Māyā[4] thus pre-exists with Brahman, but Brahman is not thereby any the less the one and only being, in like manner as the possibility of the future tree pre-exists in the seed of the tree, without the seed becoming any the less a one and only seed. Māyā is the indifferent aggregate of all the possibilities of emanatory or derived existences, pre-existing together with Brahman, as the possibility

[1] *Viśvamāyā, anādimāyā.*

[2] *Triguṇātmikā māyā, guṇatrayasāmyam māyātattvam, sukhaduḥkhamohātmakāśeshaprapañcharūpā māyā.*

[3] *Vivartyopādāna.*

[4] *Bhāvivaṭavṛikshaśaktimad vījam svaśaktyā na sadvitīyam kathyate, tadvad brahmāpi na māyāśaktyā sadvitīyam.*

CHAP. II. of the tree pre-exists in the seed. Māyā is the ancillary associate of the Archimagus. Māyā, though unconscious, is said to energise in the evolution of the world through its proximity to the inert and impassive Brahman, as the unconscious iron is set in motion through its proximity to the loadstone. Māyā is that out of which, literally speaking, the world proceeds; it is said, by a figure of speech, to emanate from Brahman. Māyā is the literal, Brahman the figurative *upādāna*, or principle out of which all things emanate.

It is Māyā[1] that presents the manifold of experience. The world, with its apparent duality of subject and object, of external and internal orders, is the figment of this fiction, the imagination of illusion. All that presents itself to the migrating soul in its series of embodiments, lies unreally above the real; like the redness or blackness of the sky, which is seen there though the sky itself is never red or black, like the waters of a mirage, like the visions of the dreaming phantasy, like the airy fabric of a daydream, like the bubbles on the surface of a stream, like the silver seen on the shell of a pearl-oyster, like the snake that the belated wayfarer sees in a piece of rope, like the gloom that encircles the owl amidst the noonday glare. All the stir of daily life, all the feverish pleasures and pains of life after life, are the phantasmagory of a waking dream. For the soul that wakes to its own nature these things cease to be, and, what is more, have never so much as been.

Brahman and Māyā eternally co-existent.

Brahman and Māyā have co-existed from everlasting, and their association and union is eternal. Apart from Avidyā or Māyā, Brahman is purely characterless and indeterminate,[2] and is not to be regarded as the principle from which things emanate, and again, is not to be regarded as not that principle; nor is it to be affirmed to be both that principle and not that prin-

[1] *Nānātvapratyupasthāpikā 'vidyā.*
[2] Śankarāchārya on Śvetāśvatara Upanishad 1, 3.

ciple at once, nor is it to be denied to be both. Self *per se* is neither *principium* nor *principiata*. When the world is said to emanate from Brahman, we are always to understand that it proceeds, not from Brahman *per se*, but from Brahman reflected upon Māyā,[1] or fictitiously limited by the limitations of the world-fiction. Māyā, in its totality, is the limitative counterfeit of Brahman,[2] or the power of Īśvara, the Māyāvin, or Archimagus, or Demiurgus. The limitations of the illimitable Brahman are derived from this limitative counterfeit—its limitations through which it manifests itself as god, and man, and animal, and plant, and so forth. It is through this union from before all time with this inexplicable illusion, that the one and only Self presents itself in the endless plurality and diversity of transient deities, of migrating spirits, and of the worlds through which they migrate. It is through this union that the one and only Self is present in every creature, as one and the same ether is present in many water-jars, as one and the same sun is mirrored on countless sheets of water. It is through this union that the one and only Self permeates and animates the world. In the words of Śankara:[3] "The image of the sun upon a piece of water expands with the expansion, and contracts with the contraction, of the ripples on the surface; moves with the motion, and is severed by the breaking, of the ripples. The reflection of the sun thus follows the various conditions of the surface, but not so the real sun in the heavens. It is in a similar manner that the real Self is reflected upon its counterfeits, the bodies of sentient creatures, and, thus fictitiously limited, shares their growth and diminution, and other sensible modes of being. Apart

Brahman fictitiously limited by Māyā is Īśvara, and passes into seeming plurality.

[1] *Tad eva chaitanyam māyāprativimbitarūpeṇa kāraṇam bhavati.* Ānandagiri on the Muṇḍaka Upanishad. Māyā is sometimes said to reflect Brahman, and sometimes to limit Brahman fictitiously.

[2] *Upādhi.*

[3] In the introduction to his Commentary on the Śvetāśvatara Upanishad.

CHAP. II. from its various counterfeits, the Self is changeless and unvaried." The one and only Self is present in the heart of every living thing, as one and the same face may be reflected upon a succession of mirrors.[1] Such are some among the many images employed by the ancient Indian philosophers, to illustrate the presence of one spiritual essence in all the innumerable forms of living things. Others will be met with in the sequel. With almost the same imagery Plotinus speaks of the one life in all things living, like the one light shining in many houses, as if itself many, and yet one and undivided; the one life shining into and vitalising all bodies, projecting pictures of itself, like one face seen upon a multitude of mirrors. Elsewhere he says that we are one in God, and again other than God, as the solar rays are one with the sun and other than the sun. And with a like simile Fichte: "In all the forms that surround me I behold the reflection of my own being, broken up into countless diversified shapes, as the morning sun, broken in a thousand dewdrops, sparkles towards itself."

The hierarchy of emanations out of Brahman and Māyā.

Māyā, then, has fictitiously associated itself to Brahman from everlasting. In the series of æons, without beginning and without end, the forms of life have at the beginning of each æon emanated in the following hierarchic succession.

Īs'vara, the Demiurgus, or world-evolving deity, the universal soul.

First appears Īśvara, the Māyin or Māyāvin, the arch-illusionist, the world-projecting deity, himself a figment of the cosmic fiction, himself an unreality; an unreality for the philosopher intent on the one and only truth, relatively a reality for the multitude, to whom the world exists with all its possibilities of pain. The totality of illusion is the body or counterfeit presentment of the Archimagus, out of which all things emanate.[2] Illusion, the world-fiction, may be viewed

[1] *Ādarśasthamukham iti yadvat.*

[2] *Kāraṇaśarīra* = the cosmic body, the body out of which things emanate, the principle of emanation.

in its several parts in the minds of the migrating sentiencies, or in its totality as the sum of pleasures, pains, and indolences. The Demiurgus, then, is the Self with the totality of illusion as its counterfeit presentment; the Self proceeding into fictitious manifestation, as the worlds and the migrating sentiencies that pass through them. The illusion of each of these sentiencies veils from it its true nature as the one and only Self; the illusion of all sentiencies taken together veils from them all their true nature as the one and only Self. The Demiurgus is identified with the sum of sentiencies in the state of dreamless sleep. His body, the principle of emanations, as the sum of the bodies of living things in the state of dreamless sleep, is the beatific vesture.[1] The Demiurgus is one, the sentiencies are many, as a forest is one and as the trees in it are many; as a piece of water is one and as the drops of water in it are many; and the one Demiurgus and the many dreamless, sleeping sentiencies are one and the same being, viewed now as whole, and now as parts. The same Brahman, the one and only Self, is present wholly in the Demiurgus, and present wholly in each dreamless, sleeping sentiency; as the same ether, one and undivided, is present to the whole forest and present to each and every tree; or as the same sky, one and undivided, is reflected upon the whole watery surface and on each portion of that surface.

Iśvara omniscient, the giver of recompense, the internal ruler.

The Archimagus is said to be omniscient, as being the witness of all lifeless and all living forms of existence. As ruling all migrating souls, and as giving to each its dole of pleasures and pains in conformity with the retributive fatality inherent in the process of things, he is Īśvara, the lord. As setting all souls in motion, and thus acting through them, he is the actuator. As dwelling in the heart of each and every living soul, and

[1] *Ānandamayakosha*, the wrapper of the migrating soul, that consists of the undifferenced beatitude of dreamless sleep.

CHAP. II. fashioning its every mental mode, he is the internal ruler.

> "The lord of all, himself through all diffused,
> Sustains and is the life of all that live."

In this last character the Demiurgus, the highest emanation of Brahman, is described in the Bṛihadāraṇyaka Upanishad:—

"That which dwells in earth, inside the earth, and the earth knows not, whose body the earth is, which actuates the earth from within,—that is thy Self, the internal ruler, immortal.

"That which dwells in water, inside the water, and the water knows not, whose body the water is, which actuates the water from within,—that is thy Self, the internal ruler, immortal.

"That which dwells in fire, inside the fire, and the fire knows not, whose body the fire is, which actuates the fire from within,—that is thy Self, the internal ruler, immortal.

"That which dwells in air, inside the air, and the air knows not, whose body the air is, which actuates the air from within,—that is thy Self, the internal ruler, immortal.

"That which dwells in wind, inside the wind, and the wind knows not, whose body the wind is, which actuates the wind from within,—that is thy Self, the internal ruler, immortal.

"That which dwells in the sky, inside the sky, and the sky knows not, whose body the sky is, which actuates the sky from within,—that is thy Self, the internal ruler, immortal.

"That which dwells in the sun, inside the sun, and the sun knows not, whose body the sun is, which actuates the sun from within,—that is thy Self, the internal ruler, immortal.

"That which dwells in moon and stars, inside the moon and stars, and the moon and stars know not, whose body the moon and stars are, which actuates the moon and stars from within,—that is thy Self, the internal ruler, immortal.

"That which dwells in all living things, inside the living things, and all living things know not, whose body all living things are, which actuates all living things from within,—that is thy Self, the internal ruler, immortal.

"That which dwells within mind, inside the mind, and the mind knows not, whose body the mind is, which actuates the mind from within,—that is thy Self, the internal ruler, immortal.

"That which sees unseen, hears unheard, thinks unthought upon, knows unknown; that other than which there is none that sees, none that hears, none that thinks, none that knows,—that is thy Self, the internal ruler, immortal."

Is'vara not a personal God but the universal soul

It must be observed that this conception of the Demiurgus or world-projecting deity is not theistic. He is nothing else than the totality of souls in dreamless sleep, present in the heart of every living thing; himself only the first figment of the world-fiction, resolved into the characterless unity of Brahman at the close of each age of the world, and issuing out of that unity at each palingenesia in the eternal procession of the æons. He is eternal, but every migrating soul is co-eternal with him, a co-eternal and only equally fictitious emanation of the one and only Self. He can hardly be conceived to have any separate personality, apart from the souls he permeates and vivifies; and his state is not one of consciousness, but that of the pure bliss of dreamless sleep. One with the sum of living beings in that state, he is yet said to allot to each of them their portion of weal and woe, but only in accordance with their merits in prior forms of embodied existence. Īśvara is feared by the many, as the deity that retracts them into his own essence at the close of each æon, and that casts the evil-doer into

Is'vara the first figment of the world-fiction.

CHAP. II.

places of torment; but the perfect sage learns that Īśvara is unreal, and passes beyond all fear of him. Īśvara is no less unreal than the migrating soul; he is the first figment of the cosmical illusion; and both Īśvara and the soul are only so far existent as they are fictitious manifestations of the one and only Self.

Hiraṇyagarbha, the spirit of dreaming sentiencies.

The next emanation in the order of descent is Hiraṇyagarbha, Prāṇa, Sūtrātman, the Golden Germ, the Breath of Life, the Thread-spirit. This divine emanation is the totality of migrating souls in the state of dreaming sleep, the sum of the dreaming consciousness of the world. His body is the sum of the invisible bodies, the tenuous *involucra*,[1] clothed in which the soul passes from body to body in the long process of metempsychosis. These invisible bodies are made up of three vestures one upon the other, the cognitional, the sensorial, and the aërial garments of the soul. Within these, as its first and innermost garment, the soul, as one with the Archimagus, is clad with the beatific vesture already spoken of; and outermost of all it has, as we shall presently see, its fifth and last garment, the nutrimentitious vesture, the visible and tangible body of the world of sense, which is born and dies and passes back into the elements, the muddy vesture of decay. Three, then, of these five wrappers clothe[2] Hiraṇyagarbha. He is called the Thread-spirit, as stringing together all dreaming souls clothed in the invisible bodies that accompany them in their migrations, as pearls are strung upon a thread to form a necklace. He is the sum of souls that illusively identify themselves with their tenuous *involucra*. It is thus that a place is provided in the cosmical conception of the poets of the Upanishads for the Hiraṇyagarbha of the ancient Rishis,

[1] *Lingaśarīra, sūkshmaśarīra.*

[2] The five wrappers of the migrating soul are styled successively in Sanskṛit the *ānandamayakosha* (this is the *kāraṇaśarīra*); the *vijñānamayakosha*, the *manomayakosha*, the *prāṇamayakosha* (these three are the *lingaśarīra*); and the *annamayakosha* (this is the *sthūlaśarīra*).

the Golden Germ that arose in the beginning, the lord of things that are, the establisher of the earth and sky, the giver of life and breath. CHAP. II.

The third and lowest of the progressive emanations is Virāj, Vaiśvānara, Prajāpati, or Purusha. His body is the whole mundane egg, the outer shell of the visible world, or the sum of the visible and perishing bodies of migrating souls. He is identified with the totality of waking consciousness, with the sum of souls in the waking state, and the sum of their gross, visible, and tangible environments. In this divine emanation a place is provided by the poets of the Upanishads for the Purusha of the ancient Rishis, the divine being out of whom, offered up as a sacrificial victim by the gods, the Sādhyas, and the Rishis, the visible and tangible world proceeded. He is the sum of souls that illusively identify themselves with their outer bodies, and thus suffer hunger, thirst, and faintness, and all the other miseries of metempsychosis. Virāj, the spirit of waking sentiencies.

The nature of spiritual entity unmanifest and manifest, in its fourfold grades, is set forth in the following lines taken from Śankarāchārya's exposition of the Aitareya Upanishad :—

" First, there is the one and only Self, apart from all duality, in which have ceased to appear the various counterfeit presentments or fictitious bodies and environments of the world of semblances; passionless, pure, inert, peaceful, to be known by the negation of every epithet, not to be reached by any word or thought.

" Secondly, this same Self emanates in the form of the omniscient Demiurgus, whose counterfeit presentment or fictitious body is cognition in its utmost purity; who sets in motion the general undifferenced germ of the worlds, the cosmical illusion; and is styled the internal ruler, as actuating all things from within.

" Thirdly, this same Self emanates in the form of

CHAP. II. Hiraṇyagarbha, or the spirit that illusively identifies itself with the mental movements that are the germ of the passing spheres.

"Fourthly, this same Self emanates in the form of spirit in its earliest embodiment within the outer shell of things, as Virāj or Prajāpati.

"And finally, the same Self comes to be designated under the names of Agni and the other gods, in its counterfeit presentments in the form of visible fire and so forth. It is thus that Brahman assumes this and that name and form, by taking to itself a variety of fictitious bodily presentments, from a tuft of grass up to Brahmā, the highest of the deities."

Ānandagiri, in his gloss on this passage of Śankarāchārya, adds that the Self fictitiously manifests itself in human and other sentiencies, as well as in the gods, and is thus, illusively, the sum of life.

Brahman *per se*, apart from fictitious manifestation, is the Nirguṇam Brahma of Indian philosophy; that is to say, the Self free from the primordia, Self apart from pleasures, pains, and indolences, the three factors of the world-fiction, the three strands of the rope that ties the soul to the miseries of metempsychosis.

Brahman in its hierarchic emanations as Iśvara, Hiraṇyagarbha, and Virāj, is the Saguṇam Brahma or Śabalam Brahma of Indian philosophy; that is to say, the Self as fictitiously implicated in the pleasures, pains, and indolences that make up the world-fiction, and are experienced by migrating souls.

Six things without beginning.

To six things there has been no beginning: souls have been passing from body to body, through æon after æon, from eternity; the Demiurgus has co-existed with and in them from eternity; there has been a distinction between the souls and the Demiurgus from eternity; the pure intelligence, the undifferenced Self, has existed from eternity; the distinction between the Demiurgus and that Self is from eternity; Māyā, the self-feigning world-fiction, has feigned itself from everlasting, and the union of Māyā with Brahman is itself eternal. The migrating souls are nothing else than the one and only Self fictitiously limiting itself to various individual minds, these individual minds being various emanations of the cosmical illusion. Self is true; the ever-moving world is false; and the migrating souls that seem to be, and do, and suffer, are nothing else than that one and only Self, clothed in the five successive vestures or *involucra*, the beatific, the cognitional, the sensorial, the vesture of the vital airs, and the nutrimentitious vesture or visible body in the world of sense. To him that sees the truth, all these bodies and their environments will disappear, merging themselves into that fontal essence; and the Self will alone remain, a fulness of unbroken and unmingled bliss.

CHAPTER III.

THE RELEASE FROM METEMPSYCHOSIS.

"To them I may have owed another gift
Of aspect more sublime; that blessed mood
In which the burthen of the mystery,
In which the heavy and the weary weight
Of all this unintelligible world
Is lightened; that serene and blessed mood
In which the affections gently lead us on,
Until the breath of this corporeal frame,
And even the motion of our human blood
Almost suspended, we are laid asleep
In body, and become a living soul:—
While with an eye made quiet by the power
Of harmony and the deep power of joy,
We see into the life of things."—WORDSWORTH.

"Moriturus Plotinus ad Eustochium dixit, se in eo esse ut quod in se haberet divinum *πρὸς τὸ ἐν τῷ παντὶ θεῖον* adduceret."—FABRICIUS.

CHAP. III.

Re-ascent to the fontal Self.

THE sum of being, as pictured by the poets of the Upanishads, may be retraced in the regressive order, from the outermost to the innermost vesture of the soul, from the outermost to the innermost body, and beyond to the spiritual reality that alone abides for ever. The lowest grade of life is that of the soul in this visible and tangible world, passing from body to body, through sphere after sphere of being, through æon after æon. The migrating soul is the one and only Self fictitiously limiting itself to this or that individual mind; and each individual mind is nothing more than one of the innumerable emanations of the cosmical illusion. To this migration there has been no beginning, and it is hard to find the end. At every stage, above and below, it is the same wearisome journey, miseries and tainted pleasures that give place to fresh miseries, to new care, hunger, thirst, bereavement, sickness, and decay. It would be intolerable to think that this never-ceasing iteration of pains is real, for then it could not be made to disappear; but to a true insight it is not real; it is but a fiction, for it comes and goes, passes into being and passes out of being; and that alone is real that neither comes nor goes, neither passes into being nor passes out of being, but simply *is*. To be is to last,—to perdure; but what is there that lasts? There is, they say, but one thing that lasts: the light within, the light in which these pains and tainted pleasures, these shifting scenes and semblances, come and go, pass into, and pass out of being. This primordial light beyond the darkness of the world-fiction, this fontal unity of characterless being, beyond the duality of subject and object, beyond the plurality of the phantasmagoric spheres of metempsychosis, is pure being, pure thought, pure bliss. This alone it is that permeates and vitalises all things, giving light and life to all that live. It is through its connection from before all ages with Avidyā, Māyā, the self-feigning world-fiction, that this light, this Self, passes into the semblances of duality and plurality, and in the shape of innumerable living beings passes through successive spheres of transmigratory experience, as through dream after dream. To wake from his dreams, to extricate himself from metempsychosis, the sage must penetrate through the unreal into the real, must refund his personality into the impersonality of the one and only Self. The way to this is a process of purificatory virtues, that may be the work of many successive lives; a renouncement of family, home, and worldly ties; the laying aside of the five successive vestures of the soul by the repression of every feeling, every desire, and every thought; the practice of apathy, vacuity, and ecstasy. A rigorous

Purificatory virtues, renunciation, meditative abstraction, ecstatic vision, re-union.

CHAP. III. process of abstraction melts away the nutrimentitious vesture of the soul into the vesture of the vital airs, this into the sensorial vesture, this into the cognitional vesture, this into the beatific vesture of the soul in union with the Demiurgus. And after this, it is only a yet more perfect inertion and yet further abstraction that can enable him to reach the last residue of all abstraction, the light within the heart, the spiritual unity of undifferenced being. After he has stripped off the successive vestures of his soul, and has reached this last, this highest mode of being, the intuition of the Self, nothing remains but that this intuition itself, as itself a mental modification, pass away, vanishing into the pure light of characterless being; that this light, this undifferenced unity, may alone remain, the isolated, only reality. The sage to whose inner faculties this vision is present lives on in the body, till the expiry of the merits that have procured his present embodiment. At last his body falls away, and his soul re-enters the one and only Self, returning to its proper state of perfect indetermination, to abide in itself as characterless being, pure intelligence, undifferenced beatitude.

> "The one remains, the many change and pass;
> Heaven's light for ever shines, earth's shadows fly;
> Life, like a dome of many-coloured glass,
> Stains the white radiance of eternity."

The Vidvekachūḍāmaṇi quoted.

On the liberation of the sage, to use the language of the Vivekachūḍāmaṇi, all things visible melt away into the original Self, as the darkness faints and melts away before the rising sun. Its fictitiously limiting mind with all its modes has been dissolved, and the soul is the Self again; the jar is broken, and the ether that was in it is one with the one and undivided ether, from which the jar once seemed to sever it. The sage has seen the Self, and passed into oneness with it, lost like a water-drop in water. His implication in metempsychosis, and his extrication from it, have been but figments of the cosmic fiction; unreal as the snake that appears and vanishes in place of the piece of rope, to the eyes of the belated traveller. He has had life after life from time without beginning, but these were but a series of dreams. At last he is awake, and his dream-lives are nullities. In pure verity it is only the Self that ever is or has been. The world has neither come into being nor passed out of being. There has been no fatal migration of the soul, no worshipper seeking recompense or mental purity, no sage yearning after liberation, and no soul has been liberated. These things were phantasmagoric figments, a play of semblances, a darkness, an absence of light. Now the light is veiled no more, and remains a pure undifferenced light, and is in truth the only thing that ever has been, and ever is.

This is the end of the knowledge of the divine Self, the consummation of theosophy.

Liberation this life, *jîvanmukti*.

Thus liberated from metempsychosis, but still living in the body, the sage is untouched by merit and demerit, unsoiled by sinful works, uninjured by what he has done and by what he has left undone, unimplicated in his actions good or evil. Good works, no less than evil works, and equally the Demiurgus that recompenses them, belong to the unreal, to the fictitious plurality of the world of semblances. As Śankarāchārya says, in his introduction to the Śvetāśvatara Upanishad, "Gnosis once arisen needs nothing farther for the realisation of its result; it requires *subsidia* only that it may arise;" and Ānandagiri says, "The perfect sage, so long as he lives, may do good and evil as he chooses, and incur no stain; such is the efficacy of a knowledge of the Self."

How the individual soul is to recognise and recover its unity with the universal soul, and thus with the one and only Self, is taught in the following verses of the Chhāndogya Upanishad, known as the Śāṇḍilyavidyā, or doctrine of the sage Śāṇḍilya. These verses are of

CHAP. III.

very frequent citation in the works of the Vedāntic schoolmen:—

The S'āṇḍilya-vidyā, Chhāndogya Upanishad iii. 14. The soul is one with the cosmic soul and with the Self.

"All this world is the Self. It arises out of, returns into, breathes in, the Self. Let the wise man be still, and meditate upon the Self.

"The soul is made of thought, and as its thought has been in this life, such shall its nature be when it departs out of this life. The wise man, therefore, must think thus:

"The universal soul[1] is operative in the inward sense, embodied in the vital air;[2] it is the pure light, the unfailing will, the ethereal essence, out of which all creations, all desires, all sweet sounds, and all sweet tastes proceed. It pervades all things, silent and unperturbed.

"This universal soul is my soul within the heart, smaller than a grain of rice, a barleycorn, a mustard-seed, a grain of millet, or the kernel of a grain of millet. This is my soul within the heart, greater than the earth, the air, the sky, greater than these worlds.

"Out of this universal soul all creations, all desires, all sweet sounds, and all sweet tastes proceed. It permeates all things, speechless, passionless. This is my soul within the heart. This is Brahman. As soon as I depart out of this life I shall win re-union with the Self.

"He that has this faith has no more doubt. These are the words of Śāṇḍilya."

When Brahman is viewed as in union with Māyā, Brahman becomes Īśvara, the cosmic soul, the world-evolving deity; and Māyā is the cosmic body, the body of the Demiurgus Īśvara. Śāṇḍilya teaches that the soul realises and recovers its unity with the cosmic soul, and with the characterless Self beyond and above the cosmic soul, by meditative ecstasy.

[1] The universal soul is Īśvara, the Self in manifestation as the creative spirit and soul of the world, the *viśvakartṛi* and *jagadātman*.

[2] Migrating along with the invisible body or tenuous *involucrum* through a succession of visible bodies.

Renunciation, ecstasy, and the liberation of the soul are spoken of as follows in the Bṛihadāraṇyaka Upanishad:—

Renunciation, ecstasy, and liberation, as characterised in the Bṛihadāraṇyaka Upanishad.

"Invisible is the path, outspread, primeval, that I have reached, that I have discovered; the sages, they that know the Self, travel along that path to paradise, liberated after this embodiment.

"They that follow after illusion enter thick darkness; they that satisfy themselves with liturgic knowledge, a thicker darkness still.

"Those spheres are joyless, overspread with thick darkness;—to those go after death those infatuated men that have no real knowledge.

"If a man know himself, that he is this universal spirit, what can he want, what can he crave, that he should go through the feverishness of a fresh embodiment?

"He whose soul is found, is gazed upon by him, amid this wild of troubles,—he is the maker of all things, the maker of the world; the world is his, for he is the world.

"Being here, we know this, and if we did not know it, it would be a great perdition:

"They that know this become immortal, others pass on again to misery.

"When he sees this Self aright, the luminous essence, the lord of all that has been, all that shall be, there is nothing that he shrinks from.

"That outside of which, day after day, the year rolls round,—that the gods adore, as the light of lights, as length of life undying.

"That over which the five orders of living things,[1] and over which the ether is outspread,—that do I know to be myself, the universal Self,—even I the sage immortal.

"They that know the breath of the breath, the eye of the eye, the ear of the ear, the thought of the thought,

[1] The five tribes of men. See above, p. 14.

CHAP. III. —they have seen the Self primeval, that has been from all time.

"It is to be seen only with the mind: there is nothing in it that is manifold.

"From death to death he goes who looks on this as manifold.

"It is to be seen in one way only, it is indemonstrable, immutable. The Self is unsullied, beyond the expanse,[1] unborn, infinite, imperishable.

"Let the patient Brahman know that, and learn wisdom. Let him not learn many words,[2] for that is a weariness of the voice.

"This is indeed the great unborn Self. This has the form of conscious life, amidst the vital airs, dwelling in the ether in the heart; the ruler of all things, lord of all things, king of all things. It becomes no greater by good works, no less by evil works. This is the lord of all, the lord of living things, the upholder of living things. This is the bridge that spans the spheres, that they may not fall the one into the other. This it is that the Brahmans seek after in reciting the Veda.

"By sacrifice, by almsgiving, by self-inflicted pains, by fasting, if he learns this, a man becomes a quietist. This it is that the holy mendicants long for, in setting out upon their wanderings. Yearning after this it was that the wise men of old desired no offspring, saying, What have we to do with children, we to whom belongs this Self, this spiritual sphere? They arose and forsook the desire of children, of wealth, of worldly existence, and set out upon their life of wandering. For the wish for children is the wish for wealth, and the wish for wealth is the wish for worldly existence, and there are both of these desires.

"This same Self is not this, not that: it is impal-

[1] The expanse is a synonym for Māyā, the self-feigning world-fiction.

[2] Words = hymns and liturgic formulas.

pable, for it cannot be handled; undecaying, for it wastes not away; unattached, for it has no ties; invulnerable, for it is not hurt by the sword or slain. Things done and things left undone cross not over to it. It passes beyond both the thought that it has done evil, and the thought that it has done good. That which it has done, and that which it has failed to do, afflict it not. CHAP. III.

"Therefore it has been said in a sacred verse: This, the eternal greatness of the sage that knows Brahman, becomes not greater by works, and becomes not lesser. Let him learn the nature of that greatness. He that knows it is no longer sullied by evil acts. Checking his senses, quiescent, passionless, ready to suffer all things, fixed in ecstasy, he sees within himself the Self, he sees the universal soul. Imperfection crosses not over to him, he crosses beyond imperfection, he burns up all his imperfections. He that knows Brahman becomes free from imperfections, free from doubt, ensphered in Self.

"This same great unborn Self is undecaying, undying, imperishable, beyond all fear. The Self is beyond all fear. He that knows this becomes the Self beyond all fear."

The perfect sage is subject to no moral law.

The imperfections beyond which the sage of perfect insight, living in the body but already free from further transmigration, has passed, are merit and demerit, the fruits of good and evil works, which serve alike only to prolong metempsychosis. Good works as well as evil are, from the higher point of view, an evil to be shunned, as they protract the migrations of the soul. It is not exertion, but inertion, and a perfect inertion, that is the path to liberation. The sage is beyond all fear, as already one with the one and only Self, and free from the fear of misery in new embodiments. He may, as we have seen that Ānandagiri says, do good and evil for the rest of his days, as he pleases, and

CHAP. III. incur no stain. Everything that he has done and everything that he is doing, all his works, save only those that are resulting in his experiences in his present body, are burnt up in the fire of spiritual intuition. And therefore in the Taittirīya Upanishad we read, "The thought no longer tortures him, What good have I left undone, what evil done?" And in another passage of the Bṛihadāraṇyaka: "Here the thief is a thief no more, the Chaṇḍāla[1] a Chaṇḍāla no more, the Paulkasa[1] no more a Paulkasa, the sacred mendicant no more a sacred mendicant: they are no longer followed by good works, they are no longer followed by evil works. For at last the sage has passed through all the sorrows of his heart." At the height reached by the self-tormenting sage, at last arrived at insight into and re-union with the one and only Self, there is no longer any distinction of personality; and at this height of insight and re-union, saint and sinner, the holy Brāhman and the impure alien and the degraded outcast, are all one in the unity of characterless being. The objection is obvious that this doctrine is immoral, and the objection has been foreseen and met. The reply is that the theosophist has had to go through a process of initiatory virtues, in order to purify his mind for the quest of reality and escape from further misery, and that after he has attained his end, and is one with the one and only Self, these virtues will adhere to him as habits, so far as others are concerned, for to himself they are unrealities like all things else excepting Brahman. This is the reply of Nṛisimhasarasvatī towards the end of the Subodhinī, an exposition of the Vedāntasāra.

But will not therefore do evil, for the purificatory virtues adhere to him as habits.

"Some one may urge: It will not surely follow from this that the living yet liberated sage may act as he chooses. We cannot allow this to be urged. It cannot be denied that the perfect sage may act as he

[1] Degraded indigenes or outcasts from the Hindu pale.

pleases, in the presence of such texts, traditions, and arguments as the following:—'Not by killing his mother, nor by killing his father.' 'He that does not mistake not-Self for Self, whose inner vision is unsullied,—he, though he kills these people, neither kills them nor is killed.' 'He that knows the truth is sullied neither by good actions nor by evil actions.' 'If he sees the unity of all things, he is unaffected alike whether he offer a hundred horse-sacrifices or kill hundreds of holy Brāhmans.' 'Sages act in various ways, good and bad, through the influence of the acts of former lives now at work in shaping their acts and their experiences in their present embodiment.' If then you say that we teach that a perfect sage may do what he likes, it is true we do teach this, but as these texts are only eulogistic of the liberated sage, it is not intended that he should act at random. As a great teacher says, 'Ignorance arises from evil-doing, and wilful action from ignorance: how can this wilful action, this doing as one likes, result from good works, when the good works pass away?' The preliminary acquirements of the aspirant to extrication from metempsychosis, his humility, sincerity, tenderness towards every form of sentient life, stick to him like so many ornaments, even after the rise of this spiritual intuition."

The mystic syllable Om as an image of Brahman.

The repetition of the sacred syllable Om is said to conduct the slow aspirant to a gradual and progressive liberation from metempsychosis. Om is a solemn affirmation, Yes. It is regarded by the Indian sages as made up of the three letters A, U, M, in euphonic combination. This mystic syllable Om is said to be the nearest similitude of Brahman;[1] it is an image of the Self, as the black ammonite serves instead of an image of Vishṇu.[2] It is said to include all speech, and as names are in some way one and the same as the things they name, it is one with all things, one with Brahman. In

[1] *Brahmaṇo nedishṭham pratīkam.*

[2] *Sālagrāma.*

CHAP. III. the Praśna Upanishad the great teacher Pippalāda says, "This syllable Om is the higher and the lower Brahman." That is to say, Om is Brahman as unconditioned, and Brahman in fictitious manifestation as the Demiurgus. In their exposition of this passage the scholiasts say that the Self, as characterless and supersensible, cannot be made an object to the thinking faculty, unless this faculty be previously purified by meditation on the mystic Om, taken and devoutly identified with Brahman, as a man may take an image and devoutly identify it with Vishṇu. Upon the mind thus purified the Self shines of itself, undifferenced. The following verses of the Taittirīya Upanishad are an invocation of this sacred utterance:—

Invocation of OM in the Taittirīya Upanishad.

"May that Indra, Om, that is the highest thing in the Vedas, that is all that is immortal, above the immortality of the Vedas, may that divine being strengthen me with wisdom.

"Let me, O god, become a holder of immortality. Let my body become able, my tongue mellifluous. Let me hear much with my ears. Thou art the sheath of Brahman, only obscured by earthly wisdom. Preserve in me what I have heard. That prosperity which brings, and adds, and quickly provides raiment and cattle and meat and drink at all times,—that prosperity bring thou to me. Wealth woolly with flocks: Svāhā.[1] Let sacred students come to me: Svāhā. Let sacred students repair to me: Svāhā. Let me become a glory among men: Svāhā. O holy one, let me enter into thee: Svāhā. In thee, with thy thousand branches, let me become pure: Svāhā.

"As the waters flow downwards, as the months pass away into the year, even so let the sacred students come to me. O maker, let them come in from every side: Svāhā. Thou art the refuge. Give me thy light. Receive me into thyself."

[1] *Svāhā* is an exclamation made in invocations of the deities.

The mystic import of Om, and the nature of the three states of the soul, above which the aspirant to extrication is to rise, and the fourth or undifferenced state of the Self one and the same in all souls, into which he is to rise, are set forth in the Māṇḍūkya Upanishad, one of the Upanishads of the Atharvaveda. This Upanishad is as follows:—

The Māṇḍūkya Upanishad. The import of OM. The four states of the soul, in waking, dreaming, dreamless sleep, and in union with pure Self.

"OM. This syllable is all. Its interpretation is that which has been, that which is, and that which is to be. All is Om, and only Om, and whatever is beyond trinal time is Om, and only Om.

"For all this world is Brahman, this Self is Brahman, and this same Self has four quarters.

The waking state.

"The first quarter is the soul in the waking state, externally cognitive, with seven members, with nineteen inlets, with fruition of the sensible, the spirit of waking souls, Vaiśvānara."

In the ascending order the first state of the Self, after it has passed into a fictitious plurality of migrating souls, is its waking state in the gross body, in which it stands face to face with outward things. Vaiśvānara or Purusha, the spirit that permeates all living bodies, is said to have seven members; the sky is his head, the sun is his eye, the air is his breath, the ethereal expanse is his body, the food-grains are his bladder, the earth is his feet, the sacrificial fire is his mouth. The nineteen inlets of the waking soul are the five organs of sense, the five organs of motion, the five vital airs,[1] the common sensory, the intellect, the self-assertive, and the memorial faculties. The individual embodied

[1] The five organs of sense are those of hearing, touch, sight, taste, and smell. The five organs of motion are those of speech, handling, locomotion, excretion, and generation. The five vital airs are that of respiration, the descending, the permeating, the ascending, and the assimilative vital airs. The four internal organs are the common sensory, *manas*; the intellect, *buddhi*; the self-assertive, *ahankāra*; and the memorial, *chitta*. These organs are made up of the elements as yet in a supersensible condition, the elements becoming sensible only after a process of concretion, technically known as quintuplication, *panchīkaraṇa*.

CHAP. III. soul is termed Viśva, the sum of embodied souls Vaiśvānara.

The dreaming state. "The second quarter is the soul in the dreaming state, with seven members, with nineteen inlets, with fruition of the ideal,—the dreaming spirit."

In the dreaming state, Śankarāchārya says, the senses are at rest, but the common sensory proceeds to work, and the images, painted upon it like pictures on a canvas, simulate the outward objects of the waking experiences. The common sensory is set in motion in this way by the illusion, the desires, and the retributive fatality, which cling to the soul through all its migrations. The individual sleeping soul is styled Taijasa, the sum of sleeping souls in their invisible bodies is Hiraṇyagarbha.

The state of dreamless sleep. "Dreamless sleep is that state in which the sleeper desires no desire and sees no dream. The third quarter is the soul in the state of dreamless sleep, being one in itself, a mass of cognition, pre-eminent in bliss, with fruition of beatitude, having thought as its inlet, and of transcendent knowledge."

In dreamless sleep the soul is said to be one in itself, the unreal duality of the waking and the dreaming consciousness having melted away into unity. The soul is, in this state, also said to be a mass of cognition, as it for the time reverts to its proper nature as undifferenced thought. All things become one, as in a dark night the whole outlook is one indistinguishable blur. The soul is now pre-eminent in bliss, as no longer exposed to the varied miseries that arise from the fictitious semblances of duality, yet it is not yet pure bliss itself, for the state of dreamless sleep is not abiding. The individual soul in this state is styled Prājña, transcendent in knowledge, and the sum of such souls is Īśvara, the arch-illusionist, the world-projecting deity. The *involucrum* of the soul at this stage is the beatific vesture, and the counterfeit presentment or body of

Īśvara is the body out of which all things emanate, the cosmical illusion. The soul is not yet at rest. As Ānandagiri says, "It cannot be admitted that in this dreamless sleep the transcendently cognitive soul is in perfect and unmingled bliss, for it is still connected with the world-fiction. If it were not so, the sleeper would be already released from further migration, and he could not rise up again as he does to fresh experiences." The soul is not at rest till it has reached its final extrication from metempsychosis. To return to the Māṇḍūkya.

"This Self is the lord of all, this the internal ruler, this the source of all things; this is that out of which all things proceed, and into which they shall pass back again.

The state of the soul as one with pure Self.

"Neither internally cognitive nor externally cognitive, nor cognitive both without and within; not a mass of cognition, neither cognitive nor incognitive, invisible, intangible, characterless, unthinkable, unspeakable; to be reached only by insight into the oneness of all spirits; that into which the world passes away, changeless, blessed, above duality;—such do they hold the fourth to be. That is Self. That is to be known."

To cite a few remarks of the scholiasts. The pure Self, the fourth and only real entity, is that in the place of which the fictitious world presents itself to the uninitiated, as the fictitious serpent presents itself in place of a piece of rope to the belated wayfarer. There is something that underlies every such figment; it is the sand of the desert that is overspread by the waters of the mirage, it is the shell that is fictitiously replaced by seeming silver, it is a distant post that in the dusk is mistaken for a man, and so on. Thus illusion everywhere points to a reality beyond itself. The three so-called quarters of Brahman previously spoken of, only fictitiously present themselves in place of the sole

CHAP. III.

reality, the fourth. They are principles that emanate, and out of which other principles emanate. Māyā, the world-fiction, is the seed, and its figments, the elements and elemental products, are the growing world-tree. The fourth, the Self, does not emanate from anything, nor does anything (save fictitiously) emanate from it; it is neither seed nor tree. It is unthinkable and unspeakable, to be enounced only in negations.[1] It is absolute. The world does not emanate from, but fictitiously presents itself in place of, Brahman.

Literal analysis of OM.

"This same Self is exhibited in the mystic syllable. Om is exhibited in letters. The quarters are the letters, and the letters are the quarters,—the letter A, the letter U, and the letter M.

"The first letter, the letter A, is Vaiśvānara, the spirit of waking souls in the waking world, because it permeates all utterance, because it has a beginning. He that knows this attains to all desires, and becomes the first of all men.

"The second letter, the letter U, is Taijasa, the spirit of dreaming souls in the world of dreams, because this letter is more excellent, or because it is the intermediate letter. He that knows this elevates the train of his ideas, becomes passionless; there is none in his family that knows not Brahman.

"The third letter, the letter M, is Prājña, the spirit of sleeping and undreaming souls, because it comprehends the other two, because the other two proceed out of it. He that knows this comprehends all things, and becomes the source of things.

"The fourth is not a letter, but the whole syllable Om, unknowable, unspeakable, into which the whole world passes away, blessed, above duality. He himself by himself enters into the Self,—he that knows this, that knows this."[2]

[1] *Nishedhadvāraiva tannirdeśaḥ sambhavati*, Ānandagiri.

[2] The repetition here as elsewhere marks the close of the Upanishad.

The doctrine of the five vestures of the soul as taught in the Taittirīya Upanishad.

The Māṇḍūkya Upanishad is thus an exposition of the significance of the sacred syllable Om, of the three unreal states, and of the one real state of Brahman. The several vestures or *involucra* of the migrating souls in the ascending order; the mode in which they and their spheres of migration emanated out of Brahman overspread with Māyā; and the scale of beatitudes by which the soul may re-ascend to its fontal essence, the one and only Self, are the themes of the second and third sections, the Brahmānandavallī and the Bhṛiguvallī of the Taittirīya Upanishad. This Upanishad belongs, as its name imports, to the so-called Black Recension of the Yajurveda. From the first section, the Śikshāvallī, treating of the initiation and purification of the aspirant to release from metempsychosis, the hymn to Om has been already presented to the reader. The scale of beatitudes the soul may mount by, is given in the same words also in the Bṛihadāraṇyaka Upanishad. The second and third sections of the Taittirīya are not so engaging and impressive as many portions of the Upanishads are; but as they contain many of the texts of most frequent occurrence in the records of Indian philosophy, a translation is subjoined. One of these texts occurs in the opening lines of the second section, the Brahmānandavallī, which is as follows:—

The Brahmānandavallī, the second section of the Taittirīya Upanishad.

"Hari.[1] OM. May he preserve us both, may he reward us both. May we put forth our strength together, and may that which we recite be efficacious. May we never feel enmity against each other. OM. Peace, peace, peace."

This is an invocation on the part of the teacher and his disciple, to remove any possible obstacles to the communication and acquisition of the traditional science of Brahman. The preserver and recompenser is the universal soul or Demiurgus.

"He that knows Brahman attains the ultimate reality.

[1] Hari is a name of Vishṇu.

CHAP. III. Therefore this sacred verse has been pronounced: Truth, knowledge, infinite, is Brahman. He that knows this Self seated in the cavity in the highest ether, has fruition of all desires at one and the same moment by means of the omniscient Self."

The Self is within the mind, inside the heart of every living thing.

The scholiasts tell us that the word ether is here another name for the world-fiction, as it is also in the text of the Bṛihadāraṇyaka: "Over this imperishable principle the ethereal expanse is woven warp and woof." The cavity is the mind, so called because knowledge, the subject knowing and the thing known, are contained in it, or because implication in metempsychosis and extrication from it depend upon it. The migrating soul is nothing else than the one and only Self fictitiously limiting itself to this or that individual mind; every individual mind being, equally with its successive environments, an emanation of the cosmical illusion. He that sees through the illusion the Self within his mind, enters into the fulness of undifferenced beatitude. He has every form of happiness at one and the same moment, not a succession of pleasures through this or that avenue of sense; such pleasures are mere products of the retributive fatality that prolongs the migration of the soul. The highest aim of all is to pass beyond such experiences to the further shore of union with Brahman, the fulness of bliss; to refund the personality of the migrating soul into the impersonality of the Self exempt from the experiences of metempsychosis. The aspirant to release from misery must learn that he and all other individuals are but particular and local manifestations of the universal soul; and that the universal soul, the Jagadātman, is the one and only Self veiled beneath the self-feigning world-fiction, and thus conscious of a seeming twofold order of subjects and objects. The world-fiction is made up of the sum of pleasures, pains, and indolences, the three *primordia rerum* of Indian cosmology. As soon as he

CHAP. III.

The soul is the Self, but does not know itself to be the Self.

recognises his true nature he shall repossess it, and on the rise of spiritual intuition the world of semblances shall dissolve and pass away. The soul is already the characterless being, the pure thought, the undifferenced bliss—how can it be said to regain it, to recover that which it already is? It recovers it by seeing it, by knowing it. In its everyday life the soul has lost itself by identifying itself with what it is not, with its temporal vestures, its fictitious envelopments. Nṛisimhasarasvatī teaches us that the soul seeking to find itself in the impersonal unity of the Self, is like a man looking for a necklace he thinks that he has lost and suffers from the loss of, the necklace being all the time about his neck. Terrified at the miseries that await his soul in its migrations, he is only trembling at his own shadow, for these miseries are unreal. His affliction ceases as soon as he learns what he truly is; his fears cease as soon as he learns the unreality of everything that only seems to be. To the highest point of view won by abstraction pursued to its last limit, the implication of the soul, and its release, in and from metempsychosis, are unreal, mere figments of the cosmic fiction. To return to the text:—

Procession of the five elements, and their quintuplication or progressive concretion.

"Out of this same Self the ether rose, from ether air, from air fire, from fire water, from water earth, from earth plants, from plants food, from food the germ of life, from the germ of life man. This is man as made up of the extractive matter of food."

Such are the five elements in their progressive concretion as they emanate from Brahman overspread with Māyā. Ether comes first with its single property of sound; it is the soniferous element, and in it all finite things exist. From ether the atmosphere proceeds, with the property of ether and with a superadded property of its own, namely, tangibility. Thus air has two properties. From air comes fire with the properties of ether and air, sound and tangibility, and with a superadded property of its own, namely, colour. Thus fire has three properties. From fire proceeds water with the properties of ether, air, and fire, and with a superadded property of its own, namely, taste. Thus water has four properties. From water emanates earth with the properties of ether, air, fire, and water, and with a superadded property of its own, namely, odour. Thus earth has five properties. It is Brahman as illusively overspread with Māyā, that manifests itself in this progressive concretion of the elements and of elemental things; and it is into Brahman that by a regressive process of abstraction the whole series may be made to disappear. Man in his visible and earthly body is made up of the materials of food. Man here stands for the whole scale of animal life, as being the highest representative, and alone capable of the worship of the gods and the knowledge of the sole reality that is veiled beneath the world. The earthly body is the first of the five vestures of the soul in order of ascent to the fontal essence: it is the nutrimentitious *involucrum.* Each lower is to be resolved into each higher garment of the soul, by a progressive insight into the fictitious nature of them all, till the aspirant passes through the last, the so-called beatific vesture, to the Self within. We are told that he is to strip every wrapper off himself one by one, as he might peel off the successive shells of a grain of rice. The several portions of the outermost shell of the soul, the earthly body, are next described in grotesque similitude to the parts of a bird:—

The first and outermost vesture of the soul is the earthly body.

"Of this, this head is the head, this right arm is the right wing, this left arm the left wing, this trunk is the body, this nether part the tail, the prop. Therefore there is this memorial verse: It is food that living creatures spring from, all they that dwell upon the earth. They live by food, and at the last they pass into food again, for food is the earliest of creatures. Therefore food is called the panacea." CHAP. III.

The body dies and restores its elements to the earth, out of which they reappear in fresh vegetable forms, to supply food again to animals and men—an Indian statement of the circulation of matter.

> "See dying vegetables life sustain,
> See life dissolving vegetate again :
> All forms that perish other forms supply,
> By turns we catch the vital breath and die ;—
> Like bubbles, on the sea of matter borne,
> They rise and break, and to that sea return."

Food, Śankarāchārya says, is called the panacea, as quenching the burning of the body,[1] that is, as repairing the waste of the system. It is a standing rule of Indian philosophy that everything passes back into that out of which it came. The body came out of, was made out of food, and it passes back into the form of food. To proceed with the text. Every item of knowledge is promised its proportionate reward, and so we read :—

"They that meditate upon food as Brahman obtain all kinds of food. For food is the earliest of created things, and it is called the panacea. From food all creatures are born, and after birth they grow by food. It is eaten by them, and it eats them, and therefore it is called food."

Within the earthly body is the invisible body that clothes the soul throughout its migrations.

Animals are said to be eaten by food, in one of the rude metaphors so frequent in the Upanishads, because the elements of their bodies after dissolution enter into the forms of vegetable life. The aspirant is now supposed to have seen into the unreality of the food-made body, and to have made it to disappear by an effort of abstraction. He is now called upon to dissolve the vesture next within, the so-called vesture of the vital

[1] *Sarvaushadham, sarvaprāṇināṃ dehadāhapraśamanam annam uchyate.*

CHAP. III.

airs. This vesture is invisible, and one of the three factors of the invisible migrating body, the tenuous *involucrum*, the other two being the sensorial and the cognitional vestures. The body has been got rid of, the vesture of vital airs must next be put away.

The second vesture, the vesture of the vital airs.

"Within this same body made of the extractive matter of food, there is another and interior body, made of the vital airs, and with that the outer body is filled up. This interior body is also in the shape of man, fashioned after the human shape of the outer body. Of this interior body the breath is the head, the pervading air is the right wing, the descending air is the left wing, ether is the trunk, and earth is the tail, the prop. Therefore there is this memorial verse: It is breath that gods breathe, and men, and cattle, for the breath is the life of living things. Therefore it is called the life of all. They that meditate upon breath as Brahman live the full life of man. This body of vital air is embodied within the food-made body."

Animals, and men, and gods live in the outer body by virtue of an inner body made of the breath of life. To this inner body there is another, the sensorial body, which fills it up; to that another, the cognitional; to that another, the beatific. They are all alike permeated and animated by the universal Self, their true being, everlasting, unchanging, beyond the five vestures. Meditation upon the vesture of vital air is rewarded with length of life, according to the maxim that the votary is assimilated to that manifestation under which he meditates upon the Self. This second wrapper being opened and laid aside by meditative abstraction, the sage proceeds to the third or sensorial vesture of his soul.

The third vesture, the vesture of the common sensory.

"Within this same body of the airs of life there is another inner body made of the common sensory, and with this the vesture of the vital airs is filled. This also is in the shape of man, fashioned after the human shape of the vesture of vital airs. Of this sensorial body the Yajush is the head, the Ṛik is the right wing, the Sāman the left wing, the Brāhmaṇas the trunk, and the Atharvāngirasa the tail, the prop. Therefore there is this memorial verse: From which words turn back with the thinking faculty, not reaching it; he that knows the bliss of the Self is for ever free from fear. This sensorial body is embodied in the body of vital airs."

After stripping off this wrapper in his quest of the reality hidden within, the aspirant proceeds to the fourth vesture of the migrating soul, its garment of intellect or cognition.

The fourth vesture, the mental or cognitional vesture.

"Within this same sensorial body there is another interior body, the cognitional body, and with this the sensorial body is filled. This also is in the shape of man, fashioned after the human shape of the sensorial vesture. Of this cognitional body faith is the head, justice the right wing, truth the left wing, ecstasy the trunk, the intellect the tail, the prop. Therefore there is this memorial verse: It is knowledge that lays out the sacrifice and performs the rites. All the gods meditate upon knowledge as the earliest manifestation of the Self. If a man learn that knowledge is the Self, and swerves not from that, he has fruition of all desires after leaving his imperfections in the body. This same cognitional vesture is embodied in the sensorial body."

The aspirant, after laying aside the first wrapper, is free from the body; after laying aside the second, third, and fourth, he is free from the invisible body, the tenuous *involucrum*, which clothes the soul in its migration from body to body. Passing beyond the visible and the invisible body, he arrives at the last vesture of the spirit, the beatific *involucrum*, that clothes the sleeping but undreaming soul.

"Within this same cognitional body there is another,

CHAP. III.

The fifth and innermost vesture, the vesture of beatitude. This clothes the soul in its third state, the state of dreamless sleep.

an inner body, the blissful body, and with this the cognitional body is filled. This also is in the shape of man, fashioned after the human shape of the cognitional body. Of this blissful vesture tenderness is the head, joy is the right wing, rejoicing the left wing, bliss the trunk, and Brahman is the tail, the prop. Therefore there is this memorial verse: If a man think that the Self is not, he becomes as if he were not: if he knows that the Self is, then they know that he is indeed. This same blissful vesture is embodied in the cognitional body."

This blissful vesture of the soul reposing in dreamless sleep is not Brahman, but it has Brahman beneath it as its prop or basis. In this vesture the soul that sleeps without dreaming is for the time at one with Brahman, and all the duality projected by illusion is for the time at an end in the pure unity of the Self. This is the last vesture to be laid aside in order to reach the ultimate truth within.

So far the doctrine of the five vestures of the migrating soul[1] has been propounded in the text of this Upanishad. A similar tenet makes its appearance in the philosophy of the neo-Platonists. Thus Proclus teaches that even before it comes into the world the soul must have animated a body, just as the dæmons and deities are embodied souls. This body is immaterial and ethereal, and emanates, like the soul itself, out of the Demiurgus. Proclus places between this immaterial body and the earthly body a series of other *involucra*, which come with it into the world, clothe it after death, and accompany it in its migrations so long as it remains in the phenomenal order of things.

The Brahmānandavallī proceeds to represent the disciple as asking his teacher who it is that is to attain to re-union with the one and only Self. The emanation of elements and elemental things from

[1] *Panchakoshavidyā.*

Brahman and Māyā, and the five wrappers of the soul, are matters that relate to the ordinary man and to the sage alike: is the re-union with the fontal essence open to both alike? The text proceeds:—

"After this arise the questions: Does a man without knowledge go after death to that veritable world? or is it only he that has knowledge, that has fruition of that veritable world?"

The sequel of the Upanishad is the reply to these questions. It is he only that surmounts the general illusion and sees the Self within by spiritual intuition, that shall pass into the Self never to return. The text first speaks of the creation of the world at the opening of each æon in the infinite series of æons, by the fictitiously-conditioned Brahman,[1] the cosmic soul, or Archimagus.

Brahman becomes Īśvara, and passes into seeming plurality.

"He desired: Let me become many, let me pass into plurality.. He performed self-torture, and having performed that self-torture, projected out of himself all this world, whatever is."

The notion of the creative action of the Demiurgus here exhibited, is the same as that in the Nāsadīyasūkta, Ṛigveda, x. 129, presented to the reader in the first chapter of this work. As the Indian scholiasts say that the words, "It was not entity, nor was it non-entity," in that hymn refer to Māyā, so they also hold that "the one that was void, covered with nothingness," which "developed itself by the power of self-torture," is Brahman in its earliest manifestation, the illusory creator, or Demiurgus, or soul of the universe. The passing of Brahman into the fictitious plurality of the phenomenal world, is frequently spoken of in the Upanishads as the self-explication of Brahman under

[1] We must be cautious not to refer what is predicable only of Īśvara to Brahman *per se*. Īśvara, the Demiurgus or Archimagus, is Brahman fictitiously associated with Māyā, and thus the fictitious creator of the fictitious world.

 names and colours, that is to say, its manifestation under visible and nameable aspects.[1] Brahman, the one and only Self, when mirrored upon Māyā, the world-fiction, is that out of which the world emanates.[2] The desires of this Demiurgus are the emanations of the world-fiction.[3] "His self-torture is a figurative expression for his prevision of the world that is to be; and after this prevision he projects out of himself the world as it is to be experienced by migrating souls, waking, dreaming, or in dreamless sleep, in space and time, in name and colour,—a world that is suitable to the residuary influence of the works of those souls in the last æon." For it must always be remembered that the series of worlds is without beginning, and that every genesis is a palingenesia. To proceed with the text:—

"Having evolved that world, he entered into it, and having entered it, he became the limited and the unlimited, the definite and the indefinite, the receptacle and not the receptacle, the living and the lifeless, the true and the false; he became the true, for whatever is they call the true. Therefore there is this memorial verse: Non-existent was this in the beginning, from that the existent proceeded. That made itself, and therefore it is called self-made or holy.[4] He is taste, for on receiving taste a man becomes blissful. For who could live, who could breathe if in this ether there were not bliss? For he gives bliss; for when a man finds a safe footing in this invisible, incorporeal, undefinable, ultimate principle, he arrives beyond all fear; but when he admits even the smallest difference in that principle, fear comes upon him. That very principle is a fear to the sage that views such difference. Accordingly there is this memorial verse: In awe of

[1] *Nāmarūpavyākaraṇa.*

[2] *Māyāprativimbitam brahma jagataḥ kāraṇam*, Ānandagiri.

[3] Śankarāchārya's Commentary on the Taittirīya Upanishad.

[4] *Sukṛita.*

this the wind blows, in awe of this the sun rises; in awe of this speed Agni and Indra, and the Death-god speeds besides those other four."

The universal soul enters into the ether in the heart of every living thing, and there lodges in fictitious limitation to each individual mind, like the ether one and undivided in every jar and other hollow thing, or like the one sun reflected upon every piece of water. Thus lodged, it is many in the many that see, that hear, that think, that know. It is the life of all. In saying that this was non-existent in the beginning, the text does not deny that Brahman existed in the beginning, but only that it existed in the fictitious modes of the phantasmagoric world. The text now presents the scale of beatitudes in human and divine embodiments, through which the migrating soul may remount on its passage to the fontal unity of Self.

The scale of beatitudes that may be ascended by the sage.

"There is the following computation of beatitude: Let there be a youth, a good youth, versed in the Veda, an able teacher, hale and strong, and let the whole earth, full of wealth, belong to him. This is one human bliss. A hundred of these human beatitudes are the one bliss of the man that has become a Gandharva, and also of a sage learned in the Veda and unstricken with desire. A hundred of these beatitudes of the man that has become a Gandharva, are the one bliss of the divine Gandharvas, and also of a sage learned in the Veda and unstricken with desire. A hundred of these beatitudes of the divine Gandharvas, are the one bliss of the forefathers of the tribes in their long-lasting sphere, and also of a sage learned in the Veda and unstricken with desire. A hundred of these beatitudes of the forefathers in their long-lasting sphere, are the one bliss of those born as gods in the sphere of the gods, and also of a sage learned in the Veda and unstricken with desire. A hundred of these beatitudes of those born as gods in the sphere of

CHAP. III. the gods, is the one bliss of those that have become gods, having gone to the gods by means of sacrifice, and also of a sage learned in the Veda and unstricken with desire. A hundred of these beatitudes of those that have become gods, is one bliss of the gods themselves, and also of a sage learned in the Veda and unstricken with desire. A hundred of these beatitudes of the gods is the one bliss of Indra, and also of a sage learned in the Veda and unstricken with desire. A hundred of these beatitudes of Indra is the one bliss of Bṛihaspati,[1] and also of a sage learned in the Veda and unstricken with desire. A hundred of these beatitudes of Bṛihaspati is the one bliss of Prajāpati,[2] and also of a sage learned in the Veda and unstricken with desire. A hundred of these beatitudes of Prajāpati is the one bliss of Brahmā,[3] and also of the sage learned in the Veda and unstricken with desire. It is the same universal soul[4] that is in the soul and that is in the sun.

"He that knows this turns his back upon the world, passes through this food-made body, passes through this body of the vital airs, passes through this sensorial body, passes through this cognitional body, and passes through this beatific body. Therefore there is this memorial verse: It is the Self from which words turn back with the mind, not reaching it; he that knows the bliss of the Self no longer fears anything. He is no longer tortured with the thought, What good thing have I left undone, what evil have I done? When he knows this, these two, the good and the evil, strengthen his spirit, for both are only Self.[5] These two only strengthen his spirit when he knows this. Such is the mystic doctrine."

[1] The spiritual teacher of the gods.

[2] Prajāpati is the same as Purusha, Virāj, or Vaiśvānara.

[3] Brahmā is Hiraṇyagarbha.

[4] The Demiurgus.

[5] That is, the good and the evil things that he has done are now seen by him to have been only fictitious manifestations of the one and only Self.

CHAP. III.

The aspirant on his way to liberation passes through and beyond all finite and local phases of bliss, into the pure, undifferenced beatitude, in which there is no longer the distinction of subject and object. He enters into the beatitude beyond duality; and good and evil for him have lost their sting, the power of giving rise to the miseries of fresh embodiments. The Bhṛiguvallī opens and closes with the same invocation as that prefixed to the Brahmānandavallī. It treats of self-torture and of meditation on the five wrappers of the soul, as subsidiary to the knowledge of Brahman.

The Bhṛiguvallī, the third section of the Taittirīya Upanishad.

"Hari. OM. May he preserve us both, may he reward us both. May we put forth our strength together, and may what we recite be efficacious. May we never feel enmity against each other. OM. Peace, peace, peace.

"Bhṛigu, the son of Varuṇa, approached his father and said, Sir, teach me about Brahman. His father said this to him: Food, breath, eye, ear, the thinking organ, speech."

Varuṇa is said to be here enumerating the several avenues to the knowledge of Brahman, these being food, *i.e.*, the outer body, the breath within, and within that the organs of sense and motion, which belong to the cognitional and sensorial vestures of the soul.

First step to the knowledge of Brahman. The earthly body is Brahman.

"And again he said to him: Seek to know that out of which these living things come forth, by which they live when they have come forth, and into which they pass again and re-enter: that is Brahman. Bhṛigu practised self-suppression, and upon performing it perceived that food is Brahman, in that all these living things arise from food, live by food when they have arisen, and pass back into and re-enter food.

Second step. The vital air is Brahman.

"After learning this he came again to his father Varuṇa and said, Sir, teach me about Brahman. He said to him, Seek to know Brahman by self-suppression: self-suppression is Brahman. He practised self-

CHAP. III.

suppression, and upon performing it perceived that vital air is Brahman, inasmuch as all these living things proceed from vital air, live by vital air, and pass back and re-enter vital air."

The self-torture[1] or self-suppression prescribed as introductory to the knowledge of Brahman, is a prolonged effort to annul the individual consciousness, to put away sense and thought, desire and will. It consists in the fixation of the muscles, the senses, and the intellect, with a view to riveting the senses and the thought upon one single object.

Third step. The common sensory is Brahman.

"Upon learning this he again came to his father Varuṇa and said, Sir, teach me about Brahman. He said to him, Seek the knowledge of Brahman by self-suppression: self-suppression is Brahman. He practised self-suppression, and on practising it learned that the common sensory is Brahman, inasmuch as all these living things issue out of, live by, and return into the common sensory.

Fourth step. The mind is Brahman.

"After learning this he again came to his father Varuṇa and said, Sir, teach me about Brahman. He said to him, Seek the knowledge of Brahman by self-suppression: self-suppression is Brahman. He practised self-suppression, and on practising it perceived that cognition is Brahman, inasmuch as all these living things issue out of cognition, live by it, and pass back into it.

Fifth step. The bliss of dreamless sleep is Brahman.

"Upon learning this he again came to his father Varuṇa and said, Sir, teach me about Brahman. He said to him, Seek the knowledge of Brahman by self-suppression: self-suppression is Brahman. He practised self-suppression, and on practising it perceived that bliss is Brahman, inasmuch as all these living things issue out of bliss, live upon it, pass back into it. This is the science that Varuṇa imparted and Bhṛigu received, a science made perfect in the supreme ether

[1] *Tapas. Tach cha tapo vāhyāntaḥkaraṇasamādhānam, manasas chendṛiyāṇāṃ chaikāgryam paramaṃ tapaḥ*, Śankarāchārya.

Chap. III.

in the heart. He that knows this is made perfect; he becomes rich in food, an eater of food; he becomes great in offspring, in flocks and herds, and spiritual power; he becomes great in fame. Let him never find fault with food: that is his observance. The vital air is food. The body is the eater of that food. The body is based on vital air, and vital air is based on the body, and thus food is based on food. He that knows this food based on food is made perfect; he becomes rich in food, an eater of food; he becomes rich in offspring, flocks and herds, and spiritual power; he becomes great in fame.

Outward observances of the meditating sage, and their rewards.

"Let him never despise food: that is his observance. Water is food, light is the eater of that food. Light is based on water, and water is based on light, and thus food is based on food. He that knows this food based on food is made perfect; he becomes rich in food, an eater of food; he becomes rich in offspring, flocks and herds, and spiritual power, and rich in fame.

"Let him make much of food: that is his observance. Earth is food, ether is the eater of that food. Ether is based on earth, and earth is based on ether, and thus food is based on food. He that knows this food based on food is made perfect; he becomes rich in food, an eater of food; he becomes rich in offspring, in flocks and herds, and spiritual power, and rich in fame.

"Let him forbid no man to enter his house: that is his observance. Let him then store up food in whatever way he can. They tell him that comes to the house that his food is ready. If the food is given at once, it shall be given at once to the giver; if it be given later, it shall be given later to the giver; if it be given only at the last, it shall be given only at the last to the giver.

He is to meditate on the various manifestations of Brahman.

"Let Brahman be meditated on as that which is preservative in speech, as that which is acquisitive and preservative in the ascending and descending vital airs,

CHAP. III.

as work in the hands, as locomotion in the feet. These are the meditations on the Self in man. Now for its manifestations in the gods. It is fertility in the rain, mightiness in lightning. It is wealth in flocks and herds; in the stars it is light. It is offspring, immortality, beatitude. In the ether it is all that is. Let him meditate upon Brahman as the basis of all that is, and he shall be firmly based. Let him meditate upon it as greatness, and he shall become great. Let him meditate upon it as thought, and he shall become a thinker. Let him meditate upon it as that which overawes, and the things that he desires shall bow before him. Let him meditate upon it as powerful, and he shall become powerful. Let him meditate upon it as that into which divine things die away, and his enemies and rivals shall perish, and his brother's sons, if they displease him, shall die. It is the same universal spirit that is in the soul and that is in the sun.

He strips off the five vestures of the soul one after another. He acquires and exercises magical powers. He sings the song of universal unity, and is absorbed into the one and all.

"He that knows this turns his back upon the world, passes through this food-made body, passes through this body of the vital airs, passes through this sensorial body, passes through this cognitional body, and passes through this beatific body. Expatiating through these worlds, with food at will, and taking shapes at will, he is ever singing this song of universal unity: O wonderful, wonderful, wonderful. I am food, I am food, I am food; I am the eater, I am the eater, I am the eater; I am the transmuter of food into the eater, I am the transmuter of food into the eater, I am the transmuter of food into the eater. I am the first-born of creation, earlier than the gods, the navel of immortality.[1] He that gives me keeps me. I am the food that eats the eater. I stand above every world, with light as of the sun. He that knows this is all this. Such is the mystic doctrine.

"Hari. OM. May he preserve us both, may he re-

[1] Hiraṇyagarbha.

ward us both. May we put forth our strength together, and may what we recite be efficacious. May we never feel enmity against each other. OM. Peace, peace, peace." CHAP. III.

In this song of universal unity the sage finds that he is one with every manifestation of Brahman, from the visible elemental things of the world of sense up to the divine emanations Purusha, Hiraṇyagarbha, and Īśvara; one also with the underlying reality, the one and only Self. At this stage he is said to possess magical powers; he can range at will from this world through the several worlds of the deities, and assume what shapes he pleases. A trace of illusion[1] adheres to him at times, so that he still sees the semblances of duality; he knows himself to be the Self that is in all things, and finds that he possesses the wonder-working powers of the Yogin or ecstatic seer; he can take upon himself any shape, visible or invisible, from the least to the greatest, and go where he chooses among the worlds of men and gods, and is said figuratively to enjoy every form of pleasure at one and the same moment. Thaumaturgy is the gift of ecstasy. The epithets that Archer Butler bestows upon the philosophy of Proclus are applicable to the philosophy of ancient India. It is sublime and it is puerile. It is marked at once by sagacity and by poverty, by daring independence and by grovelling superstition.

The great text, That art thou.

In the view of the Indian schoolmen, the greatest of all the texts of the Upanishads is the text That art thou, in the sixth Prapāṭhaka[2] of the Chhāndogya Upanishad. This is pre-eminently the Mahāvākya, the supreme enouncement. It is on the comprehension of this text that spiritual intuition[3] or ecstatic vision rises in the purified intelligence of the aspirant to extrication from metempsychosis. This text is the burden of the instruction given by Āruṇi to his son, the pedantic and

[1] Ānandagiri *in loco.* [2] Lecture. [3] *Samyagdarśana.*

CHAP. III.

opinionated Śvetaketu, already mentioned in the second chapter of this work.

The dialogue of Aruni and S'vetaketu, from the Chhāndogya Upanishad.

"Rooted in the existent are all these created things, built upon the real, based upon the real. It has been said already how these divine elements heat, water, earth, in man are threefold.[1] When a man is dying, his speech passes into his inner sensory, his inner sensory into his vital breath, his vital breath into heat, his heat into the supreme divinity. All this world is animated by the supersensible. This is real, this is Self. THAT ART THOU, Śvetaketu. Hearing this, Śvetaketu spoke again: Teach me further, holy sir. Be it so, my son, he replied.

Allegory of the sweet juices and the honey.

"As bees make honey, gathering into one mass, into unity, the sweet juices of various plants; as those juices cannot distinguish themselves the one from the other, as the juices of this plant and that: so all these creatures, though they are one in the real, know not that they are one in the real. What they are severally in this life, lion, or wolf, or boar, or worm, or moth, or gnat, or musquito, that they become again and again. All this world is animated by the supersensible. This is real, this is Self. THAT ART THOU, Śvetaketu. He said again: Teach me further, sir. Be it so, my son, he replied.

Allegory of the rivers and the sea.

"These rivers flow east and west, they are drawn from the sea east and west, and flow into the sea again.[2] They become sea and only sea. They know not there that one is this river and another that. And so with all these living things. They come out of the real, and do not know that they come out of it, and therefore they

[1] The threefold nature of the elements, as taught in the Chhāndogya, is said by the scholiasts to imply the fuller doctrine of quintuplication, or the fivefold successive concretion of the elements already described in this chapter.

[2] "They are drawn up from the sea into the clouds, fall again in the form of rain, and in the shape of the Ganges and other rivers flow back into the sea, and become one with it again."—Śankarāchārya *in loco*.

become in this life, as it may be, lion, or wolf, or boar, or worm, or moth, or gnat, or musquito. All this world is animated by the supersensible.' That is real, that is Self. THAT ART THOU, Śvetaketu. He said again: Teach me further, sir. Be it so, my son, said Āruṇi.

Allegory of the tree and its informing life.

"Here is a great tree. If a man strike the root, it still lives, and its sap exudes. If he strike it in the trunk, it still lives, and its sap exudes. If he strike it at the top, it still lives, and its sap exudes. This tree, permeated by the living soul, stands still imbibing, still luxuriant.[1] If the living soul forsake one of its branches, that branch dries up: if it forsake a second branch, that branch dries up: if it forsake a third branch, that branch dries up: if it forsake the whole tree, the whole tree dries up. Know this, my son, said Āruṇi. Informed as it is by the living soul, it is this body that dies, the soul dies not. All this world is animated by the supersensible. That is real, that is Self. THAT ART THOU, Śvetaketu. Hereupon Śvetaketu spoke again: Teach me further, holy sir. Be it so, my son, said Āruṇi.

Allegory of the seeds of the holy fig-tree.

"Take a fig from the holy fig-tree. Here it is, sir, said he. Break it open. It is broken open, sir. What dost thou see in it? These little seeds, sir. Break open one of them. It is broken open, sir. What dost thou see in it? Nothing. His father said: From this, so small that thou canst not see it, from this minuteness the great holy fig-tree grows up. Believe, my son, that all this world is animated by the supersensible. That is real, that is Self. THAT ART THOU, Śvetaketu. He said again: Teach me further, sir. Be it so, my son, said Āruṇi.

Allegory of the salt in salt water.

"Take this lump of salt, and throw it into some water, and come to me again to-morrow. Śvetaketu did so. His father said: Take out the lump of salt thou threwest into the water yesterday evening. He

[1] The tree is the body, the branches the constituents of the body. These are vitalised by the indwelling soul.

CHAP. III.

looked for it, but could not find it, for it was dissolved. His father told him to sip some water from the surface. What is it like? It is salt, he answered. Taste it further down: what is it like? It is salt. Taste it from the bottom: what is it like? It is salt. Now thou hast tasted it, come to me, said Āruṇi. Śvetaketu came and said: It remains always as it is. His father said: The salt is still there, though thou seest it not. All this world is animated by the supersensible. That is real, that is Self. THAT ART THOU, Śvetaketu. So Śvetaketu said again: Teach me further, sir. Be it so, my son, he replied.

Allegory of the highwayman and the blindfold traveller.

"A highwayman leaves a wayfarer from Kandahār blindfold in a desolate waste he has brought him to. The wayfarer brought blindfold into the waste and left there, knows not what is east, what is north, and what is south, and cries aloud for guidance. Some passer-by unties his hands and unbinds his eyes, and tells him, Yonder is the way to Kandahār, walk on in that direction. The man proceeds, asking for village after village, and is instructed and informed until he reaches Kandahār. Even in this way it is that in this life a man that has a spiritual teacher knows the Self. He is delayed only till such time as he pass away.[1] All this world is animated by the supersensible. That is real, that is Self. THAT ART THOU, Śvetaketu. Then Śvetaketu said again: Teach me further, sir. Be it so, my son, he replied.

Gradual departure of the soul at death.

"His relatives come round the dying man and ask, Dost thou know me? dost thou know me? He recognises them so long as his voice passes not away into his thought, his thought into his breath, his breath into his vital warmth, his warmth into the supreme divinity. But when his voice has passed away into thought, his

[1] The sage liberated and yet living, the *jīvanmukta*, has to wait only till his body falls away from him, to make his personality pass away for ever into the impersonality of the one and only Self.

thought into breath, his breath into warmth, his warmth into the supreme divinity, then at last he ceases to know them. All this world is animated by the supersensible. That is real, that is Self. THAT ART THOU, Śvetaketu. After this Śvetaketu spoke yet once again: Teach me further, holy sir. Be it so, my son, said Āruṇi.

Allegory of the fiery ordeal.

"They bring a man with his hands tied before the Raja, saying, He has carried something off, he has committed theft. Heat the axe for him. If the man is guilty of the deed, but falsifies himself, intending falsehood, and screens himself with a lie, he lays hold of the red-hot hatchet and is burnt, and thereupon is put to death. If he is guiltless he tells the truth about himself, and with true intent, clothing himself with the truth, he lays hold of the glowing hatchet and is not burnt, and is not put to death. As he is not burnt in that ordeal, so is the sage unhurt in the fiery trial of metempsychosis. All this world is animated by the supersensible. This is real, this is Self. THAT ART THOU, Śvetaketu."

Scholastic explanation of the great text, That art thou.

THAT ART THOU.[1] The word THAT, in the first place, denotes the totality of things in the whole, that is, the world-fiction, the Demiurgus or universal soul, and the characterless Self. These three fictitiously present themselves in union; the universal soul and the fictitious universe being penetrated and permeated by the Self, as a red-hot lump of iron is penetrated and permeated by fire. The word THAT, in the second place, points to the characterless Self apart from the fictitious universal spirit, and the fictitious universe which overlies it.

The word THOU, in the first place, denotes the totality of things in the parts, that is, the various portions of the world-fiction, the various individual minds or migrating souls to which these portions are allotted, and the

[1] This explanation is taken from Nṛisimhasarasvatī's Subodhinī.

CHAP. III. characterless Self. These three also fictitiously present themselves in union; the various phases of the world-fiction and the various migrating souls being penetrated and permeated by the Self as a lump of iron by fire. The word THOU, in the second place, points to the characterless Self, the pure bliss, that underlies the various phases of the world-fiction and the various migrating souls.

The sense of the text is therefore this: the individual soul is one with the universal soul, and the universal soul is one with the one and only Self. It is of this Self, through the operancy of the world-fiction, that all individual things and persons are the fictitious parts:—

> "Not all parts like, but all alike informed
> With radiant light, as glowing iron with fire."

The differences that mark off thing from thing and soul from soul are false, and shall pass away; the spiritual unity that pervades and unifies them is true, and shall abide for ever.

CHAPTER IV.

THE MUNDAKA UPANISHAD.

"All are but parts of one stupendous whole
Whose body nature is, and God the soul:
That changed through all, and yet in all the same,
Great in the earth as in the ethereal frame,
Warms in the sun, refreshes in the breeze,
Glows in the stars, and blossoms in the trees;
Lives through all life, extends through all extent,
Spreads undivided, operates unspent;
Breathes in our soul, informs our mortal part,
As full, as perfect, in a hair as heart;
As full, as perfect, in vile man that mourns
As the rapt seraph that adores and burns:
To him no high, no low, no great, no small:
He fills, he bounds, connects and equals all."—POPE.

"And this deep power in which we exist, and whose beatitude is all accessible to us, is not only self-sufficing and perfect in every hour, but the act of seeing and the thing seen, the seer and the spectacle, the subject and the object, are one. We see the world piece by piece, as the sun, the moon, the animal, the tree; but the whole, of which these are the shining parts, is the soul. From within or from behind a light shines through us upon things, and makes us aware that we are nothing, but the light is all."—EMERSON.

CHAP. IV.

The religion of rites and the religion of gnosis, the inferior science and the superior science.

IT is said in a Vedic text that every Brāhman[1] comes into the world bringing with him three debts. These are his debts to the Rishis of sacred studentship, that he may learn the primitive hymns by heart, and become able himself to teach them to pupils of his own to ensure their perpetual transmission; his debt of sacrifice to the gods; and his debt to the Pitris or forefathers of the

[1] *Jāyamāno vai brāhmaṇas tribhir ṛiṇavān jāyate, brahmacharyeṇa ṛishibhyo, yajnena devebhyaḥ, prajayā pitṛibhyaḥ.*

tribes, of sons to offer the food and water to their deceased father and to their progenitors. The payment of these debts is incumbent on those living in the world; and they must fulfil every prescriptive usage, and live in obedience to the religion of tradition and liturgic rites. Worship with its proper ritual is binding upon the multitude, and has its fruit in raising the worshipper to higher embodiments, or procuring for him a sojourn in a paradise of the deities. This religion belongs therefore to the world of fictions and semblances, to the phantasmagoric world of migrating souls and their spheres of recompense; and has its reality only for the unpurified and unawakened spirit, for whom it is true that the miseries of metempsychosis are real enough. These immemorial rites and ordinances have their place; they are the religion of the many, and if followed with the understanding of their mystic import, and a knowledge of the deities invoked, may elevate the worshipper to the paradise of Brahmā. This understanding and this knowledge are the "inferior science," *aparā vidyā*. The worship of the deities and the ancestral usages, however, bear also a higher fruit. The aspirant to extrication from metempsychosis may practise them with a sole view to the purification of his intellect for the reception of higher truth. He turns his back upon the world, and upon the religion of the world and all its promises. He wishes for no higher form of life, for every form of life is hateful; he wishes for no paradise, for the pleasures of every paradise are tainted and fugitive. The religion of usages and liturgic rites is a mode of activity, and, like every other mode of action, tends to misery. Activity is the root of pain, for so long as a living being acts so long must he receive the award of his good and evil works, in body after body, in æon after æon. The aspirant has already learnt, imperfectly as he may have realised it, that to the true point of view taught by the recluses in the

The religion of rites prolongs the migration of the soul.

jungle, the religion of rites and of immemorial usages, the sacrifices, and the gods sacrificed to, are alike unreal: for the sage made perfect they have no existence. There is no truth in things many, in things finite; no truth where the thinker is other than the things around him. A Vedic text says that he that meditates upon any deity as a being other than himself has no knowledge, and is a mere victim to the gods. As soon as a man turns his back on every form of life, and aspires to escape from all further embodiment, he is free from the debt of sacrifice to the deities, and the debt of progeny to the forefathers of the tribes. He may, if he will, leave these debts unpaid, and proceed at once from sacred studentship to meditation and self-discipline in the jungle. After his initiation into the Veda, the path of abnegation and knowledge is at once open to him. As there is no truth in the many, all truth is in the one; and this one that alone is is the Self, the inmost essence of all things, that vivifies all sentiencies and permeates all things, from a tuft of grass up to the highest god, up to Brahmā himself. This is the pure bliss, and it dwells within the heart of every creature, and to see this and to become one with it for ever is the highest end of aspiration. It is to be reached only by a never-failing inertion and a never-failing abstraction, by a rigid and insensible posture, by apathy, vacuity, and ecstasy. To see it, to become one with it, to melt away his personality into its impersonality, a man must renounce all ties, must repair to the solitude of the forest, must crush every desire, and check every feeling and thought, till his mind be fitted to reflect the pure light of undifferenced being, to be irradiated with, till it pass away into, "the light of lights beyond the darkness." In the course of this procedure the cosmic fiction gradually vanishes, and the Self shines forth as the sun shines out slowly as the clouds disperse. There is thus a

The religion of gnosis frees the soul from further migration.

higher religion for the few, to which the religion of the many is only the first step of preliminary purification. This higher religion, the knowledge of the Self, is the superior science, the *parā vidyā.* The sacrifices, and the deities sacrificed to, and the recompenses, have a relative reality to the unawakened multitude. They have no reality to the already purified aspirant to liberation from metempsychosis; he refuses reality to everything but the one and only real, and renounces all things that he may find that one and only real, the Self within. His only business is with the spiritual intuition. Such is the subsumption of *karmavidyā*, the knowledge of rites, under *brahmavidyā*, the knowledge of the Self; and such is the absorption of the religion of usages into the religion of ecstatic union. The inferior science is a *dharmajijñāsā*, or investigation of the several rewards of the various prescriptive *sacra;* the superior science is a *brahmajijñāsā*, or investigation of the fontal spiritual essence, Brahman.

This religion or philosophy must be learned from an authorised exponent.

The knowledge of the Self or Brahman is not a private and personal thing, or attainable by an exercise of the individual intellect. It is everywhere taught in the Upanishads that it was revealed by this or that god or other semi-divine teacher, and handed down through a succession of authorised exponents.[1] It is only from one of these accredited teachers that the knowledge of the Self is to be had; as we have already read, "A man that has a spiritual teacher knows the Self." All teaching that is out of accordance with the traditionary exposition of the Upanishads, is individual assertion and exercise of merely human ingenuity.[2]

These things premised, and with the information given in the preceding chapters, the reader is in a position to understand the Muṇḍaka Upanishad. This is one of the Upanishads of the Atharvaveda, and one of the most

[1] *Āchāryaparamparā, sampradāyaparamparā.*
[2] *Svabuddhiparikalpita, utprekshāmātra.*

important documents of primitive Indian philosophy. Explanations will be given from time to time from the traditional exposition of the scholiasts Śankarāchārya and Ānandagiri. The text is as follows:— CHAP. IV.

I. 1. "OM. Brahmā was the first of the gods that emanated, the maker of the world, the upholder of the spheres. He proclaimed the science of the Self, the basis of all science, to his eldest son, Atharvan. Mundaka Upanishad. 1st Mundaka, 1st Section.

"Atharvan in ancient days delivered to Angis that science of the Self which Brahmā had proclaimed to him, and Angis to Satyavāha the Bhāradvāja, and the Bhāradvāja transmitted the traditionary science to Angirasa. The διαδοχή.

"Śaunaka the householder came reverently to Angirasa and asked: Holy sage, what must be known that all this universe may be known?

"Angirasa replied: Those that know the Veda say that there are two sciences that are to be known, the superior science and the inferior.

"Of these, the inferior is the Rigveda, the Yajurveda, the Sāmaveda, the Atharvaveda, and the instrumental sciences, the phonetics, ritual, grammar, etymology, metrics, and astronomy. The superior science is that by which the imperishable principle is attained to.

"That which is invisible, impalpable, without kindred, without colour, that which has neither eyes nor ears, neither hands nor feet, which is imperishable, manifested in infinite variety, present everywhere, and wholly supersensible,—that is the changeless principle that the wise behold as the origin of all things. To know the Self is to know all things.

"The whole world issues out of that imperishable principle, like as a spider spins his thread out of himself and draws it back into himself again, or as plants grow up upon the earth, or as the hairs of the head and of the body issue out of the living man." Simile of the spider.

Māyā, the world-fiction, is, as has been already seen, the body of Īśvara, the Archimagus, the first and highest of emanations,—the body out of which all things pro-

CHAP. IV.

ceed, the *kāraṇaśarīra*. Īśvara projects all things and all migrating souls out of his body, and withdraws them into it again at the close of each æon, as the spider extends its thread out of its body and draws it back into it again. The simile of the spider occurs also in the Bṛihadāraṇyaka Upanishad. A curious misapprehension on the part of Hume, or rather of some informant of Hume, is noteworthy in reference to this image.

Hume's misinterpretation of this simile.

It is to be found in his Dialogues concerning Natural Religion:—"The Brahmins assert that the world arose from an infinite spider, who spun this whole complicated mass from his bowels, and annihilates afterwards the whole or any part of it, by absorbing it again and resolving it into his own essence. Here is a species of cosmogony which appears to us ridiculous; because a spider is a little contemptible animal, whose operations we are never likely to take for a model of the whole universe. But still here is a new species of analogy even in our globe. And were there a planet wholly inhabited by spiders, this inference would then appear as natural and irrefragable as that which in one planet ascribes the origin of all things to design and intelligence. Why an orderly system may not be spun from the belly as well as from the brain, it will be difficult to give a satisfactory reason." To return to the text:—

The Demiurgus and the world-fiction.

"Brahman begins to swell with fervid self-coercion. Thence the aliment begins to unfold itself, and from that aliment proceed Prāṇa, the internal sensory, the elements, the actions of living souls, and their perennial fruits.

"This Brahman,[1] Hiraṇyagarbha, and name and colour, and food, issue forth out of that being that knows all, that knows everything, whose self-coercion is prevision."

Here again we meet with the same idea as in the Nāsadīyasūkta and in the Taittirīya Upanishad. The

[1] The *sagunam brahma*, or *śabalam brahma*, the divine emanation of Brahman and Māyā, the *māyopādhikam brahma*.

one, the Self, Brahman in association with Māyā, and thus already the creative Īśvara,—that is to say, Brahman in the first quasi-personal manifestation or emanation as the Demiurgus,—is said to engage in self-torture,[1] self-suppression, or self-coercion. This self-torture of the Demiurgus is a meditation, a prevision of the world that is to be. The "aliment" is the cosmical illusion, developing itself in such a way that each migrating soul shall pass through successive lives appropriate to the residuary influences of its works in the last æon. Prāṇa or Hiraṇyagarbha, the spirit of dreaming sentiencies, emanates out of Īśvara, the all-knowing Demiurgus. "Name and colour" is a constant phrase of the Upanishads for the outward world in its visible and nameable aspects. Food as the material of the earthly body, is the latest manifestation of Brahman in the descending order of progressive concretion.

The text speaks, in the next place, of the matter of the two sciences. The inferior science, it says, has to do with metempsychosis, and with the usages and rites on the fulfilment or neglect of which higher and lower future states of life depend; the superior science treats of the knowledge of the Self as the means of releasing the aspirant from further migration.

1st Mundaka, 2d Section.

I. 2. "This is the truth: The rites which the sages saw in the Mantras were widely current in the Tretāyuga or second age of the world. Perform them regularly, you that wish for rewards. This is your path to recompense in a higher embodiment.

"When the fire is kindled, and its blaze is flickering, the sacrificer should throw the offering between the two portions of sacrificial butter, throwing it with faith.

"If the sacrifice upon the perpetual household fire

[1] *Tapas*, in this verse translated in accordance with its derivation, and at the same time with its usual sense, as *fervid* self-coercion.

CHAP. IV.

The rewards of the prescriptive *sacra* are transient. The sage must turn his back upon them all.

be not followed by the oblation at new-moon, by the full-moon rites, by the Chāturmāsya, and by the offering of first-fruits; if it be unfrequented with guests; or if it be unaccompanied with the oblation to all the deities; or if it be presented with any error in the form; the sacrificer forfeits the seven ascending worlds of recompense.

"Fire has seven wavy tongues,—the black, the terrific, the thought-swift, the red, the purple, the scintillating, and the tongue of every shape, divine.

"If a man offers his sacrifices while these tongues of fire are flashing, and offers them in proper season, his very sacrifices become the solar rays to lead him up to the abode of the one lord of all the gods.

"The shining sacrifices bear the sacrificer upward through the solar rays, crying, Come hither, come hither; greeting him with kindly voice, and doing honour to him, saying, This is your recompense, the sacred sphere of Brahmā.

"But these sacrifices with their ritual and its eighteen parts are frail boats indeed; and they that rejoice in sacrifice as the best of things, in their infatuation shall pass on again to decay and death.

"They that are infatuated, dwelling in the midst of the illusion, wise in their own eyes, and learned in their own conceit, are stricken with repeated plagues, and go round and round, like blind men led by the blind.

"They are foolish, and living variously in this illusion, think that they have what they want: and since they that trust in sacrifices are too greedy of higher lives to learn the truth, they fall from paradise on the expiry of their reward.

"In their infatuation they think that the revealed rites and works for the public good are the best and highest thing, and fail to find the other thing that is higher and better still. When they have had their reward in the body in some upper mansion in paradise, they return to a human embodiment, or to a lower life than that of man.

"They among them that practise austerity and faith in the forest, quiescent, versed in the knowledge of the gods, and living upon alms,—these put away the stain of good and evil works, and go after death to the sphere of the imperishable deity, the abiding spirit, Hiraṇyagarbha.

He must repair to an accredited teacher.

"Surveying these spheres won by works, the seeker of Brahman should learn to renounce all things. No uncreated sphere of being is to be gained by works. Therefore he should take fuel in his hands, and repair to a sacred teacher, learned in the Veda, intent upon the Self, that he may learn the uncreate.

"The spiritual guide, when he comes to him with reverence, with a humble heart and with his senses repressed, must truly expound to him the science of the Self, as he knows the undecaying spirit, the sole reality."

The aspirant to extrication from metempsychosis must turn his back upon every sphere of recompense, even upon the paradise of the gods that is won by sacrificial rites, and upon the paradise of Hiraṇyagarbha or Brahmā, that is attained to by those that add to their outward worship a knowledge of the deities and of the import of the rites. These latter reside in the paradise of Brahmā till the close of the æon. All these spheres of fruition are transitory; they reproduce each other like seed and plant; they are empty and unsatisfying, perishing like a reverie or dream, like the waters of a mirage, like the bubbles and foam upon the surface of a stream. To return to the text. The first section of the second Muṇḍaka treats of Brahman and the superior science.

2d Muṇḍaka, 1st Section. Simile of the fire and the sparks.

II. 1. "This is the truth: As its kindred sparks fly out in thousands from a blazing fire, so the various living souls proceed out of that imperishable principle, and return into it again.

CHAP. IV.

"That infinite spirit is self-luminous, without and within, without origin, without vital breath or thinking faculty, stainless, beyond the imperishable ultimate."

The imperishable ultimate is the cosmical illusion. Brahman is in truth untouched by the world-fiction. It is only fictitiously that this overspreads Brahman, as the waters of the mirage fictitiously overspread the sànds of the desert. All living things are only the one Self fictitiously limited to this or that fictitious mind and body, and return into the Self as soon as the fictitious limitation disappears. As soon as the jar is broken the ether from within it is one with the ether without, one with ether one and undivided. The text next speaks of the several unreal effluences or emanations from the Self as illusorily overspread with the cosmical illusion. Each such emanation is false; in the words of the Chhāndogya Upanishad, "a modification of speech only, a change, a name."

"From that proceed the vital breath, the thinking principle and all the organs of sense and motion, and the elements, ether, air, fire, water, and the earth that holds all things."

Purusha or Vaiśvānara, the universal soul that emanates from Hiraṇyagarbha, dwells in every living body, and every living body is made up of the elements just spoken of. The text accordingly proceeds to characterise this Purusha. The scholiast identifies him with Vishṇu.

Purusha characterised, as in the Purusha-sūkta.

"Fire is his head, the sun and moon his eyes, the regions his ears, the open Vedas are his voice, the air is his vital breath, the whole world is his heart, the earth springs from his feet, for this is the inner soul of all living things."

The whole world is said to be the heart of Purusha, because it is all an effluence of the mind,[1] into which it is seen to melt away in the state of dreamless sleep,

[1] *Antaḥkaraṇa*, the aggregate of *buddhi*, *manas*, *ahankāra*, and *chitta*.

and out of which it re-issues when the sleeper awakes, as sparks fly up out of fire. The mind is in the heart. Purusha is the soul internal to all living things, for in every living thing it is he that sees, hears, thinks, and knows.

"Fire proceeds from him, and the sun is the fuel of that fire. From the moon proceeds the cloud-god Parjanya; from the cloud-god the plants upon the earth; from these the germ of life. Thus the various living things issue out of Purusha.

"The Ṛik, the Sāman, and the Yajush, the initiations, the sacrifices, the offerings of victims, and the presents to the Brāhmans, the liturgic year, the sacrificer, and the spheres of recompense, those in which the moon purifies, and those in which the sun purifies the elevated worshipper,—all these things issue out of Purusha.

"The gods in various orders, the Sādhyas, men, and beasts, and birds, the breath and vital functions, rice and barley, self-torture, faith, truth, continence, and the prescriptive usages,—all issue out of Purusha."

The imagery of the Nāsadīyasūkta was reproduced in the first section of the first Muṇḍaka, that of the Purushasūkta is reproduced in these verses. The cosmological conception of the poets of the Upanishads seems to have had its first beginnings in the later part of the Mantra period of Vedic literature.

"The seven breaths proceed from him, the seven flames, the seven kinds of fuel, the seven oblations, the seven passages of the vital airs, the vital airs that reside in the cavity of the body, seven in each living thing.

"It is from him that the seas and all the mountains proceed; it is from him that the rivers flow in various forms; it is from him that plants grow up, and their nutritious material by which the inner invisible body is clothed with the visible elemental frame.

"All this world, with its sacrifices and its knowledge, is Purusha. Self is supreme, immortal. My friend,

CHAP. IV.

The vision of the Self within the heart is the only salvation.

he that knows this Self that is seated in the heart of every living thing, scatters off the ties of illusion even in this present life."

The second section of the second Muṇḍaka sets forth the means of a fuller knowledge of Brahman. The aspirant is to meditate upon it as the characterless essence that shines forth in every mode of mind, the one and only Self illusorily manifested in the plurality of migrating souls.

2d Muṇḍaka, 2d Section.

II. 2. "This Self is self-luminous, present, dwelling in the heart of every living thing, the great centre of all things. All that moves, and breathes, and stirs is centred in it. You know this as that which is and that which is not; as the end of aspiration, above the knowledge of all living things, the highest good:

"As bright; as lesser than the least and greater than the greatest; as that on which all the spheres of recompense are founded, together with the tenants of those spheres. This same imperishable Brahman is the vital air, the inner sensory, the voice. This same Brahman is true, this is immortal. That is the mark. Hit it with thy mind, my friend.

Use of the mystic syllable OM.

"Let a man take the great weapon of the Upanishads for his bow, and let him fix upon it his arrow sharpened with devotion. Bend it with the thoughts fixed upon the Self, and hit the mark, the undecaying principle.

"The mystic utterance OM is the bow, the soul the arrow, the Self the mark. Let it be shot at with unfailing heed, and let the soul, like an arrow, become one with the mark.

"It is over this Self that sky and earth and air are woven, and the sensory, with all the organs of sense and motion. Know that this is the one and only Self. Renounce all other words, for this is the bridge to immortality.

"This Self dwells in the heart where the arteries are concentred, variously manifesting itself. OM: thus meditate upon the Self. May it be well with you that you may cross beyond the darkness.

"This Self knows all, it knows everything. Its glory is in the world. It is seated in the ether in the irradiated heart, present to the inner sensory, actuating the organs and the organism, settled in the earthly body. The wise fix their heart, and by knowledge see the blissful, the immortal principle that manifests itself.

The ties of the heart are loosed by seeing the Self, the light of the world.

"When a man has seen that Self unmanifest and manifest, the ties of his heart are loosed, all his perplexities are solved, and all his works exhausted.

"The stainless, indivisible Self is in that last bright sheath, the heart: it is the pure light of lights that they that know the Self know.

"The sun gives no light to that, nor the moon and stars, neither do these lightnings light it up; how then should this fire of ours? All things shine after it as it shines, all this world is radiant with its light.

"It is this undying Self that is outspread before, Self behind, Self to the right, Self to the left, above, below. All this glorious world is Self."

The aspirant is bidden to renounce all other words. He is to renounce the inferior science, the knowledge of the gods and of the various rites with which they are worshipped; for these things only prolong the series of his embodied lives. The knowledge of Brahman is said to be the bridge to immortality, as it is the way by which the sage is to cross over the sea of metempsychosis to reunite his soul with the Self beyond. The Self or Brahman is said to reside in the heart, in the midst of all the arteries. By this it is only meant that the modifications of the mind seated within the heart shine, or as we should say, rise into the light of consciousness, in the light of the Self. The mind is in the heart, and there receives the light of the one and only Self, that itself is everywhere, *ubique et in nullo loco.* It is only in semblance that the Self, which is

CHAP. IV. everywhere, can be said to come and go, to dwell here or there. The indwelling of the Self is its manifestation in the mental modes. A lotus-shaped lump of flesh in the heart is styled the *brahmapura*, the abode of Brahman. It is here that the Self is said to witness, that is, to give light to, every feeling, thought, and passion of the soul. It is here that it sees unseen, hears unheard, thinks unthought upon; but its vision, its hearing, and its thought are unintermittent and undifferenced. It does not see as we see, or hear as we hear, or think as we think, but as a pure light of characterless intelligence. It gives light to all, and receives light from nothing. It is the pure light beyond the darkness of the world-fiction; the pure bliss of exemption from evil, pain, and weariness. All the things that present themselves in nameable and coloured phases seem to be, and this only *is*.

The first section of the third Muṇḍaka opens with the simile of the two birds upon one tree. They represent the migrating soul and Íśvara the cosmic soul, residing together in the body of each and every living thing. This section is said to treat of the qualifications required in an aspirant to liberation, before he can enter on the pursuit of ecstasy and intuition of the Self.

3d Muṇḍaka, 1st Section. Allegory of the two bird on one tree.

III. I. "Two birds always together and united nestle upon the same tree; one of them eats the sweet fruit of the holy fig-tree, the other looks on without eating.

"In the same tree the migrating soul is immersed, and sorrows in its helpless plight, and knows not what to do; but its sorrow passes as soon as it sees the adored lord, and that this world is only his glory.

"When the sage sees the golden-hued maker of the world, the lord, the Purusha that emanates from Brahman, he shakes off his good and evil works, and without stain arrives at the ultimate identity."

The body is a tree that bears the fruits of actions

in a former life. The migrating soul, clothed in the tenuous *involucrum*, resides in the body, and eats the various fruits of its good and evil actions in earlier embodiments. Not so the Demiurgus, the golden-hued, that is, the self-luminous, universal soul, ever pure, intelligent, and free. He actuates all the migrating souls and all the spheres through which they migrate, but takes no part in the experiences they pass through. The soul, laden with illusions, and with cravings after temporal felicity, is fated to pass through all the varied anguish of hunger, thirst, faintness, sickness, partings, bereavements, decay, and death, in body after body in vegetal, animal, or human shape, through countless ages; till at last the good works that it has done in a series of lives may bring it in a human embodiment into the presence of a spiritual guide, who shall teach it the way of release from further migration, through self-torture, ecstasy, and intuition in which it identifies itself, first with the universal soul, and then with the one and only Self.

"This Īśvara is the living breath that variously manifests itself in all living things. Knowing him, the sage ceases to speak of many things; his sport is in the Self, his joy is in the Self, his action is relative to the Self, and he is the best of those that know the Self.

Mental purity is required of the aspirant to liberation.

"For this Self is to be reached by persevering truthfulness, self-coercion, precise intuition, and continence. This Self, which ascetics behold after the annulment of their imperfections, is within the body, luminous and pure.

"It is truth that prevails, not falsehood. The road is laid out by truth, the divine path by which the Rishis free from all desire proceed to the treasure of truth.

"That Self is great and luminous, unthinkable; it is supersensible beyond the supersensible, farther than the

CHAP. IV.

farthest, and yet near, within the body, seated within the cavity of the heart of those that see it.

"It is not apprehended by the eye, nor by the voice, nor by the other organs of sense and motion, nor by self-coercion, nor by sacrificial rites. He whose mind is purified by the limpid clearness of his knowledge, sees in meditation that undivided Self.

"This supersensible Self is to be known by the mind, in the body in which the vital air has entered to its fivefold functions; every mind of living things is overspread with the vital airs, and when this mind is purified the Self shines forth.

"He whose mind is purified wins whatever sphere of recompense he aspires to, and whatever pleasures he desires. Therefore let him that wishes for prosperity worship him that knows the Self."

A pure mind is the only mirror that reflects the Self.

Truthfulness, the repression of the senses and the volitions, and continence, are part of the purification of the mind required in the seeker of spiritual insight and ecstatic union. They are among the qualifications of the aspirant. In its natural state the mind is stained with desires, aversions, and passions relative to external things, and like a tarnished mirror or a ruffled pool, is unprepared to mirror the Self that is ever present to it. The senses must be checked and the volitions crushed, that the impurity and turbid discoloration of the mind may be purged away, and that it may become an even and lucid reflecting surface, to present the image of the Self. This image of the Self[1] is itself a mode of mind, but it is the last of the modes of the mind, arising only when the mind is ready to melt away into the fontal unity of the characterless Self. As this mode passes away, the personality of the sage passes away with it into the impersonality of Brahman. The magical powers of the Yogin or ecstatic seer are again asserted. All that is promised to the follower of the prescriptive

[1] *Phalitam brahma.*

sacra, of the religion of the many, is promised to him, if he desire it, before his re-absorption into the spiritual essence. The promise is intended as a farther incitement to the seeker of release from the miseries of metempsychosis.[1] Here again, as elsewhere, the Muṇḍaka Upanishad is remarkable for the clearness with which it states the relation of the philosophy of the recluses of the forest to the religion of those living in the world. This religion is retained as part of the fictitious order of things; real for the many, as bearing fruit in the unreal series of embodied lives, and unreal for the few that turn their back upon the world, and refuse reality to all things but the spiritual unity that permeates them. The old religion, unreal as it is, is needed for the purification of the unreal mind, and has its place prior to the quest of the sole reality. It has its place and passes away: for the perfected sage it is a figment.

The last section of the Muṇḍaka Upanishad is as follows:—

III. 2. "He knows the supreme Brahman, the base on which the world is fixed, which shines forth in its purity. The wise that have put away desire and worship this sage, pass beyond all further re-embodiment. *3d Muṇḍaka, 2d Section.*

"He that lusts after pleasures and gives his mind to them, is born by reason of them into sphere after sphere of recompense; but if a man has already all that he desires and has found the Self, all his cravings melt away even in his present embodiment.

"This Self is not attainable by learning, by memory, by much sacred study, but if he choose this Self it is attainable by him: the Self itself manifests its own essence to him. *The Self manifests itself to the perfect sage.*

"This Self is not attainable by a man that lacks fortitude, nor without concentration, nor by knowledge

[1] *Saguṇavidyāphalam api nirguṇavidyāstutaye prarochanārtham uchyate.* Ānandagiri.

CHAP. IV.

without the renunciation of the world; but if a sage exert himself with these appliances, his soul enters the abode of Brahman.

"When they that have this inner vision, satisfied with knowledge, perfected in the spirit, their imperfections passed away, their faculties quiescent,—when they have reached this Self, when they have fully reached the all-pervading principle,—with perfect insight and with spirits unified, they enter into the all of things.

"All these quietists, familiar with the object of intuition in the Upanishads, purified in mind by renunciation and ecstatic union, are liberated in the hour of death, being one with the supreme immortal principle.

"The fifteen constituents of their bodies re-enter their several elements; their senses return into their several presiding deities; their works and their conscious soul are all unified in the imperishable Self.

He loses himself in it, as a river loses itself in the sea.

"The sage, quitting name and colour, enters into the self-luminous spirit beyond the last principle,[1] in like manner as rivers flow on until they quit their name and colour, and lose themselves in the sea.

"He that knows that highest Self becomes that highest Self only. There is none in his family ignorant of the Self. He passes beyond misery, he passes beyond the taint of good and evil works, he is released from his heart's ties, and becomes immortal.

"Therefore it has been said in a memorial verse: Let a sage reveal this knowledge of Brahman to those only that have fulfilled the prescriptive rites, who know the Veda, intent on the Self, who sacrifice to that one Rishi, the fire-god Agni, and have duly achieved the self-torture of carrying fire upon their heads.

"This true Self was proclaimed of old by Angiras the Rishi. Let none that has not undergone that discipline presume to study it. Glory to the great Rishis. Glory to the great Rishis."

[1] The world-fiction.

They, says Śankarāchārya, that rise to the ecstatic vision become one in the unity of the one and only Self. The images of the sun are seen no longer when the watery surfaces evaporate. The jar is broken, and the ether that was in it is again one with the ether one and undivided. On the rise of the ecstatic vision all the difficulties of the sage are past; to raise fresh impediments is beyond the power of the gods themselves. He has passed through the darkness into light. His personality passes into impersonality, his mortality into immortality. He has found himself, and is for ever one with the one and all.

Fichte quoted. Perfect peace from conscious participation in the divine life that lives in all things.

Fichte,[1] in like but higher terms, rich with the thought of centuries, speaks of his recognition of his nature as one of the many manifestations of the one abiding spiritual essence, the life of which is the progressive life of all things. "I have indeed dwelt in darkness during the past days of my life. I have indeed heaped error upon error, and imagined myself wise. Now for the first time do I wholly understand the doctrine which from thy lips, O wonderful spirit, seemed so strange to me, although my understanding had nothing to oppose to it; for now for the first time do I comprehend it in its whole compass, in its deepest foundation, and through all its consequences. Man is not a product of the world of sense, and the end of his existence cannot be attained in it. His vocation transcends time and space, and everything that pertains to sense. What he is and to what he is to train himself, that must he know: as his vocation is a lofty one, he must be able to lift his thoughts above all the limitations of sense. He must accomplish it: where his being finds its home, there his thoughts too seek their dwelling-place; and the truly human mode of thought, that which alone is worthy of him, that in which his whole spiritual strength is manifested, is that whereby he

[1] Dr. W. Smith's Popular Works of Fichte, pp. 368, sqq.

raises himself above those limitations, whereby all that pertains to sense vanishes into nothing,—into a mere reflection, in mortal eyes, of the one self-existent infinite. Thou art best known to the childlike, devoted, simple mind. To it thou art the searcher of the heart, who seest its inmost depths; the ever-present true witness of its thoughts, who knowest its truth, who knowest it although all the world know it not. The inquisitive understanding which has heard of thee, but seen thee not, would teach us thy nature; and as thy image shows us a monstrous and incongruous shape, which the sagacious laugh at, and the wise and good abhor. I hide my face before thee, and lay my hand upon my lips. How thou art and seemest to thy own being, I shall never know, any more than I can assume thy nature. After thousands of spirit-lives, I shall comprehend thee as little as I do now in this earthly house. That which I conceive becomes finite through my very conception of it; and this can never, even by endless exaltations, rise into the infinite. In the idea of person there are imperfections, limitations: how can I clothe thee with it without these? Now that my heart is closed against all earthly things, now that I have no longer any sense for the transitory and perishable, the universe appears before my eyes clothed in a more glorious form. The dead, heavy mass which only filled up space is vanished; and in its place there flows onward, with the rushing music of mighty waves, an eternal stream of life, and power, and action, which issues from the original source of all life,—from thy life, O infinite one, for all life is thy life, and only the religious eye penetrates to the realm of true beauty. The ties by which my mind was formerly united to this world, and by whose secret guidance I followed all its movements, are for ever sundered; and I stand free, calm, and immovable, a universe to myself. No longer through my affections, but by my eye alone, do I apprehend outward objects and am connected with them; and this eye itself is purified by freedom, and looks through error and deformity to the true and beautiful, as upon the unruffled surface of water shapes are more purely mirrored in a milder light. My mind is for ever closed against embarrassment and perplexity, against uncertainty, doubt, and anxiety; my heart against grief, repentance, and desire."

CHAPTER V.

THE KATHA UPANISHAD.

"If the red slayer think he slays,
Or the slain think he is slain,
They little know the subtle ways
I keep, and pass, and turn again.
Far or forgot to me is near,
Shadow and sunlight are the same;
The vanished gods to me appear,
And one to me are shame and fame.
They reckon ill who leave me out,
Me when they fly I am the wings;
I am the doubter and the doubt,
And I the hymn the Brahman sings.
The strong gods pine for my abode,
And pine in vain the sacred seven;
But thou, meek lover of the good,
Find me, and turn thy back on heaven."

—EMERSON.

CHAP. V.

The story of Nachiketas and the regent of the dead.

THE reader is by this time becoming familiar with the general conception of the primitive Indian philosophers, and with the grotesque imagery and rude sublimity with which it is exhibited in the Upanishads. Epithet is added to epithet, and metaphor to metaphor, and sentence stands by sentence in juxtaposition, rather than in methodical progression, till we are at a loss to pass any judgment, and feel alternately attracted and repelled. The thoughts of these thinkers formed themselves out of other antecedents, and other predispositions, and in another medium, than any of which we have had experience. In the present chapter the work of exposition will proceed by the presentation of the Kaṭha Upanishad, a perspicuous and poetical Upanishad of the Yajurveda. This Upanishad opens with the legend of the revelation of the *brahmavidyā*, or knowledge of the one and only Self by Yama, the regent of the dead, to Nachiketas the son of Vājaśravasa. CHAP. V.

Katha Upanishad. First Vallī.

I. "Vājaśravasa, with the desire of recompense, offered sacrifice, and gave all that he possessed to the priests. He had a son named Nachiketas.

"While the presents were in course of distribution to the priests and to the assembly, faith entered into Nachiketas, who was yet a stripling, and he began to think:

"These cows have drunk all the water they will ever drink, they have grazed as much as they will graze, they have given all the milk that they will ever give, and they will calve no more. They are joyless spheres of recompense that a sacrificer goes to, who gives such gifts as these.

"He therefore said to his father: Father, to whom wilt thou give me? He said it a second time and a third time, until his father exclaimed: I give thee to Death.

"Nachiketas thought: I pass for the first among many disciples, I pass also for the middlemost among many: what has Yama to do that he will do with me to-day?"

Seeing his father's regretful looks, and fearing that he would break his promise to the regent of the dead, Nachiketas begs him not to waver.

"Look back and see how those of old acted, and how those of later days. Man ripens and is reaped like the corn in the field, and like the corn is born again."

His father sends him to the realm of Yama. The death-god is absent, and Nachiketas is neglected. On Yama's return his wife and servants admonish him:

"When a Brāhman comes into the house he is like a fire, and therefore men offer him the customary propitiation. Bring water for his feet, Vaivasvata.[1]

[1] A patronymic of Yama the son of Vivasvat.

CHAP. V.

"A Brāhman that stays without eating food in the house of an inattentive host lays waste all his hopes and expectations, the merits that he has earned by intercourse with good men, by friendly speech, and by sacrifices and works for the public good,[1] as well as all his children and his flocks and herds.

Yama bids Nachiketas to choose three gifts.

"Hearing this, Yama said to Nachiketas: Three nights hast thou lodged in my house fasting, thou a Brāhman guest that shouldst be worshipped. Hail, Brāhman, and may it be well with me. Choose therefore three wishes, a wish for each such night.

The first gift, that he may return to his father.

"Nachiketas said: God of death, I choose as the first of these three wishes that my father Gautama may be easy in his mind, that he may be gracious towards me, that his anger may be turned away from me, that thou send me back to him, and that he may know me again and speak to me.

"Yama replied: Auddāliki,[2] the son of Aruṇa, by my permission shall be as tender towards thee as of old. He shall sleep peacefully at night, and his anger shall pass away when he sees thee released from the power of Death.

"Nachiketas said: In the sphere of paradise there is no fear. Thou art not there, and there man fears not decay. A man passes beyond both hunger and thirst, leaves misery behind, and rejoices in the sphere of paradise.

"Thou, Death, knowest the sacred fire that is the means of winning a sojourn in paradise. Teach me about it, for I have faith. They that are insphered in paradise partake of immortality. I choose this as the second wish.

The second gift, a knowledge of the Nāchiketa fire.

"Yama said: I know the fire that leads to paradise, and tell it to thee: therefore listen. Know that that fire that wins the endless sphere for him that knows it, the basis of the world, is seated in the heart."

[1] Such as tanks, wells, roads, bridges, gardens.
[2] A name of Vājaśravasa.

The fire the knowledge of which is recompensed by a sojourn in Svarga, the paradise of the gods, is a figurative name for Vaiśvānara, Purusha, or Virāj, the divine soul that dwells in all that live in earthly bodies. Yama proceeds to teach Nachiketas the nature of that divine Vaiśvānara. The sage is to meditate upon himself as one with that mystic fire; the seven hundred and twenty bricks that form the sacrificial hearth are the days and nights of the year, and so on. He will then become one with Vaiśvānara.

"He revealed to him that fire, the origin of these spheres of migration, and what were the bricks, and how many, and how laid out, in building the sacrificial hearth; and Nachiketas repeated everything after him as he had said it. So Death was pleased, and spoke again.

"Feeling gratified, the large-minded Yama said, I give thee now and here another gift: this fire shall be called by thy name. Take also this necklace of gems of various colours.

"He that thrice performs the Nāchiketa fiery rite, taking counsel of three,—of his father, his mother, and his spiritual teacher,—and fulfilling the three observances of sacrifice, sacred study, and almsgiving, passes beyond birth and death. He that knows and gazes upon the lustrous and adorable emanation of Hiraṇyagarbha, the divine being that proceeds from Brahmā (or Īśvara), passes into peace for ever.

"He that has performed three Nāchiketa rites, and knows these three things,—the bricks, their number, and the arrangement of them,—he that thus piles up the Nāchiketa fire, shakes off the ties of death before he dies, leaves his miseries behind, and rejoices in the sphere of paradise.

"This is thy fire, Nachiketas, the knowledge of which wins paradise. This thou hast chosen as thy second boon, and men shall call this fire thine. Choose the third wish, Nachiketas."

CHAP. V.

Identification with Purusha or Vaiśvānara, with its consequent exemption from personal experiences in body after body till the close of the æon, is the promise to those that meditate on the allegory of the Nāchiketa fire. In this there is no final release from metempsychosis, as the soul of the rewarded votary will have to enter afresh on its transit from body to body and sphere to sphere at the opening of the next æon. The third gift requested by Nachiketas is teaching relative to the renunciation of all things and the quest of the real and immortalising knowledge of Brahman. The form in which the request is preferred points to the existence of doubt and dissentiency on spiritual questions in the age of the Upanishads. A similar indication occurs in the second verse of the Śvetāśvatara Upanishad: "Is time to be thought the source of things, or the nature of the things themselves, or the retributive fatality, or chance, or the elements, or the personal soul?" Another occurs in the sixth Prapāṭhaka of the Chhāndogya Upanishad, with a reference to Buddhistic or pre-Buddhistic teaching of the emanation of migrating souls and the spheres through which they migrate from an aboriginal void or blank: "Existent only, my son, was this in the beginning, one only, without duality; but some have said: Non-existent only was this in the beginning, one only, without duality, and the existent sprang out of the non-existent; but how could it be so, how could entity come out of nonentity?" To return to the Kaṭha Upanishad.

Disquieting doubt of awaking reflection.

"Nachiketas said: When a man is dead there is this doubt about him: some say that he is, and others say that he is no more. Let me learn how this is from thy teaching, and let this be the third boon."

The third gift, a knowledge of the soul, and of its real nature.

Some people say there is, and some say there is not, a Self[1] other than the body, the senses, and the mind,

[1] *Śarīrendriyamanobuddhivyatirikto dehāntarasambandhy ātmā*, Śankarāchārya.

that passes onward into another body. This is a matter that is beyond human observation and human reasoning, and yet we must know it if we would know the highest end of man.

"Yama said: The gods themselves have been puzzled about this long ago, for it is no easy thing to find out. This is a subtile nature. Choose another boon, Nachiketas, press me not; but release me from this gift.

"Nachiketas answered: As for thy saying, Death, that the very gods have been perplexed about this long ago, and that this is no easy thing to learn,—there is no other teacher to be found like thee, no other boon that shall be equal to this.

"Yama said: Choose sons and grandsons gifted with a hundred years of life, many flocks and herds, elephants, and gold, and horses: choose a wide expanse of soil, and live thyself as many autumns as thou wilt.

"If thou thinkest of any other gift as great, choose that. Choose riches and long life, and rule over a wide territory, and I will give thee the enjoyment of thy desires.

"Ask what thou wilt, ask for whatever pleasures are hardest to get in the world of men. Ask for these nymphs, their heavenly chariots and heavenly music, for such as these are not to be won by men; have thyself waited upon by these, for I will give them; but ask me not about dying.

This preferable even to the pleasures that the gods enjoy.

"Nachiketas answered: These are things that may or may not be to-morrow, and things that waste the strength of all the faculties; and every life alike is short. I leave to thee the chariots, and the singing and the dancing.

"A man is not to be satisfied with wealth. We shall obtain wealth. If we have seen thee we shall live so long as thou rulest, but no more. The boon that I choose is preferable to this.

"For what decaying mortal in this lower world, after

CHAP. V.

coming into the presence of the undecaying and immortal gods,—what mortal that has knowledge, and that reflects upon the fleeting pleasures of beauty and love, would be enamoured of long life?

"Tell us, Death, about that great life after death that the gods are themselves in doubt about. Nachiketas chooses no other boon than this boon that penetrates that mystery."

So far Yama has tested the readiness of Nachiketas to renounce the pleasures of the world. Finding him ready to put away all ties, he judges that he is a fit disciple, and proceeds to contrast the two pursuits of men, the pursuit of the pleasurable, which prolongs the series of embodied lives, and the pursuit of the good, which leads to a final release from metempsychosis. Nachiketas has already chosen the pursuit of the good.

Second Vallî. The pleasurable and the good.

II. "The good is one thing, the pleasurable another. Both these engage a man, though the ends are diverse. Of these, it is well with him that takes the good, and he that chooses the pleasurable fails of his purpose.

"Both the good and the pleasurable present themselves to man; and the wise man goes round about them both and distinguishes between them. The sage prefers the good to the pleasurable; the unwise man chooses the pleasurable that he may get and keep.

"Thou, Nachiketas, hast thought upon these tender and alluring pleasures, and hast renounced them. Thou hast not chosen the path of riches, which most men sink in.

"Far apart are these diverse and diverging paths, the path of illusion and the path of knowledge. I know thee, Nachiketas, that thou art a seeker of knowledge, for all these various pleasures that I proposed have not distracted thee.

The liturgic experts are blind leaders of the blind.

[1] "They that are infatuated, dwelling in the midst

[1] This verse occurs also in the second section of the first Muṇḍaka. See above, p. 101.

of the illusion, wise in their own eyes, and learned in their own conceit, are stricken with repeated plagues, and go round and round, like blind men led by the blind.

"Preparation for the hereafter does not suggest itself to the foolish youth neglecting everything in his infatuation about riches. Thinking that this life is, and that there is no life after this, he comes again and again into subjection to me.

The seekers of the Self are few.

"The good, the Self, is not reached by many that they should hear it; and many hearing of it know it not. Wonderful is he that teaches it, and wise is he that attains to it; wonderful is he that knows it when he is taught by the wise.

"This Self is not proclaimed by an inferior man; it is not easy to know when variously thought upon. When it is taught by one that is one with it, there is no dissentiency about it. It is supersensible beyond the infinitesimal, and is unthinkable.

"This idea of the Self that thou hast gained is not to be attained by the discursive intellect, but it is easy to know it when revealed by another, dearest disciple. Thou art truly steadfast. May I find another questioner equal to thee, Nachiketas!

"I know that the treasure of recompense is fleeting, for that lasting Self is not gained by transient works; and therefore I have piled up the Nāchiketa fire, and have won with perishable goods a lasting sphere."

There is an apparent inconsistency between the former and the latter portions of this last verse. The scholiast explains that the lasting sphere that Yama has attained by means of the Nāchiketa sacrifice is the regency of the dead. This is said to be lasting, not as everlasting like the Self, but only as enduring throughout an æon until the next dissolution or collapse of all things into the aboriginal unity of Brahman. In the verse that next follows Yama commends Nachiketas for refusing

CHAP. V.

to be satisfied with the sphere of the highest divinity already promised to his knowledge of the Nāchiketa rite, and for insisting on the pursuit of a knowledge of Brahman, the one and only Self.

Renunciation and meditative abstraction the only path of safety.

"Though thou hast seen the consummation of desire, the basis of the world, the lasting meed of sacrifice, the farther shore where fear is left behind,—great and glorious and wide-spread, a place to stand upon,—yet, Nachiketas, thou hast renounced it all, wise in thy fortitude.

"By spiritual abstraction the sage recognises the primeval divine Self, invisible, unfathomable; put out of sight by things of sense, but seated in the heart, dwelling in the recesses of the mind; and on recognising it he bids farewell to joy and sorrow.

"When a mortal man has heard this, and grasped it on all sides, and parted Self from all that is not Self, and reached this subtile essence, he rejoices at it, for he has won pure bliss. I know thee, Nachiketas, to be a habitation open to that spiritual essence.

"Nachiketas said: Tell me about that which thou seest, which is apart from good and apart from evil, apart from the create and the uncreate, apart from that which has been and that which is to be.

The mystic syllable OM must be employed by the seeker of the Self.

"Yama said: I will tell thee briefly the utterance that all the Vedas celebrate, which all modes of self-coercion proclaim, and aspiring to which men live as celibate votaries of sacred science. It is OM.

"This mystic utterance is Brahmā, this mystic utterance is Brahman. He that has this has all that he would have.

"This is the best reliance, this is the highest reliance; he that knows this reliance is glorified in the sphere of Brahmā."

The repetition of the mystic monosyllable and meditation upon it, is said to raise the less skilful aspirants[1]

[1] The *mandādhikārin* and *madhyamādhikārin*.

to the paradise of Brahmā, the highest of the deities, the first emanation out of the divine Self. To the higher order of aspirants[1] it serves as a help on the way to knowledge of Brahman, and extrication from the miseries of metempsychosis, as being an image or a substitute for the characterless Self.

CHAP. V.

"This Self is not born, and dies not; it is omniscient. It proceeds from none, and none proceeds from it; it is without beginning and without end, unfailing, from before all time. It is not killed when the body is killed.

"If the slayer think to slay, and if the slain think that he is slain, they neither of them know the Self that they are. This neither slays nor is slain.

Antithetic epithets of the Self.

"Lesser than the least and greater than the greatest, this Self is seated in the heart of every living thing. This the passionless sage beholds and his sorrows are left behind; in the limpid clearness of his faculties he sees the greatness of the Self.

"Motionless it moves afar, sleeping it goes out on every side. Who but I can know that joyful and joyless deity?

"It is bodiless and in all bodies, unchanging and in all changing things. The sage that knows himself to be the infinite, all-pervading Self, no longer sorrows."

The scholiasts remark that contradictory attributes are simultaneously predicable of the Self, as, on the one hand, it is the characterless Self *per se*, and as, on the other hand, it is the Self present in this or that fictitious embodiment. The Self may thus be likened to a colourless gem reflecting the various hues of the things that are nearest to it, or to a magic crystal,[2] presenting to the spectator the various things he may choose to think about. The pure indifference alone is true, the differences are illusory, mere figments of the cosmical illusion.

[1] *Uttamādhikārin.*

[2] *Chintāmaṇi.*

CHAP. V.

The Self manifests itself to the purified aspirant.

[1]"This Self is not attainable by learning, by memory, by much sacred study; but if he chooses this Self it is attainable by him: the Self itself manifests its own essence to him.

"Neither he that has not ceased from evil, nor he that ceases not from sensations, nor he that is not concentrated, nor he whose mind is not quiescent, can reach this Self by spiritual insight.

"Who in this way knows where that Self is, of which Brāhman and Kshatriya are the food and death the condiment?"

All personal distinctions are merged in the characterless impersonality of the Self. Brāhman[2] and Kshatriya, and death itself that swallows all, are swallowed up and reabsorbed into it, at the close of every æon. To return to the text.

Third Vallī. The individual soul and the soul of the world.

III. "The universal and the individual souls residing in the cavity, in the ether of the heart, in the same body, drink in the recompense of works. Sages that know the Self, householders that keep up the five sacred fires,[3] and worshippers who have thrice performed the Nāchiketa rite,—alike pronounce that these universal and the individual souls are like shade and sunshine."

Properly speaking, it is only the individual soul that has fruition of its works in body after body. The visible body is the place of pleasures and pains.[4] The universal soul, or Īśvara, abides together with it in the heart, the regulator of its actions and witness of its experiences, as is set forth in the simile of the two birds in the first section of the third Muṇḍaka. The individual soul differs from the universal as shade from

[1] This verse occurs also in the second section of the third Muṇḍaka. See above, p. 110.

[2] *Brahman*, manifested as Īśvara, is here spoken of as the *viśvasaṃhartṛi*, as retracting all things into its own essence at each *pralaya* or period of universal collapse.

[3] The five fires known as Anvāhāryapachana, Gārhapatya, Āhavanīya, Sabhya, and Āvasathya.

[4] *Sukhaduḥkhāyatana*, *bhogāyatana*.

sunshine, the individual soul migrating from body to body, and the universal soul being free from such migration. CHAP. V.

"We know and can pile up the Nāchiketa fire, the bridge that leads the sacrificers to the sphere of the highest deity; and we also know the undecaying, highest Self, the farther shore beyond all fear for those that will to cross the sea of metempsychosis."

There now follows the celebrated simile of the chariot.[1] The migrating soul is compared to a person in a chariot; the body is the chariot, the mind is the charioteer, the common sensory or will the reins, the senses the horses. The soul drives in this chariot either along the path of metempsychosis, or along the road of liberation from further embodiments.

Allegory of the chariot.

"Know that the soul is seated in a chariot, and that the body is that chariot. Know that the mind is the charioteer, and that the will is the reins.

"They say that the senses are the horses, and that the things of sense are the road. The wise declare that the migrating soul is the Self fictitiously present in the body, senses, and common sensory.

"Now if the charioteer, the mind, is unskilful, and the reins are always slack, his senses are ever unruly, like horses that will not obey the charioteer.

"But if the charioteer is skilful, and at all times firmly holds the reins, his senses are always manageable, like horses that obey the charioteer.

"If the mind, the charioteer, lacks knowledge, and does not firmly hold the will, and is always deficient in purity, the soul fails to reach the goal, and returns to further transmigration.

The goal is release from metempsychosis by reunion with the Self.

"But if the charioteer has knowledge, and firmly holds the will, and is at all times pure, the soul then arrives at the goal, and on reaching it is never born again.

"The soul whose charioteer is skilful and holds

[1] *Ratharūpaka.*

CHAP. V. firmly the reins of the will, reaches the further term of its migration, the sphere of Vishnu the supreme.

"For their objects are beyond and more subtile than the senses, the common sensory is beyond the objects, the mind is beyond the sensory, and the great soul Hiraṇyagarbha is beyond the mind.

"The ultimate and undeveloped principle[1] is beyond that great soul, and Purusha,[2] the Self, is beyond the undeveloped principle. Beyond Purusha there is nothing; that is the goal, that is the final term.

"This Self is hidden in all living things, it shines not forth; but it is seen by the keen and penetrating mind of those that see into the supersensible.

"Let the sage refund his voice into his inner sense, his inner sense into his conscious mind; let him refund his mind into the great soul, and let him refund the great soul into the quiescent Self.

The path of release is fine as the edge of a razor.

"Arise, awake, go to the great teachers and learn. The wise affirm this to be a sharp razor's edge hard to walk across, a difficult path.

"When a man has seen the Self, inaudible, intangible, colourless, undecaying, imperishable, odourless, without beginning and without end, beyond the mind, ultimate and immutable,—when he has seen that, he escapes the power of death.

"The sage that hears and recites this primeval narrative that Death recited and Nachiketas heard is worshipped as in the sphere of Self.

"If the purified sage rehearse this highest mystery before an assembly of Brāhmans, or to those present at a Śrāddha ceremony, it avails to endless recompense, it avails to endless recompense."

Self is said to be hidden within all living things, as lying veiled beneath those fictitious presentments of the senses that make up the experience of common life.

[1] Māyā, Avidyā, the world-fiction, the cosmical illusion.
[2] Purusha is here synonymous with Brahman.

The aspirant to extrication from metempsychosis is to melt away the visible and nameable semblances that hide it from him; to cease to see the figments, and to see only that which they replace; as a man may cease to see the waters of the mirage, and may come to see the sands of the desert in place of which they have fictitiously presented themselves to his illusive vision. The varied phases of fictitious life, and the varied elemental environments of migrating souls, are to be set aside by progressive abstraction and ecstatic vision; they are like so many webs of finer and finer tissue woven across and across the Self, and veiling it from heedless eyes. In the descending order each successive manifestation is more and more concrete; in the ascending order each is more and more simple, fine, or subtile. In the progress of abstraction each later is melted away into each earlier manifestation; the mind of the aspirant rises to more and more subtile and supersensible emanations, until he arrives at that which lies beyond them all, the Self that emanates from nothing, and cannot be melted away into any principle from which it has emanated. In a new metaphor he is then said to have awakened from his dreaming vision of the figments of the world-fiction to the intuition of his true nature as one with the characterless and impersonal spiritual essence. To return to the text.

The liberated theosophist wakes up out of this dream-world into real being.

Fourth Vallî.

IV. "The self-existent Īśvara has suppressed the senses that go out towards the things of sense. These senses then go out, not inwards to the Self. Here and there a wise man with the craving for immortality has closed his eyes and seen the Self.

"The unwise follow after outward pleasures and enter into the net of wide-spread death; but the wise, who know what it is to be immortal, seek not for the imperishable amidst the things that perish."

The net of death is metempsychosis, the endless succession of birth and death, decay and sickness. To be

CHAP. V.

immortal is not to be as the gods are, who live till the close of a period of evolution, but to be at one with the transcendent Self. The state of the gods is said to be a relative immortality:[1] they are implicated in metempsychosis until they liberate themselves by self-suppression and ecstatic meditation.

"What is left over as unknown to that Self by which the soul knows colour and taste and smell and sound and touch? This is that."

This is that, this is the imperishable principle in man, as to the existence of which the gods themselves are said to have been puzzled, the principle about which Nachiketas has inquired, the spiritual reality that manifests itself in the world of semblances.

The sage eludes the net of death, and has no fear.

"He that knows that this living soul that eats the honey of recompense, and is always near, is the Self, and that it is the lord of all that all that has been and all that is to be, no longer seeks to protect himself from anything. This is that.".

The sage that knows that his true nature is imperishable, and that his bodily life is only a source of misery, is exempt from fear, and there are no longer any perils against which he can seek to protect himself. He has won—

> "A clear escape from tyrannising lust,
> And full immunity from penal woe;"

and is one with the universal soul, the deity that makes the world, and one with Brahman.

"He sees the Self who sees Hiraṇyagarbha, that emanated from the self-coercion of Īśvara, that came forth before the elements, that has entered into the cavity of the heart, and there abides with living creatures. This is that.

"He sees the Self who sees Aditi, one with all the gods, who emanated out of Hiraṇyagarbha, and has

[1] *Āpekshikam amṛitatvam. Ābhūtasamplavam avasthānam amṛitatvaṃ hi bhāshyate.*

entered into the cavity of the heart, and there abides with living creatures. This is that. CHAP. V.

"Agni, the fire that is hidden in the fire-drills as the unborn child within the mother, to be adored day by day by men as they wake and as they offer their oblations,—this is that."

Agni the fire-god, worshipped in the Vedic sacrifices, is here identified with Hiraṇyagarbha, as also the fire within the heart meditated upon by the self-torturing mystic or Yogin. Hiraṇyagarbha is said to be one with Brahman, as an earring is one with the gold of which it is made.

"All the gods are based upon that divine being Hiraṇyagarbha, out of whom the sun rises, into whom the sun sets. No one is beyond identity with that divine being. This is that.

"What the Self is in the world, that is it outside the world; and what it is outside the world, that it is in the world. From death to death he goes who looks on this as manifold."

It is illusion that presents the manifold of experience

The Self manifested in every form of life, from a tuft of grass up to the highest deity, and passing in semblance from body to body, is the same with the Self outside the world, Brahman *per se*, the characterless thought beyond the fictions of metempsychosis. He that sees in his individual soul an entity apart from the universal soul, and other than the one impersonal Self, retains his fictitious individuality, and must pass from body to body so long as he retains it. Let a man therefore see that he is one with the one reality, the characterless thought, that is, like the ether that is everywhere, a continuous plenitude of being. It is only illusion[1] that presents the variety of experience, a variety that melts away into unity on the rise of the ecstatic vision. The many pass, the one abides.

"It is to be reached only with the inner sense; there

[1] *Nānātvapratyupasthāpikā 'vidyā.*

CHAP. V.

is nothing in it that is manifold. From death to death he goes who looks on this as manifold.

"Purusha, the Self, is within the midst of the body, of the size of a thumb, the lord of all that has been and of all that is to be. He that knows this seeks no longer to protect himself. This is that.

Purusha or Brahman is pure light.

"Purusha, of the size of a thumb, is like a smokeless light, the lord of all that has been and of all that is to be. This alone is to-day and is to-morrow. This is that.

"He that looks upon his bodily manifestations as other than the Self, passes into them again and again, as rain that has fallen on a hill loses itself among the heights.

"The soul of the sage that knows the unity of souls in the Self, is like pure water poured out upon a level surface."

The Self is figuratively said to be of the size of a thumb, inasmuch as it is manifested in the mind, and the mind is lodged in the cavity of the heart; in the same way as the ether within a hollow cane may be said to be of the same size as the hollow, whereas in propriety this ether is one with the ether present everywhere, one and undivided. The soul of the sage that sees the unity of all things is compared to pure water upon a level surface, as having returned to its proper nature of pure undifferenced thinking. It is a uniformity of thought in which every particular character of thought has been suppressed.

Fifth Valli.

V. "The sage who meditates upon his body as an eleven-gated city for the Self, without beginning, and of changeless thought, ceases to sorrow, is already liberated, and liberated once for all. This is that.

Various manifestations of Purusha or Brahman.

"This is the all-permeating Self; it is the sun in the firmament, the air in middle space, the fire on this earth as its altar; it is the guest in the house; it dwells in men, it dwells in the gods, it dwells in the sacrifices, it dwells in the sky; it is born in the waters in the shapes of aquatic animals, it is born on the earth as barley, rice, and every other plant, it is born in the sacrificial elements, it is born on the mountains in the form of rivers. It is the true, the infinite. CHAP. V.

"It impels the breath upwards, it impels the descending air of life downwards. All the senses bring their offerings to this adorable being seated in the midst of the heart.

"When the spirit that is in the perishing body is parted from it, what is left of the body? This is that.

"No mortal lives by his breath or by the descending vital air. They live by another principle in which these vital airs reside."

Vedāntic proofs of the existence of the Self.

The scholiasts remark of the last three verses that they give the proofs of the existence of the Self. These proofs are these:—The activities of the vital airs (on which, in Indian physiology, the functions of the viscera are said to depend), and the functions of the senses and the muscles, are for the sake of some conscious principle ulterior to themselves; the activity of unconscious things being instrumental to the ends of conscious beings, as the activity of a chariot is instrumental to the ends of the person driving in it. Again, the body implies a conscious tenant, as it loses all sense of pleasure and pain on the departure of that tenant. Again, the body is composite, and everything composite exists for the sake of something ulterior to itself,—a bed for the sake of the sleeper, a house for the sake of the inmates, and so forth. That there is an ultimate principle of reality beyond the plurality of experience, is proved by the fact that the last residuum of all abstraction is entity. After all differences have one by one been thrown away, the mind remains to the last filled with the idea of being. And this ultimate reality is proved to be spiritual, by that power of intuition to which the aspirant to extrication may rise even in this

CHAP. V.

life. He comes to see the light within the heart, the light of consciousness in which the modes of mind are manifested. He puts away the duality of subject and object as the fictitious outflow of the world-fiction,[1] and recovers the characterless bliss of unity, the fulness of joy that is the proper nature of the soul as Self. Every phase of happiness [2] in everyday experience is only a fictitious portion of that total blessedness, and everything that is dear to us is dear only as it is one with us in the unity of the beatific Self.[3] To return to the text.

What becomes of the soul at death.

"Lo, Gautama, I will again proclaim to thee this mystery, the everlasting Self, and how it is with the Self after death.

"Some souls pass to another birth to enter into another body, and some enter into vegetable lives, according to their works, and according to their knowledge.

"The spirit that is awake in those that sleep, fashioning to itself enjoyment after enjoyment,—this is the pure Self, this is the immortal; on this the spheres of recompense are based; beyond this none can pass. This is that.

The Self is like a permeating fire, or like a pervading atmosphere.

"As one and the same fire pervades a house and shapes itself to the shape of everything, so the one Self that is in all living things shapes itself to all their several shapes, and is at the same time outside them.

"As one and the same atmosphere pervades a house and shapes itself to the shape of everything, so the one Self that is in all living things shapes itself to all their several shapes, and is at the same time outside them.

Simile of the sun unsullied by the impurities it looks down upon.

"As the sun, the eye of all the world, is unsullied by visible external impurities, so the one Self that is within

[1] *Niraste 'vidyākṛite vishayavishayivibhāge vidyayā svābhāvikaḥ paripūrṇa eka ānando 'dvaite bhavati.*

[2] *Laukiko hy ānando brahmānandasyaiva mātrā.*

[3] *Ātmaprītisādhanatvād gauṇī anyatra prītiḥ.*

all living things is not soiled by the miseries of migration, and is external to them. CHAP. V.

"The wise see within their own heart the one and only lord, the Self that is in all living things, that makes its one form to become many; and everlasting bliss is for them and not for others.

"The wise see within their own heart the one thing that perishes not in all things that perish; the one thing that gives light in all things that have no light; the one being that gives the recompense to many; and peace eternal is for them and not for others.

Everlasting peace is for them only that find the light of the world in their own hearts.

"This is that, so think they; this is the unspeakable, the bliss above all bliss. How shall I come to know that bliss? does it shine forth, does it reveal itself?

"[1]The sun gives no light to that, nor the moon and stars; neither do these lightnings light it up; how then should this fire of ours? All things shine after it as it shines, all this world is radiant with its light.

"VI. This everlasting holy fig-tree stands with roots above, with branches downwards. Its root is that pure Self, that immortal principle. All the spheres of recompense have grown up upon it, and no man can pass beyond it. This is that. Sixth Vallī.

"All this world, whatever is, trembles in that living breath; it has come forth and stirs with life. They that know this, the great awe, the uplifted thunderbolt, become immortal.

"[2]In awe of this, fire gives heat; in awe of this, the sun scorches; in awe of this speed Indra and Vāyu, and the Death-god speeds besides those other four.

"If a man has been able to see this in this life before his body falls away from him, he is loosed from future embodiments. If not, he is fated to further embodiments in future ages and future spheres of recompense.

[1] This verse occurs also in the second section of the second Muṇḍaka. See above, p. 106.

[2] A similar verse occurs in the Taittirīya Upanishad. See above, p. 82.

"This Self is seen in the heart as in a mirror, in the sphere of the forefathers as in a dream, in the sphere of the Gandharvas as on a watery surface, in the sphere of Brahmā as in light and shade."

The world-tree and the seed from which it springs.

Brahman, it has been seen, is the seed of the world-tree, and Māyā is the power of growth residing in the seed. Here Brahman is said to be the root of the world-tree. The world of semblances is a tree, and may be cut down with the hatchet of ecstatic vision. It grows up upon Brahman as its root, out of the world-fiction Māyā as its seed. Hiraṇyagarbha is the sprouting seed. It is watered by the cravings of migrating souls, whose actions through the law of retribution prolong the existence of the spheres of metempsychosis. Its fruits are the pleasure and pains of living things. The spheres of recompense are the nests in which deities and migrating souls dwell like birds. It rustles with the cries, the weeping, and the laughter, of the souls in pain or for the moment happy. It is like a holy fig-tree in constant agitation, tremulous to the breeze of emotion and of action. Its pendulous branches are the paradises, places of torment, and spheres of good and evil recompense. It is in constant growth and change, varying from moment to moment. It is unreal as the imagery of a reverie, as the waters of a mirage, and vanishes away in the light of intuition of the one and only truth, the Self beyond it. The Self in its earliest manifestation as Īśvara is the great awe; the being in fear of whom the sun and moon and stars, and all the powers of nature, perform their never-ceasing ministrations. The sage is urged to strive with all his force to rise to the intuition of the Self, before he quits his present body. In this life he can see the light within his heart in the polished mirror of a purified mind. In the sphere of the Pitṛis or forefathers of the tribes, to which the soul of the worshipper of the deities proceeds, he can see it faintly and dimly only as in a dream, for in that sphere the soul is engrossed in the enjoyment of its reward. In the sphere of the Gandharvas, he can see it only fitfully reflected as on a ruffled sheet of water. In the sphere of Brahmā, the highest deity, it may indeed be seen as a thing is seen in the sunlight and in the shade, but this sphere is promised only to the rarest merit, and the sage may fail to win it. To return to the text.

CHAP. V.

"The wise man knows that the senses are not himself, and that they rise and set as they have severally issued forth, and knowing this he grieves no more.

"The inner sensory is beyond the senses, the mind is higher than the inner sensory, the great soul Hiraṇyagarbha is higher than the mind, and the undeveloped principle[1] is higher than that great soul.

"The supreme Purusha[2] is beyond the undeveloped principle, pervading all things, characterless; and the migrating soul that knows this Purusha is loosed from metempsychosis, and passes into immortality.

The Self is to be seen only as mirrored on the purified mind of the aspirant.

"Its form is not in anything visible; no man has seen this Self with his eyes: it is seen as revealed by the heart, the mind, the spiritual intuition. They that know this Self become immortal.

"When the five senses and the inner sense are at rest, and when the mind ceases to act, they call this the highest state.

Ecstatic vision, and the recovery of immortality.

"They account this motionless suspension of the senses to be the ecstatic union. This is the unintermittent union, for union has its furtherances and hindrances.

"The Self is not to be reached with voice, or thought, or eye. How shall it be known otherwise than as he knows it who says only that it is?

"It is,—only thus is the Self to be known, and as that which is true in both that which is and that which is not. Its real nature reveals itself only when it is known as that which is.

[1] Māyā. [2] Brahman.

CHAP. V.

"When all the desires that lie in his heart are shaken off, the mortal becomes immortal, and in this life rejoins the Self.

"When all his heart's ties already in this life are broken off, the mortal becomes immortal. This is the whole of the sacred doctrine."

Apathy, vacuity, and trance, the steps of access to the Self.

The aspirant must become passionless. If he desire anything he will act to get it, and action is followed by recompense in this or in a future body. All desire arises from the illusion by which a man views his animated organism as himself. Action, good and evil alike, serves only to prolong the miseries of migration, by giving rise to retributive experience. The aspirant must learn the falsity of plurality, the fictitious nature of the duality in experience, and the sole reality of the supersensible and unitary Self. He must crush every sense and suppress every thought, that his mind may become a mirror to reflect the pure, characterless being, thought, and bliss. Its everyday experience is a dream of the soul, and it is only by suppressing this experience that it awakes to its proper nature. It is true that the Self is not to be reached by desire or thought; but if it be argued that it is not, for if it were it would be reached, the reply, says Śankarāchārya, is as follows. The Self is, for it may be reached as the ultimate principle from which all things have emanated. Refund by progressive efforts of abstraction each successive entity in the world of semblances into the entity out of which it emanated; ascend through the series of emanations to the more and more rarefied, the less and less determinate; do this, and you will find, at the end of this process, the idea of being. The final mode of mind is not nonentity but entity.[1] The mind, after thus resolving all things into the things from which they came, is itself

[1] *Yadāpi vishayapravilāpanena pravilāpyamānā buddhis tadāpi sā satpratyayagarbhaiva vilīyate.*

resolved; yet as it melts away it melts away in the form of existence and full of the idea of being; and the mind is our only informant as to what is and is not. Again, another reply is, that if non-existence were the root of the world, all the things of the world that have successively come into manifestation would manifest themselves as non-existent. This is not the case; these things manifest themselves as existent, as an earthenware vessel manifests itself as made of earth. It is only as apart from that which underlies them that these things are non-existent, "a modification of speech only, a change, a name." The Self is "true in both that which is, and that which is not," it is true in its proper nature as the fontal characterless essence, and true underneath the figments of the world-fiction that illusively overspread it. The desires are said to lie in the heart. The feelings, passions, thoughts, and volitions are modes of mind, and the mind is lodged in the heart. When these modes are blown out like a lamp, the personality passes away into the impersonality of Brahman. To proceed with the text.

The soul's path of egress and ascent to the courts of Brahmā.

"There are a hundred and one arteries to the heart, and one of these issues up through the head. Going upwards by that artery a sage ascends to immortality. The other arteries proceed in all directions."

The coronal artery, *sushumnā*, is the passage by which the soul of the aspirant to extrication from metempsychosis ascends to the sphere of Brahmā, there to sojourn till it wills its reabsorption into the pure spiritual essence Brahman. The other arteries are the passages through which the soul issues out to new embodiments.

"Of the size of a thumb, the Purusha, the Self within, is ever seated in the hearts of living things. The sage should patiently extract it from his body, as he might extract the pith out of a reed; and he should learn that that Self is pure and immortal, pure and immortal.

"Thus Nachiketas received this gnosis revealed by

CHAP. V.

the god of death, together with all the precepts for ecstatic union; he reached the Self, and became free from good and evil, and immortal; and so will any other sage become who thus knows the fontal spiritual essence.

"May he preserve us both, may he reward us both. May we put forth our strength together, and may that which we recite be efficacious. May we never feel enmity against each other. OM. Peace, peace, peace. Hari. OM."

The formula with which the Kaṭha Upanishad closes has already several times occurred in these pages. It is intended to secure the co-operation of the universal soul or Demiurgus, and the safe tradition and reception of its doctrines of gnosis and ecstatic vision by teacher and disciple.

The allegory of the chariot compared with the Platonic figure in the Phædrus.

One of the most striking passages in this Upanishad is the allegory of the chariot in the third section. The migrating soul is said to be seated in the body as in a chariot. The mind is the charioteer, the will is the reins, the senses are the horses, and the journey is either towards fresh embodiments or towards release from metempsychosis. This allegory of the chariot has often been compared with the Platonic figure in the Phædrus, in which the souls of gods and of men in the ante-natal state are pictured as a charioteer in a chariot with a pair of winged horses. The charioteer is the reason. In the chariots of the gods both horses are excellent, with perfect wings; in the human chariot one of the horses is white and fully winged, the other black and unruly, with imperfect or half-grown wings. The white horse typifies the rational impulse, and the black violent and rebellious horse represents the sensual and concupiscent elements of human nature. In these chariots gods and men ascend to the vision of the intelligible archetypes of things, men for ever slipping down again to intercourse only with the things of sense, to feed upon opinion, and no longer upon truth.

"Now the winged horses and charioteers of the gods are all of them good and of good breed, while those of men are mixed. We have a charioteer who drives them in a pair, and one of them is excellent and of excellent origin, and the other is base and of base origin; and necessarily it is hard and troublesome to manage them. The teams of the gods, evenly poised, glide upwards in obedience to the rein; but the others have a difficulty, for the horse that has evil in him, if he has not been thoroughly broken in by the charioteer, goes heavily, inclining towards the earth, and depressing the driver."

The gods ascend to the heaven above the heavens, the place of pure truth, and there contemplate the colourless and figureless ideas. "This is the life of the gods, but of the other souls that which follows the gods best and is likest to them lifts the head of the charioteer into the outer region, and is carried round in the revolution of the worlds, troubled with the horses, and seeing the ideas with difficulty. Another rises above and dips below the surface of the upper and outer region, and sees and again fails to see, owing to the restiveness of its team. The rest of the souls are also longing after the upper world, and they all follow; but not being strong enough, they sink below the surface as they are carried round, plunging, treading on one another, striving to be first. There is confusion, and conflict, and the extremity of effort, and many of them are lamed or have their wings broken through the ill-driving of the charioteers; and all of them, after a long toil, depart without being initiated into the spectacle of being, and after their departure are fain to feed upon the food of opinion. The reason why the souls show this great eagerness to see the field of truth is that pasturage is found in that meadow suited to the highest part of the soul, and to the growth of the pinions on

CHAP. V. which the soul flies lightly upwards. And the law of Nemesis is this, that the soul which, in company with the gods, has seen something of the truth, shall remain unharmed until the next great revolution of the world, and the soul that is able always to do so shall be unharmed for ever. But when a soul is unable to keep pace, and fails to see, and through some mishap is filled with forgetfulness and vice, and weighed down, and sheds its plumage, and falls to the earth beneath the weight, the law is that this soul shall not in its first birth pass into the shape of any other animal, but only into that of man. The soul that has seen most of truth shall come to the birth as a philosopher, or lover of beauty, or musician, or amorist; that which has seen truth in the second degree shall be a righteous king, or warrior, or lord; the soul that is of a third order shall be a politician, or economist, or trader; the fourth shall be a lover of hard exercise, or gymnast, or physician; the fifth shall have the life of a soothsayer or hierophant; to the sixth the life of a poet or some kind of imitator will be suitable; to the seventh the life of an artisan or husbandman; to the eighth that of a professor or a people's man; to the ninth that of a tyrant. In all these varieties of life he who lives righteously obtains a better lot, and he who lives unrighteously a worse one." The soul of him that has never seen a glimpse of truth will pass into the human form, but into some lower form of life. "The intellect of the philosopher alone recovers its wings, for it is ever dwelling in memory upon those essences, the vision of which makes the gods themselves divine. He is ever being initiated into perfect mysteries, and alone becomes truly perfect. But as he forgets human interests and is rapt in the divine, the many think that he is beside himself and check him; they fail to see that he is inspired."

CHAPTER VI.

THE BRIHADARANYAKA UPANISHAD.

"The thing visible, nay the thing imagined, the thing in any way conceived as visible, what is it but a garment, a clothing of the higher celestial, invisible, unimaginable, formless, dark with excess of bright. This so solid-seeming world, after all, is but an air-image over Me, the only reality; and nature, with its thousand-fold production and destruction, but the reflex of our own inward force, the phantasy of our dream; or what the earth-spirit in Faust names it, the living visible garment of God:—

"In being's flood, in action's storm,
I walk and work, above, beneath,
Work and weave in endless motion,
Birth and death,
An infinite ocean;
A seizing and a giving
The fire of living:
Tis thus that at the roaring loom of time I ply,
And weave for God the garment thou seest him by."

—CARLYLE.

MANY of the most impressive utterances of the primitive Indian philosophy are to be found in the Bṛihadāraṇyaka Upanishad, a long treatise on the science of Brahman, forming the last portion of the Śatapathabrāhmaṇa, the legendary and liturgic dissertation annexed to the Vājasaneyisamhitā, or so-called White Recension of the Yajurveda. A passage treating of renunciation, ecstasy, and the liberation of the soul has been already laid before the reader in the third chapter of this work. The present chapter will present the greater part of the narratives and dialogues of this Upanishad that relate to the revelation of the Self, CHAP. VI.

CHAP. VI. with a few words of explanation from the scholiasts interposed from time to time.

The Bṛihadāraṇyaka Upanishad.

The earlier part of the Bṛihadāraṇyaka Upanishad, setting forth the mystic significance of the Aśvamedha or horse-sacrifice, and relating the generation of the world by Prajāpati or Purusha, may be passed over. The first extract selected is the dialogue between Gārgya and Ajātaśatru. It is as follows:—

Dialogue of Ajātaśatru and the Gārgya.

"Once upon a time there lived the proud son of Balākā, a Gārgya, an able reciter of ancient learning. On a particular occasion he visited Ajātaśatru, the Raja of Kāśi, and said: Let me expound Brahman to you. Ajātaśatru replied: I will give you a thousand head of cattle as a return for your instruction, for people go about with the idea that a liberal man is the best disciple.

"The Gārgya said: I meditate upon the Purusha, the divine spirit that is in the sun, as the Self. Ajātaśatru said: Nay, never teach me of such a Self as that. I meditate upon the Self as that which stands beyond, the head of all things, the king of all things. He that meditates upon the Self in this manner stands beyond, the head of all things, the king of all things."

The being that the Gārgya identifies with the Self is his own individual soul, Brahman as it is manifested in the sun and in the eye, and that through the eye has entered into the hearts of living things, and seems to know and act and suffer in the world of semblances. He finds the Self in his own body and senses. Ajātaśatru at once rejects this presentation of the Self as inadequate; he himself already meditates upon the Self in a higher manifestation. [1]It is a Hindu maxim that a man rises to that grade of being under which he meditates upon Brahman. The Gārgya proceeds to enumerate a variety of other manifestations under which he meditates upon the sole spiritual essence.

[1] *Yathā yatho 'pāste tad eva bhavati.*

As in the first instance he found Brahman in the sun and in the organ of vision, of which the sun-god is the tutelary deity, so next he finds Brahman in the moon and in the inner sense or common sensory, of which the moon-god is the tutelary deity. CHAP. VI.

"The Gārgya said: I meditate upon the Purusha, the divine being that is in the moon, as the Self. Ajātaśatru said: Nay, never teach me of such a Self as that. I meditate upon the Self as the great, white-robed Soma, the king. If a man meditate upon the Self in this wise, his soma libation is pressed out and poured forth day by day, and his food does not fail.

"The Gārgya said: I meditate upon the Purusha, the divine being that is in the lightning, as the Self. Ajātaśatru said: Nay, never teach me of such a Self as that. I meditate upon the Self as the glorious being. He that meditates upon the Self in this wise becomes glorious, and his progeny becomes glorious.

"The Gārgya said: I meditate upon the Purusha, the divine being that is in the ether, as the Self. Ajātaśatru said: Nay, never teach me of such a Self as that. I meditate upon that which fills all things and is inoperative as the Self. He that meditates upon the Self in this wise has the fulness of offspring and of flocks and herds, and his posterity is never cut off in this world.

"The Gārgya said: I meditate upon the Purusha, the divine being that is in the air, as the Self. Ajātaśatru said: Nay, never teach me of such a Self as that. I meditate upon the Self as Indra the unassailable, and as the never-vanquished host of the Maruts. He that meditates upon the Self in this wise becomes an invincible victor, the vanquisher of the aliens.

"The Gārgya said: I meditate upon the Purusha, the divine being that is in fire, as the Self. Ajātaśatru said: Nay, never teach me of such a Self as that. I meditate upon the Self as the sustainer. He that meditates upon the Self in this way becomes a sus-

CHAP. VI. tainer of things, and his posterity become sustainers of things.

"The Gārgya said: I meditate upon the Purusha, the divine being that is in water, as the Self. Ajātaśatru replied: Nay, never teach me of such a Self as that. I meditate upon the Self as that which is in conformity with prescriptive ordinances. If a man meditate upon the Self in this wise, the fruit of such conformity accrues to him, and a religious son is born to him.

"The Gārgya said: I meditate upon the Purusha, the divine being that is seen upon a mirror, as the Self. Ajātaśatru said: Nay, never teach me of such a Self as that. I meditate upon the Self as the shining being. If a man meditate upon the Self in this way, he shines, his children shine, and he outshines all men that he meets with.

"The Gārgya said: I meditate upon the sound of my footsteps as the Self. Ajātaśatru said: Nay, never teach me of such a Self as that. I meditate upon the Self as the breath of life. If a man meditate upon the Self in this wise, he lives out his whole life in this world, and his breath does not fail him before his day.

"The Gārgya said: I meditate upon the Purusha, the divine being that is in the regions of space, as the Self. Ajātaśatru said: Nay, never teach me of such a Self as that. I meditate upon the Self as the companion that never leaves me. If a man meditate upon the Self in this way, he has friends, and his friends are never parted from him.

"The Gārgya said: I meditate upon the Purusha, the divine being that is my shadow, as the Self. Ajātaśatru said: Nay, never teach me of such a Self as that. I meditate upon death as the Self. If a man meditates upon the Self in this way, he lives out all his days in this life, and death does not come to him before his hour.

"The Gārgya said: I meditate upon the Purusha, the

divine being that is in the mind, as the Self. Ajātaśatru said: Nay, never teach me of such a Self as that. I meditate upon the Self as that which has peace of mind. If a man meditate upon the Self in this manifestation, he has peace of mind in this life, and his children have peace of mind. After this the Gārgya held his peace."

Bālāki the Gārgya knows the Self in its particular and local manifestations, as it presents itself fictitiously in the shape of the gods, in the forces of nature, and in the hearts and minds of living things. He does not know the Self as it is in its own nature, the Self *per se*, the Self unmanifested, the *nirguṇam brahma*, the *mukhyam brahma;* and Ajātaśatru the prince, finding that the Gārgya is put to shame and has nothing more to say, has to instruct the Brāhman in his own Brāhmanic lore.

"Ajātaśatru asked, Is this all you have to say? The Gārgya replied, It is all. Ajātaśatru said: The Self is not learnt by anything you have said so far. The Gārgya said: Let me wait upon you as your disciple.

Ajātaśatru teaches the Gārgya the doctrine of the three states of the soul, and of the Self beyond those states.

"Ajātaśatru said: It is preposterous that a Brāhman should come to a Kshatriya to be taught about the Self, but I will teach you. So he stood up and took him by the hand, and they went to a place where a man was lying asleep. The Raja called to him by the names, Great white-robed King Soma, but he did not rise. He patted him with his hand and woke him, and the man stood up.

"Ajātaśatru said: When this man was fast asleep where was his conscious soul, and where has it come from back to him? The Gārgya did not know what to say.

"Ajātaśatru said: When the conscious soul was asleep within him, it was in the ether in his heart, and had withdrawn into itself the knowledge that arises from the intimations of the senses. When the soul withdraws these into itself, it is said to sleep in the dreamless state; its sense is withdrawn into itself, its speech is withdrawn, its sight is withdrawn, its hearing is withdrawn, its inner sense is withdrawn.

"But when the soul enters into the dreaming state the retributive experiences present themselves, and the man seems to himself to be, it may be a great Raja, or it may be a great Brāhman, or he passes into bodies higher or lower than those of man. If he seems to be a great Raja, he seems to have his subjects, and to live as he pleases in his kingdom. In this way it is that he has withdrawn the outer senses into the inward sense, and lives as he wills within his own person.

"But when the soul returns to dreamless sleep and is no longer cognisant of anything, it retires by way of the seventy-two thousand arteries that proceed out of the heart and ramify throughout the body, into the body and reposes in it. It passes into the state of highest bliss and sleeps at peace like a child, like a great prince or Brāhman. It is thus that the spirit rests in dreamless sleep.

"All the senses, all the spheres of recompense, all the gods, and all living things proceed in all their diversity out of this Self, in like manner as a spider issues out of itself in the form of its threads, and as the little sparks fly on all sides out of a fire. The mystic name of this Self is the true in the true: the senses are true, and the Self is the truth of them."

Ajātaśatru thus teaches Bālāki that Brahman is the one and only Self, that manifests itself in the seeming plurality of souls in their three states of dreamless sleep, dreaming sleep, and waking experience. The peaceful state of the undreaming sleeper, in which the duality of subject and object has for the time melted away, is the highest manifestation of the one divine life that lives in all things. In this state the soul recovers its native purity; it is like water that has been purified from previous discolorations. To sleep without dreaming is to be released awhile from the miseries of metempsychosis. To be for ever in such a state would be final peace and blessedness, the devoutly-to-be-wished-for consummation. In the state of dreamless sleep the Self is said to permeate the whole body, as fire penetrates and permeates a redhot mass of iron. In the state of dreaming sleep the senses are withdrawn through the arteries into the mind [1] within the heart, and the inner sensory [2] presents a series of images that simulate the objects of perception. On awaking, the organs of sense and motion are sent out of the mind to their several stations in the body through the network of the arteries. In dreaming and in waking the modes of the mind shine, that is, rise into consciousness, in the light of the Self that dwells in the heart. In dreamless sleep there are no modes of mind to be lighted up, for the mind is for the time melted away. The Self is said at that time to permeate the body, only in the sense that it is ready to reillumine the mind so soon as it shall reappear. Brahman is said to be the true in the true. Brahman is that out of which all things arise, that upon which they abide in false presentment, and that into which they disappear again. All things are the five elements, or made of the five elements, in their supersensible or their sensible manifestation. The mind and the senses are themselves made of the supersensible elements. The elements are designated name and colour; name and colour are said to be the true, and Brahman is that which is true in this true.

The next dialogue in the Bṛihadāraṇyaka Upanishad is that between the Ṛishi Yājñavalkya and his wife Maitreyī. Yājñavalkya is on the point of quitting the ties of home to become a religious mendicant, that he may be able to ponder on the emptiness of life and to seek reunion with the one and only being, the impersonal Self.

[1] *Buddhi.* [2] *Manas.*

CHAP. VI.

Dialogue of Yājñavalkya and his wife Maitreyī.

"Yājñavalkya said: Maitreyī, I am about to leave this home-life; come, let me divide the property between thee and my other wife, Kātyāyanī.

"Maitreyī said: If all this earth were mine and full of riches, should I be any the more immortal? No, replied Yājñavalkya; your life would be like the life of other wealthy people; but as for immortality, there is no hope of that from riches.

"Maitreyī said: What am I to do with a thing that will not make me immortal? Tell me, holy lord, the thing that thou knowest. Yājñavalkya said: I love you indeed, and I love what you now say; come, sit down, and I will tell you, and you must think deeply about what I say.

Things that are dear are dear for the sake of the Self.

"He said: A husband is loved, not for love of the husband, but the husband is loved for love of the Self that is one within us all. A wife is loved, not for love of the wife, but a wife is loved for love of the Self. Children are loved, not for love of the children, but children are loved for love of the Self. Wealth is loved, not for love of wealth, but wealth is loved for love of the Self. The Brāhmanic order is loved, not for the love of that order, but for the love of the Self. The Kshatriya order is loved, not for the love of that order, but for the love of the Self. The spheres of recompense are loved, not for the love of those spheres, but for the love of the Self. The gods are loved, not for the love of the gods, but the gods are loved for love of the Self. Living things are loved, not for love of the living things, but for love of the Self. The world is loved, not for love of the world, but the world is loved for love of the Self that is one in all things. Ah! Maitreyī, it is the Self that one must see, and hear about, and think about, and meditate upon. All this world is known by seeing the Self, by hearing about it, thinking about it, meditating upon it."

It is the Self that is to be seen.

These expressions look strange and not very lucid,

but the words must be taken to represent a nascent feeling that there is a universal and impersonal element in every form of interest, attachment, love, and worship, and that in these the individual rises above his usual limitations. All other love, say the scholiasts, is imperfect; the love of the Self that is one in all things, alone is perfect; all other love has fictitious limitations, the love of the Self alone is illimitable. And therefore it is that the Self is what one has to see, and that the aspirant must turn his back on all things that he may come to see it. First he is to hear about it in the teaching of his spiritual guide and in the words of revelation; next it is to be thought about in the exercise of the understanding; next it is to be meditated upon in prolonged ecstasy; and, last of all, the inner vision rises clear within the purified mind, so soon as all the semblances of the world have been melted away into their fontal unity by a never-failing effort of abstraction. Then and not till then he shall have reached the only satisfying love and blessedness. The words, It is the Self that one must see, and hear about, and think about, and meditate upon,[1] form one of the texts of highest importance and most frequent citation in the philosophy of the Upanishads. To return to the text.

"The Brāhmanic order would reject any one who should view the Brāhmanic order as elsewhere than in the Self. The Kshatriya order would reject any one who should regard the Kshatriya order as elsewhere than in the Self. The spheres of recompense would reject any one who should regard the spheres as elsewhere than in the Self. The gods would reject any one who should view the gods as elsewhere than in the Self. All living things would reject any one that should view the living things as elsewhere than in the Self. All things would reject any one that should view all things as elsewhere than in the Self. This Brāhmanic order,

[1] *Ātmā vā're drashṭavyaḥ śrotavyo mantavyo nididhyāsitavyaḥ.*

CHAP. VI.

this Kshatriya order, these spheres, these gods, these living things, this all, are the Self.

All things are one in the Self, as partial sounds in one total sound, as of a drum, a conch-shell, a lute.

"All various things are the one and only Self, in the same manner as when they beat a drum a man cannot catch the various external sounds, but the one total sound is caught by listening to the drum or to the beating of the drum;

"In the same manner as when they blow a conch-shell a man cannot catch the various external sounds, but the one total sound is caught by listening to the conch-shell or to the blast upon the shell;

"In the same manner as when they touch a lute a man cannot catch the various external sounds, but the one total sound is caught by listening to the lute or the performance on the lute.

The Vedas are an exhalation of the Self.

"Smoke issues forth on every side from a fire laid with moist fuel. Even so the Ṛigveda, Yajurveda, Sāmaveda, Atharvāngirasa, the legendaries, the sayings of the ancient sages, the theogonies, the sacred texts and memorial verses of the Upanishads, the aphorisms, the explanations of the texts,—rise as an exhalation out of that great being. All these are exhalations of that Self.

"The Self is that into which all things pass away, even as the ocean is the one thing into which all waters flow; as the touch is the sense in which all modes of tactual feeling meet; as the sight is the sense in which all feelings of colour meet; as the hearing is the sense in which all feelings of sound meet; as the common sensory is the organ in which all the volitions find their unity; as the heart is the place where all the modes of mind are unified; as the hands are the organs in which all forms of manual activity are at one; as the feet are those in which all modes of locomotion are centred; as the voice is the organ in which all repetitions of the Veda are at one.

"A lump of salt thrown into water melts away into

the water, and no one can take it out, but wherever any one takes up the water it is salt. Even so, Maitreyī, is this great, this endless, impassable being a pure indifference of thought. A man comes out of these elements, and passes back into them as they pass away, and after he has passed away there is no more consciousness. This is what I have to tell you, Maitreyī, said Yājñavalkya."

No more consciousness for the liberated sage.

This dialogue of Yājñavalkya and Maitreyī is repeated with variations farther on in the Bṛihadāraṇyaka, and the last verse is there: "This Self has nothing inside it or outside it, in the same way as a lump of salt has nothing inside it or outside it, but is one mass of savour. The Self is a pure indifference of thought. A man rises from these elements, and passes back into them again as they pass away, and there is no consciousness after he has passed away." The figure of the salt and the salt water is one of the commonplaces of the philosophy of the Upanishads, and has already occurred, as the reader will recollect, in the dialogue between Āruṇi and Śvetaketu in the Chhāndogya Upanishad. The body, the senses, and the mind are said to be emanations of the sensible and of the supersensible elements. Every individual soul is the Self itself in fictitious limitation to such and such a mind and body. At the end of every æon the bodies and the minds of all living things, as well as their environments, are dissolved and return into Māyā, and their souls return into unity with Brahman. Every personality melts away into the impersonality of Brahman, as the lump of salt is lost in the uniformity of the salt water. All living things are bubbles and foam that return to the water they issued from. All the bodies and minds of living things are like pools that reflect the sun; the pools disappear, and the sun alone remains. Or, to reproduce another Indian simile, they are like flowers of various hues, that impart their own colour to the pure and colourless crystal of

CHAP. VI. the Self; the flowers are withdrawn, and the crystal is pure and colourless again. There is no consciousness for the soul freed for the time or freed for ever from the body, the senses, and the mind; there is only the state of characterless bliss beyond personality and beyond consciousness, unthinkable and ineffable. To return.

"Maitreyī said: Holy sir, thou hast bewildered me by saying that there is no consciousness after one has passed away. Yājñavalkya answered her: I have said nothing bewildering, but only what may well be understood.

The duality of subject and object is unreal.

"For where there is as it were a duality, one sees another, one smells another, one hears another, one speaks to another, one thinks about another, one knows another; but where all this world is Self alone, what should one smell another with, see another with, hear another with, speak to another with, think about another with, know another with? How should a man know that which he knows all this world with? Wherewithal should a man know the knower?"

The dialogue of Yājñavalkya is followed by the Madhuvidyā or allegory of honey, in which the following verses may be noticed:—

"The body is the honey of all living things, and all living things are the honey of this body; and this same luminous immortal Purusha that is in the body and this same luminous immortal Self are one. Purusha is Self. This is immortal, this is Brahman, this is all that is.

"This same Self is the lord over all living things, the king of all living things. All living things, all the gods, all the spheres, all the faculties, all souls are concentred in the Self, as the spokes of a wheel are all fixed in the axle and the felly.

"This is the honey that Dadhyach the son of Atharvan

CHAP. VI.

The Demiurgus passes illusively into a plurality of souls and environments of souls.

proclaimed to the Aśvins. Seeing this, the Ṛishi has said: This Self shaped itself after the shape of everything, that it might unfold its essence. Indra[1] appears multiform by his illusions, for his horses are yoked, hundreds and ten. This Self is the horses (the senses), this is the ten (organs of sense and motion), this is the many thousands, the innumerable (living souls). This same Self has nothing before it or after it, nothing inside it or outside it. This Self is Brahman and is omniscient. Such is the doctrine."

The fourth book of the Bṛihadāraṇyaka Upanishad introduces us to a public disputation on the import of various elements of sacrificial worship, and on the knowledge that liberates the soul, between the Ṛishi Yājñavalkya and the Brāhmans present at a sacrifice offered by Janaka, the Raja of Videha or Tirhut. The ceremony was thronged with visitors, who came either at the invitation of the prince, or of their own accord, to see the spectacle, some Brāhmans having come from the lands of the Kurus and Panchālas in the distant north. The story is as follows:—

The disputation at the sacrifice celebrated by Janaka, the Raja of Videha. A drove of cattle is the prize.

"Janaka, the Raja of Videha, performed a sacrifice, and gave numerous gifts to those that came to it. Brāhmans from the countries of the Kurus and Panchālas had come to be present at it. A desire arose in the mind of Janaka to know which of all these Brāhmans was the most proficient in the repetition of the sacred text. He accordingly had a thousand head of cattle driven into a pen, the horns of each being overlaid with ten measures of gold.[2]

Yājñavalkya takes the prize without waiting for the disputation.

"He said: Holy Brāhmans, let him that is most learned of you all drive off these cattle. Not one of them took upon himself to do so. Yājñavalkya said to

[1] Indra is Īśvara. Īśvara appears in a fictitious plurality of forms, by illusively entering into and identifying himself with the plurality of bodies and minds that proceed out of the elements that emanate from Māyā.

[2] Cf. Odyssey, iii. 426; Tibullus Eleg., iv. 1, 15.

CHAP. VI.

his disciple, Good Sāmaśravas, drive these cattle to my house; and the youth did as he was bid. The Brāhmans were angry, thinking, Why should this man think himself more learned than any of us all? Now Janaka had a Hotṛi priest named Aśvala, and Aśvala asked Yājṅavalkya, Yājṅavalkya, art thou more learned than any one of us? He answered, I offer my profound obeisance to the most learned, but I must have the cattle; and thereupon Aśvala took courage to put questions to him.

As'vala challenges him to explain the symbolical import of the several factors of the sacrifice.

"Yājṅavalkya, he said, thou knowest how all these sacrificial elements are pervaded by death and under the dominion of death: what shall the sacrificer escape beyond the reach of death withal? He replied: He shall escape beyond death by seeing that the Hotṛi priest and the voice are one and the same with Agni, the god invoked by means of them. It is the voice that is the Hotṛi priest at the sacrifice, and this same voice is the fire-god Agni, and is the Hotṛi priest. This is the escape, this is the escape beyond death.

"Yājṅavalkya, he said, thou knowest how all these sacrificial elements are things that exist in day and night, and under the dominion of day and night: what shall the sacrificer escape beyond the reach of day and night withal? He replied: He shall escape beyond day and night by seeing that the Adhvaryu priest and the eye are one and the same with Āditya. It is the eye that is the Adhvaryu priest at the sacrifice, and this same eye is the sun-god Āditya, and is the Adhvaryu priest. This is the escape, this is the escape beyond day and night.

"Yājṅavalkya, he said, thou knowest how all these sacrificial elements are things that exist in the waxing and the waning of the moon, and under the dominion of the waxing and the waning of the moon: what shall the sacrificer escape beyond the reach of the waxing and the waning of the moon withal? He replied: He shall escape beyond the two semi-lunations by seeing that the Udgātṛi priest and the vital breath are one and the same with Vāyu. The vital breath is the Udgātṛi priest at the sacrifice, and this same breath is the wind-god Vāyu, and is the Udgātṛi priest. This is the escape, this is the escape beyond the periods of the waxing and the waning of the moon.

"Yājñavalkya, he said, thou knowest how yonder sky seems unsupported. By what ascent shall the sacrificer ascend to the paradise that is his recompense? He replied: He shall ascend to paradise by seeing that the Brahman priest and the inner sense are one with Chandra. The inner sense is the Brahman priest at the sacrifice, and this same inner sense is the moon-god Chandra, and is the Brahman priest. This is the escape, the escape beyond the sky. Such are the modes of liberation, and the preparations at the sacrifice."

Aśvala's questions relate to the mystic significance of the various persons and things employed in the great sacrifice of Janaka. They are questions in the kind of knowledge which may be added to the performance of the time-hallowed ritual; and the ritual, and the knowledge of this kind added to it, may elevate the worshipper to higher and higher spheres of recompense, but they are of no avail towards the highest end of all, the final escape from metempsychosis. The next interrogator, Ārtabhāga, proceeds to examine Yājñavalkya on the nature of the bondage of the soul, its implication in metempsychosis. The soul is in bondage so long as it attributes reality to the objects of its sensible experience, and the nature of its experience is determined by the senses and the things of sense.

Ārtabhāga calls upon him to enumerate the elements of sensible experience.

"Next Ārtabhāga the Jāratkārava began to question him. Yājñavalkya, he said, how many organs of sense and motion are there, and how many objects of those organs? Yājñavalkya replied: There are eight such

CHAP. VI. organs and eight such objects. He asked: What are the eight organs, and what are the eight objects?

"Yājñavalkya said: Smell is an organ, and the exhaling substance is its object; for a man is sensible of odours by the sense of smell.

"The voice is an organ, and the utterable word is its object; for a man utters words by means of the voice.

"The tongue is an organ, and the sapid thing is its object; for a man is sensible of taste by means of the tongue.

"The eye is an organ, and colour is its object; for a man sees colours with the eye.

"The ear is an organ, and sound is its object; for a man hears sounds with the ear.

"The common sensory is an organ, and the pleasurable is its object; for a man lusts after the pleasurable with this sensory.

"The hands are an organ, and the thing handled is the object; for a man handles things with the hands.

"The skin is an organ, and the tangible is its object; for a man is sensible of touch by means of the skin. These are the eight organs and the eight objects of the organs.

"Yājñavalkya, he said, thou knowest how all this world is food for death, what divine being is death the food of? Yājñavalkya replied: Fire is the death of death, and fire is the food of water.[1] A man may overcome death.

The mind and senses of the liberated sage are dissolved at death.

"Yājñavalkya, he said, when the sage that has won release from metempsychosis dies, do his organs issue upwards to pass into another body or not? Yājñavalkya replied: They do not; they are melted away at the

[1] All things in the spheres of recompense, the world of metempsychosis, may be destroyed by fire; fire itself again may be destroyed, that is, extinguished, by water. All these things being perishable, the soul, as imperishable, may be disengaged from them, and may overcome death, that is, may achieve its extrication from metempsychosis.

moment of his death. He is inflated, and swells, and lies a swollen corpse.

"Yājñavalkya, he said, when the liberated sage dies, what is it that does not leave him? The Rishi replied: His name; his name is endless: the Viśvadevas are endless, and therefore he wins an endless recompense.

"Yājñavalkya, he said, where does a man that has not won this release go when he dies, and his voice passes back into fire and his vital breath into the air, his eyes into the sun, his common sensory into the moon, his ears into the regions of space, his body into the earth, the ether in his heart into the ether without, the hair of his body into plants, the hair of his head into trees, and his blood into water? Yājñavalkya said: Give me thy hand, good Ārtabhāga; we will find out the answer to thy question, but this is no matter to discuss in public. So they went out and conferred together, and said that it was the law of retribution that they had been speaking of, and pronounced it to be this law that sent the soul from body into body. A man becomes holy by holy works, and unholy by unholy works in previous lives.

The soul of the unphilosophic man enters a new body in obedience to the law of retribution.

"Hereupon Ārtabhāga the Jāratkārava held his peace."

At the death of an ordinary man his several organs of sense and motion, as forming part of the tenuous involucrum of his soul, pass out and enter into a new body, and he is born again. At the death of the perfect sage they sink back into the original unity of Brahman, as waves sink back into the sea. The answer to the question, Where does the soul that has not won its release go after the dissolution of his present body? is that it goes into some new embodiment, higher or lower in the scale according to its works in former lives. By the law of retribution the soul becomes holy, that is, is born into higher grades of life, by good works, by conformity to the prescriptive *sacra;* and it becomes un-

CHAP. VI. holy, that is, is born into vegetal, animal, or other lower grades of life, by unholy works, that is, by neglect of immemorial usages. The reader must beware of attaching to the text a higher moral and spiritual significance than properly belongs to it.

Bhujyu examines Yājñavalkya on the recompense of the horse-sacrifice.

"Next Bhujyu, the grandson of Lahya, began to question him. Yājñavalkya, he said, when we were itinerating as sacred students in the country of the Madras, we came to the house of Patanchala the Kāpya. He had a daughter possessed of a spirit more than human, a Gandharva. We asked the Gandharva who he was, and he said that he was Sudhanvan, an Āngirasa. In talking to him about the uttermost parts of the world, we asked what had become of the descendants of Parikshit. Now I ask thee, Yājñavalkya, what has become of the Pārikshitas?

"Yājñavalkya said: They have gone to the sphere to which they go who have celebrated an Aśvamedha or sacrifice of a horse. Bhujyu asked: And where do the celebrants of an Aśvamedha go? This world, said Yājñavalkya, is equal to thirty-two daily journeys of the sun-god's chariot. This is surrounded on every side by a land of twice that size. That land again is surrounded by a sea twice as extensive. Beyond this sea there is an ethereal space of the width of a razor's edge or a mosquito's wing. There Indra, taking the shape of a bird, conveyed the Pārikshitas to the air, the air holding the Pārikshitas within itself forwarded them to the sphere where all former celebrants of an Aśvamedha reside. The Gandharva therefore revealed to you that it was the air through which the Pārikshitas passed. Air is each and every thing, and air is all things. He that knows it as such overcomes death.

"Hereupon Bhujyu Lāhyāyani was silent.

"Next Ushasta Chākrāyaṇa began to question him. Yājñavalkya, he said, tell me plainly what that present and visible Brahman is, that is the Self within all living

CHAP. VI.

Ushasta calls upon him for an ocular demonstration of the Self. He replies that the Self is the *unseen* seer.

things? Yājñavalkya replied: The Self that is thine is the Self within all living things. What Self, Yājñavalkya, is in all things? Yājñavalkya answered: That which breathes with the breath is the Self that is thine, and that is in all living things. That which descends with the descending air of life is the Self that is thine, and that is in all living things. That which circulates with the circulating air of life is the Self that is thine, and that is in all living things. That which ascends with the ascending air of life is the Self that is thine, and that is in all living things. This is thy Self that is in all things that are.

"Ushasta Chākrāyaṇa said: Thou hast only taught me as a man might say a cow is so and so, a horse is so and so. Point out to me plainly what that present and visible Brahman is, that is the Self within all living things. Yājñavalkya replied again, The Self that is thine is the Self within all living things. Ushasta asked again, What Self is in all things? Yājñavalkya answered him: I cannot point it out. Thou canst not see the seer of the sight; thou canst not hear that that hears the hearing; thou canst not think the thinker of the thought; thou canst not know the knower of all knowledge. This is thy Self that is in all things that are, and everything else is misery.

"Hereupon Ushasta Chākrāyaṇa ceased from farther questioning."

So far, says Śankarāchārya, the text of this dialogue has treated of the bondage of the soul, its implication in metempsychosis, and has taught that the migrating soul is, if only it be truly viewed, the Self itself. The text now proceeds to treat of the renunciation of all things and spiritual intuition, as the means by which the soul may win its release from further transmigration.

Kahola questions him about the one Self in all things living.

"Next Kahola Kaushītakeya began to question him. Yājñavalkya, he said, tell me plainly what that present and visible Brahman is, that is the Self within all living

CHAP. VI. things. Yājñavalkya said, This Self of thine is the Self that is within all things. What Self, Yājñavalkya, is in all things? Yājñavalkya answered him: The Self that is beyond hunger and thirst, and grief and stupor, and decay and death. Knowing the Self to be such, Brāhmans have risen and laid aside the desire of children, the desire of wealth, and the desire of spheres of recompense, and have wandered forth as sacred mendicants. For the desire of children is the same as the desire of wealth, and the desire of wealth is the same as the desire of the spheres of recompense; for there are both of these kinds of desire. Therefore[1] let a Brāhman learn wisdom, and stand fast in the power of wisdom; and having made an end of wisdom and the power of wisdom, let him become a quietist; and when he has made an end of quietism and non-quietism, he shall become a Brāhman, a Brāhman indeed. Whatever kind of a Brāhman he may have been, he becomes a veritable Brāhman now.

The visionary sage is the true Brāhman.

"Hereupon Kahola Kaushītakeya held his peace.

Gārgī questions him. Over what is the cosmic web woven?

"Next Gārgī the daughter of Vachaknu began to question him. Yājñavalkya, she said, thou knowest how all this earth is woven upon the waters warp and woof; what are the waters woven upon warp and woof? Upon the air, Gārgī, replied the Ṛishi. What is the air woven upon warp and woof? Upon the regions of middle space, Gārgī. What are the regions of middle space woven upon warp and woof? Upon the spheres of the Gandharvas, Gārgī. What are the spheres of the Gandharvas woven upon warp and woof? Upon the solar spheres, Gārgī. What are the solar spheres woven upon warp and woof? Upon the lunar spheres,

[1] The translation of this part of the verse follows the gloss of Śankarāchārya. Quitting the traditional explanation, the words might be translated, "Let a Brāhman renounce learning and become as a child; and after renouncing learning and a childlike mind, let him become a quietist; and when he has made an end of quietism and non-quietism, he shall become a Brāhman, a Brāhman indeed."

Gārgī. What are the lunar spheres woven upon warp and woof? Upon the starry spheres, Gārgī. What are the starry spheres woven upon warp and woof? Upon the spheres of the gods, Gārgī. What are the spheres of the gods woven upon warp and woof? Upon the spheres of Indra, Gārgī. What are the spheres of Indra woven upon warp and woof? Upon the spheres of Prajāpati, Gārgī. What are the spheres of Prajāpati woven upon warp and woof? Upon the spheres of Brahmā, Gārgī. What are the spheres of Brahmā woven upon warp and woof? He said to her: Gārgī, push not thy questioning too far, lest thy head fall off. Thou goest too far in putting questions about the divine being that transcends such questioning; push not thy questioning too far.

"Hereupon Gārgī the daughter of Vachaknu ceased to speak."

Here as elsewhere in the Upanishads, the various spheres of recompense through which the soul has to go up and down in its migrations in obedience to the law of retribution, are said to be woven warp and woof, like so many veils of finer and finer tissue, across and across the one and only Self. The whole world of semblances is only a vesture that hides from the soul, the underlying spiritual essence of which it is only one of the innumerable fictitious emanations.

The soul is one of the countless sparks of the fire, one of the countless wavelets of the sea, one of the countless images of the sun upon the waters; and it is only the inexplicable power of the illusion that exercises itself from before all time, that hides from it its pure and characterless nature, its unity with the primitive essence, thought, and bliss. The true Self is hidden from the eyes and thoughts of living souls by veil after veil of illusory presentation, by sphere after sphere of seeming action and suffering; the successive figments of the primitive world-fiction, the principle of

CHAP. VI.

unreality that has unreally associated itself from before all æons with the principle of reality.

So far the various speakers in the dialogue have talked about the spheres of recompense lower in ascent than the sphere of Hiraṇyagarbha. Beyond Prajāpati or Purusha, beyond the souls in the waking state, is Hiraṇyagarbha, the Sūtrātman, the spirit that permeates all dreaming souls; and beyond Hiraṇyagarbha and the dreaming souls is Īśvara, the internal ruler, the spirit that is present in all souls in their dreamless sleep, that directs every movement of every living thing, and metes out to the migrating sentiencies their varied lots from the lowest to the highest, in accordance with the law of retribution. Accordingly the dialogue proceeds to treat of the thread-soul Hiraṇyagarbha, and the internal ruler Īśvara within the thread-soul.

Uddālaka questions him on the nature of the thread-soul Hiraṇyagarbha.

"Next Uddālaka the son of Aruṇa began to question him. Yājñavalkya, he said, we once lived in the country of the Madras, in the house of Patanchala the Kāpya, studying the nature and import of sacrificial rites. He had a wife possessed of a spirit more than human, a Gandharva. We asked the Gandharva who he was, and he said, I am Kabandha the son of Atharvan. He also said to Patanchala the Kāpya, and to us liturgists: Kāpya, dost thou know what the thread is by which this embodiment and the next embodiment and all living things are strung together? Patanchala the Kāpya said, I do not know it, venerable spirit. He said again to Patanchala the Kāpya, and to us liturgists: Kāpya, dost thou know that which actuates this embodiment and the next embodiment and all living things from within? Patanchala the Kāpya said, Great spirit, I know it not. The Gandharva said again to Patanchala the Kāpya, and to us liturgic students: Kāpya, he that knows that thread and that internal actuator within the thread-soul, knows Brahman, knows the spheres of recompense, knows the gods, knows the Vedas, knows all living things, knows the Self, knows all things. He revealed the thread-soul and the internal actuator that is within it to us, and I know them. Now if thou, Yājñavalkya, hast driven away the cattle that are the prize of the most learned Brāhman, without knowing that thread-soul and that internal ruler, thy head shall fall off. Yājñavalkya said, Gautama, I know that thread-soul and that internal ruler. Uddālaka rejoined, Any one can say, I know them; tell me what thou knowest.

"Yājñavalkya said: Gautama, the air is that thread-soul. This embodiment and the next embodiment and all living things are strung together by the air. It is for this reason that they say of a dead man that his limbs are unstrung, for his limbs are strung together by the air as by a thread. Just so, Yājñavalkya, said Uddālaka; now tell me about the internal actuator."

He questions him on the nature of the cosmic soul or Demiurgus.

Śankarāchārya tells us that the air is here a metonym for the supersensible rudiments, or elements in their primitive state, as yet uncondensed by progressive concretion. It is out of these supersensible elements that the tenuous *involucra*, or invisible bodies of migrating souls, are formed. These invisible bodies clothe the soul in its transit from body to body, and the retributive influences of the good and evil works of former lives adhere to them. Yājñavalkya proceeds to answer Uddālaka by a description of the Demiurgus, the universal soul that permeates and vivifies all nature and all migrating personalities. This cosmic soul is the first manifestation of Brahman; it is Brahman itself in its first illusory presentment, as fictitiously overspread with Māyā, or, as it is otherwise said, with the whole world-fiction as a body, the cosmic body out of which all things lifeless and living emanate. It is in virtue of the presence and light of this universal soul within them that the deities of earth,

CHAP. VI. and water, and fire, and other natural agents, pass from rest to motion and from motion to rest again. This universal soul is also present in every living thing, from the grass below the feet to Brahmā the god high over all; and it is in virtue of his presence and his light that they pass from rest to motion, and from motion back to rest. He is invisible, and vision is his being; unknowable, and knowledge is his being; as heat and light are the being of fire. As the universal soul he is exempt from the varied experiences of metempsychosis, which are the modes of individual life, and which he allots, in conformity always with the law of retribution, to the innumerable migrating souls.

The Demiurgus is the internal ruler or actuator, the first and highest manifestation of the Self: He informs and animates the elements.

"Yājñavalkya said: That which dwells in earth, inside the earth, and earth knows not, whose body the earth is, which actuates the earth from within,—that is thy Self, the internal ruler, immortal.

"That which dwells in water, inside the water, and the water knows not, whose body the water is, which actuates the water from within,—that is thy Self, the internal ruler, immortal.

"That which dwells in fire, inside the fire, and the fire knows not, whose body the fire is, which actuates the fire from within,—that is thy Self, the internal ruler, immortal.

"That which dwells in air, inside the air, and the air knows not, whose body the air is, which actuates the air from within,—that is thy Self, the internal ruler, immortal.

"That which dwells in wind, inside the wind, and the wind knows not, whose body the wind is, which actuates the wind from within,—that is thy Self, the internal ruler, immortal.

"That which dwells in the sky, inside the sky, and the sky knows not, whose body the sky is, which actuates the sky from within,—that is thy Self, the internal ruler, immortal.

"That which dwells in the sun, inside the sun, and the sun knows not, whose body the sun is, which actuates the sun from within,—that is thy Self, the internal ruler, immortal.

"That which dwells in the regions of space, inside the regions, and the regions know not, whose body the regions are, which actuates the regions from within,—that is thy Self, the internal ruler, immortal.

"That which dwells in the moon and stars, inside the moon and stars, and the moon and stars know not, whose body the moon and stars are, which actuates the moon and stars from within,—that is thy Self, the internal ruler, immortal.

"That which dwells in the ether, inside the ether, which the ether knows not, whose body the ether is, which actuates the ether from within,—that is thy Self, the internal ruler, immortal.

"That which dwells in darkness, inside the darkness, which the darkness knows not, whose body the darkness is, which actuates the darkness from within,—that is thy Self, the internal ruler, immortal.

"That which dwells in light, inside the light, which the light knows not, whose body the light is, which actuates the light from within,—that is thy Self, the internal ruler, immortal.

"Such are the elemental manifestations of the internal ruler; now for his manifestations in animated nature.

He informs and animates all living things.

"That which dwells in all living things, inside all living things, which no thing living knows, whose body all living things are, which actuates all things living from within,—that is thy Self, the internal ruler, immortal.

"That which dwells in the breath of life, inside the breath, which the breath knows not, whose body the breath is, which actuates the breath from within,—that is thy Self, the internal ruler, immortal.

"That which dwells in the voice, inside the voice,

CHAP. VI. which the voice knows not, whose body the voice is, which actuates the voice from within,—that is thy Self, the internal ruler, immortal.

"That which dwells in the eye, inside the eye, which the eye knows not, whose body the eye is, which actuates the eye from within,—that is thy Self, the internal ruler, immortal.

"That which dwells in the ear, inside the ear, which the ear knows not, whose body the ear is, which actuates the ear from within,—that is thy Self, the internal ruler, immortal.

"That which dwells in the inner sense, inside the inner sense, which the inner sense knows not, whose body the inner sense is, which actuates the inner sense from within,—that is thy Self, the internal ruler, immortal.

"That which dwells in the sense of touch, inside the touch, which the touch knows not, whose body the sense of touch is, which actuates the sense of touch from within,—that is thy Self, the internal ruler, immortal.

"That which dwells in the consciousness, inside the consciousness, which the consciousness knows not, whose body the consciousness is, which actuates the consciousness from within,—that is thy Self, the internal ruler, immortal.

The Demiurgus is Brahman manifested in the world.

"That which sees unseen, hears unheard, thinks unthought upon, knows unknown; that other than which there is none that sees, none that hears, none that thinks, none that knows;—that is thy Self, the internal ruler, immortal. Everything else is misery.

"Hereupon Uddālaka the son of Aruṇa ceased from questioning."

From Brahman as manifested in the form of the Demiurgus or universal soul that permeates and animates all things, the dialogue next passes to Brahman as beyond manifestation, the present and visible Brahman within the heart of every living thing, the pure light, the characterless fontal essence. CHAP. VI.

"Next Gārgī the daughter of Vachaknu spoke again: Reverend Brāhmans, I will ask this man two questions. If he can answer them, no one of you all can outvie him in exposition of the Self. They said, Ask him, Gārgī.

Gārgī examines him again. Over what is the web of the world-fiction woven?

"Yājñavalkya, said Gārgī, I rise to put two questions to thee. I rise as some Raja of Kāśi or Videha might rise to encounter thee, a father of heroes, with his bow strung, and with two sharp threatening arrows of cane in his hand. Answer me these questions. Yājñavalkya said, Put the questions to me.

"Yājñavalkya, she said, across what is that principle woven warp and woof, which they say is above the sky, below the earth, and within which this earth and yonder sky exist, and all that has been, is, and is to be?

"Yājñavalkya said: That principle that they say is above the sky, below the earth, and within which this earth and yonder sky exist, and all that has been, is, and is to be,—is woven warp and woof across and across the ethereal expanse.[1]

"Gārgī said: Glory to thee, Yājñavalkya, that thou hast answered this my first question; now prepare thyself to meet the second. He said, Put it to me, Gārgī.

"She said: Yājñavalkya, across what is that principle woven warp and woof, which they say is above the sky, below the earth, and within which this earth and yonder sky exist, and all that has been, is, and is to be?

"Yājñavalkya answered her again: That principle that they say is above the sky, below the earth, and within which this earth and yonder sky exist, and all that has been, is, and is to be,—is woven warp and woof across and across the ethereal expanse. And I

[1] Ethereal expanse is here a synonym of Māyā.

CHAP. VI.

pray, said she, across what is the ethereal expanse woven warp and woof?

It is woven over the Self, the principle that gives fixity and order to this moving world.

"Yājñavalkya said: Brāhmans say that that across which the ethereal expanse is woven is the imperishable principle, neither great nor small, neither long nor short, neither glowing like fire nor fluid like water, shadowless, without darkness, neither aerial nor ethereal, without contact with anything, colourless, odourless, without eyes or ears or voice or inward sense, without light from without, without breath or mouth. It has no measure; it has nothing within it or without it. It consumes nothing, and is consumed of none.

"Under the dominion of this imperishable principle, Gārgī, the sun and moon stand fixed in their places; under the governance of this imperishable principle the earth and sky stand fixed in their places.

"Under the dominion of this imperishable principle, Gārgī, the moments and hours, and days and nights, and fortnights and months, and seasons and years, stand fixed in their periods; under the governance of this imperishable principle, Gārgī, some of the rivers flow eastward from the snowy mountains, some westward, and others in other directions.

"Under the dominion of this imperishable principle men praise those that give freely; the gods are dependent on the sacrifices, and the ancestral spirits upon the obsequial offerings.

"If a man presents oblations and sacrifices or tortures himself for many thousand years in this life, and knows not this imperishable principle, his recompense is one that has an end. If, Gārgī, a man quits this life without knowing this imperishable principle, he is helpless; but if he knows this principle he is indeed a Brāhman.

"This same imperishable principle, Gārgī, is that which sees unseen, hears unheard, thinks unthought-upon, knows unknown; there is no other than this that sees, no other than this that hears, no other than this that thinks, no other than this that knows. It is across this imperishable principle, Gārgī, that the ethereal expanse is woven warp and woof.

"Then Gārgī exclaimed: Venerable Brāhmans, you may think it a great matter if you can save yourselves by making obeisance to this Ṛishi. Never will any one of you all outvie this Ṛishi in the exposition of the Self."

The Self is uniform, characterless vision and thought.

In the words of Śankarāchārya, the Self is unseen, inasmuch as it cannot be made an object, but it is that which sees, inasmuch as it is a pure and unceasing act of vision itself. Elsewhere[1] he tells us that the Self is the object of the notion and the name "I." It cannot be heard, but it is that which hears, being a pure and unceasing act of hearing. It cannot be thought upon, but it is that which thinks, being a pure and unceasing act of thought. It cannot be known, but it is that which knows, being itself the pure and unceasing act of knowledge. It sees with a sight that does not come and pass away, like our sight, but with a sight that always is, a sight that is its being, as the sun shines for ever with a light that is its own being. It is the Self that sees through the eyes, hears through the ears, thinks through the thought, knows through the mind, of all living things. This is the present and visible Brahman, present in the heart of every creature, visible to the purified soul of the ecstatic seer. This is the Self that seems and only seems to act and suffer in the acting and suffering souls, as the moon seems to move as the clouds scud past it. This is the one and only Self beyond the hunger, thirst, and misery of metempsychosis, and over this the world-fiction and all the figments that issue out of it are woven warp and woof. This is the goal, the final term. This, ever-present

[1] As in the Śārīrakamīmānsābhāshya, i. 1. 1, and the Vivekachūḍāmaṇi, verse 127.

CHAP. VI.

though it be, it is veiled from the hearts and eyes of the multitude, and reveals itself only to the spiritual vision of the perfect sage. He alone can find himself one with the universal soul, and one with the impersonal Self.

The dialogue now proceeds to point out how the gods are all of them only local and particular manifestations of the one life that lives in all things. It is one and the same divine being that fictitiously presents itself in every living being, to fulfil a variety of functions under all the variety of name and form and attribute and power.

Vidagdha questions him. All things are full of gods, and gods are only local manifestations of the Self.

"Next Vidagdha the son of Śakala began to question him. Yājṅavalkya, he said, how many gods are there? Yājṅavalkya answered him according to the following Nivid or enumerative text. There are, he said, as many as are enumerated in the Nivid of the Vaiśvadevaśastra, three and three hundred, and three and three thousand. Even so, said Vidagdha; how many gods are there then, Yājṅavalkya? Three and thirty, replied the Ṛishi. Even so, said Vidagdha; how many gods are there then, Yājṅavalkya? Six, he replied. Even so, said Vidagdha; and again, how many gods are there then, Yājṅavalkya? Three, he said. Yes, said Vidagdha; and how many gods are there then, Yājṅavalkya? Two, he said. Yes, said Vidagdha; and again, how many gods are there, Yājṅavalkya? One and a half, he said. Yes, said Vidagdha; how many gods are there, Yājṅavalkya? One, he answered. Yes, said Vidagdha; and what are those three gods and three hundred gods, and those three gods and three thousand gods?

"Yājṅavalkya said: The glories of these are three and thirty. Which are those thirty-three? asked the son of Śakala. The eight Vasus, replied the Ṛishi, the eleven Rudras, and the twelve Ādityas are thirty-one, and Indra and Prajāpati make thirty-three.

"Who are the Vasus? Fire, the earth, the air, the

welkin, the sun, the sky, the moon, and the stars, are the Vasus. In these all places of recompense are contained, and therefore they are called the Vasus. CHAP. VI.

"Who are the Rudras? These ten organs of sense and motion in the living soul, together with the common sensory which is the eleventh organ. When they issue upwards out of this mortal body they make men weep, and for this reason they are called the Rudras.

"Who are the Ādityas? The twelve months of the year are the Ādityas, for these take all things together with them in their course; and for the reason that they take all things with them they are called the Ādityas.

"Who is Indra, and who is Prajāpati? Indra is the thunder, and Prajāpati is the sacrifice. What is the thunder? The thunderbolt. What is the sacrifice? The sacrificial victims.

"Who are the six gods? They are fire, earth, air, welkin, sun, and sky. They are six, for all things are these six.

"Who are the three gods? They are these three worlds, earth, air, and sky; for all these gods are in these three. Who are the two gods? They are food and vital air, or Purusha and Hiraṇyagarbha. Who is the god that is one and a half? The wind that blows.

"Hereupon they cried out: This wind that is blowing seems to be one, how sayest thou that it is one and a half? Yājñavalkya replied: It is one and a half (*adhyardha*) because everything grows up (*adhyardhnoti*) in it. Who is the one god? asked Vidagdha. Yājñavalkya said: It is the breath of life. It is the Self. They call it That.

"He who knows that Purusha, that living being, whose body is the earth, whose eye is fire, whose inward sense is light, in whom all are one who live in the body, he indeed has knowledge. Yājñavalkya, said the son

CHAP. VI.

of Śakala, I know that Purusha, in whom all that live in the body are one, about whom thou speakest: it is this very living soul that is in the body. Tell me then, son of Śakala, said the Ṛishi, what is the divinity[1] of that embodied soul? It is the assimilated portion of food, said Vidagdha."

Vidagdha puts question after question to Yājñavalkya, till the Ṛishi again proclaims that all things in the world, and the ethereal expanse, or world-fiction, out of which they proceed, are woven web upon web across the one underlying reality, the spiritual essence, Brahman.

"This Self is not this, not that: imperceptible, for it cannot be perceived; indiscerptible, for it cannot be parted asunder; illimitable, for nothing can be placed beside it; inviolable, for it cannot be hurt or injured.

Vidagdha fails to answer him in turn, and perishes.

Now I ask thee what is that Purusha, that spiritual essence, revealed in the mystic doctrines, that transcends those other Purushas or embodied souls; and if thou canst not tell me, thy head shall fall off. The son of Śakala did not know that Purusha, so his head fell off; and as his disciples were carrying home his bones to burn them on the funeral pyre, thieves stole them, taking them to be some other thing.

"Meanwhile Yājñavalkya said: Holy Brāhmans, any one of you who wishes may question me, or you may all of you put questions to me; or I will put questions to any one of you that you may choose, or to all of you. But the Brāhmans had no heart to answer him.

Yājñavalkya's parable. Man is a forest-tree. When he is cut down, what root has he to grow again from?

"So Yājñavalkya put a question to them in these verses. Man, he said, is indeed like a tree of the forest; his hair is the leaves, his skin the outer bark. The blood trickles from his skin, as the sap trickles from the bark; wound him, and the blood will flow like sap from a tree that is split open. His flesh is the inner bark,

[1] *Divinity* here means informing or plastic principle. Vidagdha says that the body is built up out of materials assimilated from food.

the flesh about his bones is the membrane about the woody fibres, his bones are the wood within, and his marrow is the pith. The tree is cut down, and the tree grows up anew from its root; a mortal is cut down by death, but what root has he to grow up from anew? Say not from procreation, for that comes not from the dead but from the living. The seed-sprung tree that has seemed to die springs up again apace, but if they tear up the tree by the roots it cannot grow again. Man is cut down by death, what root has he to grow again from? You may say that he is already born again, but this not so; who then can again beget him?" CHAP. VI.

The Brahmans were unable to answer Yājñavalkya, not knowing that the soul, as it passes from body to body, has one continuous life, as being one with, and only in fictitious semblance severed from, the one and only Self that is the root of the world. After thus putting his successive opponents to silence, and overawing the whole assembly, the Ṛishi remains in undisputed possession of the prize, the thousand head of cattle. He sums up the whole matter in the following words, which close the discussion:—

"The Self is thought and bliss, the wealth of the sacrifice, the final goal of the sage that knows it, and perseveres in ecstatic union with it." The sum of the whole matter. Ecstatic union is the goal.

In the next book of the Bṛihadāraṇyaka Upanishad we have an account of two later interviews between the Ṛishi Yājñavalkya and the Raja Janaka. Princes are frequently mentioned in the Upanishads as taking a leading part in theosophic discussions.

"Janaka of Videha was sitting giving audience, and Yājñavalkya came before him. He said: Yājñavalkya, what have you come for? Do you want more cattle, or do you want subtle disputations? He said: I want both, great king." Yājñavalkya visits Janaka. Their conversation. The passage through the vestures of the soul to the Self beyond all fear.

Yājñavalkya proceeds to question Janaka about the

CHAP. VI. instruction he has received from his various spiritual directors, and points out how each of them has only taught him about the Self in some one or other of its local and particular manifestations, a knowledge of which leads only to transitory recompenses, not to extrication from metempsychosis.

"Then Janaka of Videha came down from his seat and said: Glory to thee, Yājñavalkya; teach me more. The Ṛishi said: Great king, thou art thoroughly equipped with these mystic instructions that thou hast received, as is a man who has provided himself with a carriage or a boat, being about to start on a long journey. Great and rich, versed in the Vedas and informed of mystic doctrines as thou art, when thou quittest this life whither wilt thou go? I do not know, said Janaka, where I shall go. Then I will tell thee where thou wilt go, said the Ṛishi. Say on, holy sir, replied the prince.

"This Purusha that is in the right eye is named Indha, but for the sake of mystery men call him Indra; for the gods love mystery and hate familiarity.

"The Purusha in the left eye is his wife Virāj. Their meeting-place is the ether in the heart, their nourishment is the blood within the heart, their coverlet is the network of arteries in the heart, their path of transit is the artery that goes upward out of the heart. The arteries, minute as a hair split a thousand times, converge into the heart, and the food proceeds along these; so that the tenuous involucrum has a more refined kind of nutriment than the body.

"When the sage has passed through the body to the tenuous involucrum, and through the tenuous involucrum to the beatific vesture in the heart, the forward vital air is the eastern quarter, the vital air to the left is the south, the hinder vital air is the west, the upward vital air is the north, the upper vital air is the space above, the nether vital air is the space below. The vital airs are the regions of space."

"In the beatific vesture and in the state of dreamless sleep the sage returns to unity with the vital air, that is, with the universal soul. In the state of ecstasy he makes this universal soul to disappear into the characterless Self, of which Yājñavalkya proceeds to speak.

CHAP. VI.

"This same Self is not this, not that; imperceptible, for it cannot be perceived; indiscerptible, for it canno be parted asunder; illimitable, for nothing can be placed beside it; inviolable, for it cannot be hurt or injured. O Janaka, thou hast reached the point where there is no more fear. Janaka of Videha said: May this salvation come to thee also, Yājñavalkya, for teaching me about this spiritual reality that is beyond all fear. Glory to thee: here is this kingdom of Videha, and here am I, and both are thine."

The text, O Janaka,[1] thou hast reached the point where there is no more fear, is one of those most frequently quoted in the works of the Indian schoolmen. The point beyond all fear is the pure spiritual essence, Brahman, on reaching which there is no further fear of birth and the miseries of life and death. The Ṛishi has lifted the veil of illusion, and thus enabled Janaka to see the sole reality, the one and only Self, and to recognise, and by recognition recover, his own unity with it. The story of Yājñavalkya's next interview with Janaka is as follows:—

Yājñavalkya visits Janaka again. Their conference. What is the light of man?

"Yājñavalkya went again before Janaka, the Raja of Videha, and thought as he went that this time he would not say anything. Janaka of Videha and Yājñavalkya had, however, formerly talked together at a sacrifice to the fire-god Agni, and Yājñavalkya had promised Janaka to grant the next request that he might have to make of him. Janaka now chose as his request permission to ask any question he liked, and Yājñavalkya granted it. The Raja first asked him:—

[1] *Abhayam vai Janaka prāpto 'si.*

CHAP. VI.

"Yājṅavalkya, what light has man? The light of the sun, great king, said the Ṛishi. It is by the light of the sun that he sits down, or goes about and does his work, and comes home again. The Raja said: It is as thou sayest, Yājṅavalkya.

"But when the sun has set, Yājṅavalkya, what light has man? The light of the moon, the Ṛishi answered. It is in the light of the moon that he sits down, or goes about and does what he has to do, and comes home again. It is as thou sayest, Yājṅavalkya, said the Raja.

"But, Yājṅavalkya, when the sun has set and the moon has set, what light has man? A fire, he answered, is his light. It is by the light of a fire that he sits down, or goes about and does what he has to do, and comes home again. The Raja said: "It is as thou sayest, Yājṅavalkya.

"But, Yājṅavalkya, when the sun has set, and the moon has set, and the fire has gone out, what light has man? The voice,[1] he answered, is his light: it is by the light of the voice that he sits down, or goes about and does what he has to do, and comes home again; for when a man cannot see his hand before him, he walks in the direction that a voice is heard in. The Raja said: It is as thou sayest, Yājṅavalkya.

"But, Yājṅavalkya, when sun and moon are set, and the fire is out, and all sounds are hushed, what light has man? He answered: The Self within him is his light: it is by the light of the Self that he sits down or goes about, does what he has to do, and comes home again."

In explanation of this last verse, Śankarāchārya says: "In every state the mind has some light to act in, a light that is other than the body and the senses. In the

[1] "In a cloudy night in the rainy season a man cannot see his hand before him. He is guided in his movements by the voices he hears about him, or it may be by the barking of a dog, the braying of an ass, or other signs of village life."—*Śankarāchārya.*

waking state it acts through the bodily organs in the light of sun, or moon, or fire. In the dreaming state, in the state of dreamless sleep, and in the waking state, when there is neither sun nor moon nor firelight to guide it in its actions, it still continues to act, and does so in some light that is incorporeal and immaterial. In dreaming a man sees himself meeting with or parting from his friends, and on waking from sleep without a dream he still is conscious that he has slept in peace and without a cognisance of anything. This immaterial light is the light of the Self, which is other than the body and the senses, and illumines them like the exterior light, and itself requires no light from outside itself. This is the light within." To return to the text.

The true light is the light within the heart.

"What Self is that? asked the prince. The Ṛishi said: It is this conscious soul amidst the vital airs, the light within the heart. This Self, one and the same in every mind and every body, passes through this life and the next life in the body, and seems to think and seems to move. The same Self, entering the dreaming state, passes beyond the world of waking experience, beyond the varied forms of metempsychosis.

"This self-same Self is born, and as it enters into a body is involved in the good and evil deeds that attach to the members and the senses; it passes up at death out of the body, and leaves them behind.

The three states of the migrating soul—waking, dreaming, and dreamless sleep.

"This same Self has two stations: any given present embodiment, and the embodiment that is next to follow. And there is a third place: the state intermediate between the two—the place of dreams. Standing in the place of dreams, it sees both these stations, this embodiment and the embodiment next to come. In the place of dreams it steps on to the path it has made itself to the next embodiment, and sees the pains and pleasures that have been in earlier lives and are to be in after-lives. When it proceeds to dream, it takes to

CHAP. VI.

In sleep the soul creates a dream-world.

itself the ideal residues of its waking experience in former lives; it lays aside the body; it fashions for itself an ideal body, and dreams in its own light, and then the Self is its own light. In the dreaming state there are no chariots, no horses, no roads; but it presents to itself chariots, horses, and roads. There are in that state no pleasures, no joys, no raptures; but it creates for itself pleasures, joys, and raptures. There are no houses, no pools, no rivers; but it projects before itself houses, pools, and rivers, for it is still in action.

"Therefore there are these verses. In sleep it lays aside the body, and itself unsleeping looks upon the visions of its sleep. It takes its radiant imagery with it, and again enters the place of waking experience, for it is the luminous Self, the one spirit that is ever passing onward.

"Keeping alive with the vital air its vile nest the body, it soars beyond its nest: it goes where it lists, the immortal, luminous Self, the one spirit that is ever passing onward.

"In the place of dreams[1] it passes upward, passes downward, in its own light: it projects a variety of shapes before itself, dallying with women, laughing, or it may be seeing perils.

"Men see the garden[2] that it strolls in, but no man sees the Self itself. They say they cannot rouse it when it is asleep.

"That part of the body to which this does not come back again is hard to heal; it is blind, or deaf, and lifeless. Some, indeed, say that the place of dreams is not an intermediate position, but the same as the place of waking experience, because it sees the same things

[1] In its dreams the soul rises to the position of a god, or descends to the state of one of the lower animals. This it does in reminiscence of a former embodiment, or in anticipation of a future one, higher or lower, as it may be, than its present human embodiment.

[2] The dream-world.

in its dreams as it sees when awake; but this is not so. In dreaming, the Self is its own light. Janaka exclaimed: Holy sir, I will give thee a thousand kine. Teach me again, that I may be liberated from metempsychosis.

"Yājṅavalkya said: This same Self, after rejoicing and expatiating in its dreams, and seeing good and evil, passes into the peaceful state of dreamless sleep; and thence again flits back into the place of dreams it came from, back to other dreams. It is not followed by the good or evil that it sees itself do in its dreams, for the Self is not really in union with the bodily organs. It is as thou sayest, Yājṅavalkya, said the prince. Holy sir, I give thee a thousand kine. Teach me again, that I may be liberated.

"Yājṅavalkya said: This same Self, after rejoicing and expatiating in the waking state, and seeing good and evil, flits again into the place of dreams.

Simile of the fish.

"This Self passes from dreams to waking life, and from waking life back to dreams; in the same way as a fish swims from one bank of a river to the other, from riverside to riverside.

Simile of the falcon.

"This Self passes into the state of dreamless sleep, and in that state desires no pleasures and sees no dreams; in the same way as a kite or falcon, tired of flying about in the firmament above, folds its wings and cowers in its nest.

"There are in man arteries thin as a hair split a thousand times, filled with fluids white, blue, yellow, green, and red."

These ramify in all directions through the body, the tenuous involucrum is lodged in them, and the ideal residues of the experiences of former embodiments adhere to the tenuous involucrum, and accompany it in its passage from body to body. These ideal residues furnish the imagery of dreams, and dreams point back to the former lives of the soul, or forward to its future

CHAP. VI.

lives. The tenuous involucrum is the body of the sleeping soul.

"Now whatever peril a man sees when he is awake, he may also see in his sleep. Enemies kill him or take him captive, or a wild elephant chases him, and he falls into a pit.

"Whatever peril he sees awake, he sees asleep through the force of illusion; but when, in the same way as in his dreams he had seemed to be a god or a king, he comes to know that he is all that is,—this is his highest position.

Liberation is perfect satisfaction, and exemption from all fear.

"This intuition of his oneness with all that is, is his state of exemption from desire, and freedom from the good and evil that prolong the migration of the soul; his state in which there is no more fear. The soul in the bosom of the Self is conscious of nothing within or without him, even as a man in the arms of his beloved wife ceases to be conscious of anything within him or without him. This oneness with all that is, is the state of the fulfilment of all desires, the state of satisfaction in oneself and of exemption from desires, the state in which there is no more sorrow.

All differences vanish in the unitary indifference of the Self.

"In this state a father is no more a father, a mother is no more a mother, the spheres of recompense are no longer spheres of recompense, the gods no longer gods, the Vedas no longer Vedas. Here the thief is a thief no more, the Chaṇḍāla a Chaṇḍāla no more, the Paulkasa no more a Paulkasa, the holy mendicant no more a holy mendicant, the anchorite an anchorite no more. He is no longer followed by his good works, no longer followed by his evil works; for now at length he has passed beyond all the sorrows of his heart."

CHAPTER VII.

THE SENSATIONAL NIHILISM OF THE BUDDHISTS—THE COSMOLOGY OF THE SANKHYAS.

"Suppose yourselves gazing on a gorgeous sunset. The whole western heavens are glowing with roseate hues. But you are aware that in half-an-hour all the glorious tints will have faded away into a dull ashen grey. You see them even now melting away before your eyes, although your eyes cannot place before you the conclusion that your reason draws. And what conclusion is that? That conclusion is that you never, even for the shortest time that can be named or conceived, see any abiding colour, any colour which truly is. Within the millionth part of a second the whole glory of the painted heavens has undergone an incalculable series of mutations. Before any one colour has had time to be that colour, it has melted into another colour, and that other colour has in like manner melted into a third, before it has attained to any degree of fixedness or duration. The eye indeed seems to arrest the fleeting pageant, and to give it some continuance. But the senses, says Heraclitus, are very indifferent witnesses of the truth. Reason refuses to lay an arrestment on any period of the passing scene, or to declare that it is, because in the very act of being it is not; it has given place to something else. It is a series of fleeting colours, no one of which *is*, because each of them continually vanishes in another."—FERRIER.

CHAP. VII.

The doctrine of the blank, the first antithesis. The original nothingness of the Buddhists.

So far the primitive thesis of Indian philosophy has been presented to the reader; it is time to present the primitive antithesis, and also the new position taken up by a later school of Indian thinkers with the purpose of superseding this antithesis, and of gaining a firmer footing by means of a cosmology approaching more nearly the convictions that work unrecognised in the popular mind. As has been said already, in the absence of historical data, the only methodical exposition of early Indian philosophy that is possible, must be the presentation of theses and antitheses that in their succession made up its process.

CHAP. VII.

The primitive thesis, the original Indian cosmological conception, is that of the fictitious nature of the world, and of the various forms of life that migrate through it in body after body, in age after age, and of the sole reality of the one impersonal Self. The primitive antithesis is that there is no such impersonal Self, nor spiritual reality underlying the world of passing semblances. Sensations and the ideal residues of sensations are the only things that are; and these are only semblances or fleeting shows, that come out of and pass back into a fontal nullity, void, or blank. The things of sense are fictitious presentments, but not fictions that replace at the same time that they conceal, a reality beneath: the mirage of life is an aerial vision that covers no expanse, unless it be an expanse of nothingness. The things of sense are only sensations variously assorted, rising and passing away at every moment like the shifting colours of a sunset cloud.[1] All things are in unceasing flow, and the soul itself is only a series of sensations and ideal residues of sensations. There is no inner light, no perduring Self within; the sensations and ideas flit by lit up with their own light, and each several stream of these is a migrating soul. The soul in every successive life has nothing but misery to look forward to; and the highest end of aspiration is a lapse into the void, a return to the primeval nothingness, a final extinction. In the philosophy of the Upanishads, the mind of the perfect sage is said to be blown out like a lamp as he returns to union with the one and only Self. In the philosophy of the Indian sensational nihilists, the successive mental modes are the mind, and the mind is the only soul. This mind or soul is extinguished as the sage returns to the aboriginal nothingness of things. The liberation promised in the Upanishads is a return to the pure

[1] This simile occurs in the second chapter of Mādhavāchārya's Sarvadarśanasangraha, to which the reader may refer for further details.

state of the soul as characterless being, thought, and blessedness. The liberation promised by the Indian nihilist is a return to the void beyond the miseries of the phantasmagory of metempsychosis. It is Nirvāṇa, extinction, return into the fontal nullity. All things have come out of nonentity, and shall pass back into nonentity; and as soon as it has fully learnt its unreality, the soul shall pass back into the primordial nothingness.

The doctrine of the emanation of the world from an aboriginal nullity as old as the Upanishads. It was the primitive antithesis to the doctrine of emanation from the original Self.

This doctrine of the emanation of migrating souls and the spheres of recompense out of an original nonentity, is as old as the Upanishads, and appears in a text of the sixth lecture of the Chhāndogya Upanishad: "Existent only, my son, was this in the beginning, one only, without duality. Some indeed have said, Non-existent only was this in the beginning, one only, without duality, and the existent proceeded out of the non-existent. But how should this be so? how should entity emanate out of nonentity? This then was existent only in the beginning, one only, without duality."

This passage refers either to philosophical forerunners of the Buddhists, or to the Buddhists themselves. It is easy to see how the teaching of the primitive Brahmanical philosophers would at once provoke opposition. In the earliest and the rudest age, as in the latest and richest in hereditary culture, there will always be people that fail to see the necessity of finding a positive reality at the root of things, and mistake a shallow wit for a deeper wisdom; to whom the light within is a piece of transcendental moonshine. These primitive Indian sensationalists have so far the advantage over the sensationalists of the present day, that they do not tacitly substantialise their sensations, or invent such strange abstractions as a background of permanent possibilities of sensations, to replace the realities they seek to explode. In this Indian proclamation of an

The Buddhist teaching.

CHAP. VII.

The inner light is moonshine, the Self is zero.

aboriginal vacuum or blank, which either already was or afterwards became Buddhism, the inner light, the impersonal Self or Brahman, is replaced by zero. The pessimism, metempsychosis, and Māyā, Avidyā, the primitive world-fiction, are retained. There is the same dread of every future state of life, and the same teaching that inertion, not exertion, is the path of extrication; and that the sage must loose himself from every tie, turn his back upon the world, and make all things disappear by a prolonged effort of abstraction, by a rigid and insensible posture of body, and by apathy and vacuity of mind. The phantasmagory of metempsychosis is a series of sensations and ideas, reproducing each other like plant and seed and seed and plant. The successive scenes present themselves that the migrating souls may find the recompense of their good and evil works, in higher and lower embodiments through æon after æon, in conformity with the law of retribution. The migrating souls are themselves as unreal as the spheres through which they pass. The soul[1] is identified with the mind[2] of the Brahmanical philosophers; and the mind is said to exhibit itself illusively in the twofold aspect of subject and object of consciousness. The process of things is thus pictured as so many series of sensations variously grouped, presenting themselves to so many migrating sentiencies; these sentiencies themselves being in turn only so many series of sensations and ideal residues. Everything is momentary, everything is fluxional, like the fugitive colours of a sunset cloud. The sensations and ideas pass on, lit up with their own light; and beyond them there is nothing but the void, the primordial nothingness. There is no longer any real Self to be clothed upon with the successive *involucra* of the Brahmanical philosophy. The investitures of the Self, the Koshas of the Upanishads, become the aggregates of experien-

All things momentary and fluxional. Sensations shine in their own light, *i.e.*, all consciousness is sensational.

[1] *Ātman.* [2] *Buddhi.*

tial elements, the Skandhas of the Buddhist philosophy. Buddhism is the philosophy of the Upanishads with Brahman left out. There is no light of lights beyond the darkness of the world-fiction. The highest end and final hope of man is a return into the vacuum, the aboriginal nothingness of things. This is Nirvāṇa, the extinction of the soul; and the path to it is the path of inertion, apathy, and vacuity.

This then is the primitive antithesis. *Asadvāda*, *Śūnyavāda*, the theory of the unreality of all things, the tenet of the void or blank, is set up in opposition to Brahmavāda, the doctrine of the fontal spiritual essence. This antithetic doctrine of the emanation of all things out of nonentity, is explained and redargued by Śankarāchārya in his gloss on the aphorisms of the Vedānta.[1] The Vedānta is the philosophy of the Upanishads in its later and systematic shape. The Upanishads are themselves often called Vedāntas, or final portions of the Veda.

Śankarāchārya's statement and refutation of Buddhist nihilism.

"The Buddhists," he says, "try to prove that what is comes out of what is not, according to a formula they have that nothing that comes out of another thing can come out of it without the previous suppression of that thing. Thus it is only from a seed that has already ceased to exist that a plant begins to germinate; only from milk that has ceased to exist that curds are produced; only from a piece of clay that has ceased to exist that a pot is made by the potter. They say that if things emanated out of an imperishable principle such as the impersonal Self, anything might emanate from anything; there being no particularity, as there is no limit to the power of such a principle. The plant, the curds, and the pot come into being out of the already non-existent seed, milk, and clay. They hold then that entity emanates out of nonentity.

"The reply we make is that entity cannot emanate

[1] Śārīrakamīmānsābhāshya, ii. 2, 26.

CHAP. VII. out of nonentity; what is cannot come out of what is not. If every cause is alike already non-existent, it is senseless to talk of particular things only emanating out of other particular things. Grant the seed, the milk, the clay, and so forth, to be already nonentities, being suppressed to make way for the plant, the curds, the pot that come into being out of them, and there will be no difference between these several nonentities, they being all characterless alike; just as there is no difference between the horns of a hare, the flowers in the sky, and the like pieces of absurdity. Thus the Buddhist plea that everything in particular must emanate out of something in particular, the plant out of a seed and nothing but a seed, and so on, comes to nothing, If things can come out of a characterless nullity, the plant, the curds, the pot, and so forth may come out of such mere nullities as the horns of a hare and the flowers in the sky, and every one sees that this is not the case.

"If, on the other hand, the Buddhist contends for a difference between this, that, and the other nullity, just as this, that, and the other lotus differ, this being blue, that red, and the other white; his nothings will become somethings, as much as the lotuses themselves are somethings. A nothing cannot give birth to a something, for the very good reason that a nothing is a nothing. The horns of the hare and the flowers of the sky are nothings, and as nothings they give birth to nothing.

"If entity came out of nonentity, every entity that has come into being would be nonentitative, and this is not the case, for every one can see that each and every entity is entitative in its own particular modes of being. Everything is of the same nature as that out of which it has had its origin. No one imagines the pots that have been made of clay, and retain the nature of clay, to have been woven out of threads, or imagines textile fabrics to have been fashioned out of clay. Every one is sufficiently aware that earthenware things are only new forms of earth.

"As for the Buddhist assertion that things that are come out of things that are not, nothing coming into being prior to the suppression of the thing it came out of,—this is false. Every one sees that things can only be made out of things that continue to exist; bracelets out of gold that continues to have its being in the bracelets, and so on. If you suppress the proper nature of the seed, the power of germination and the future plant are suppressed along with it. The plant proceeds just out of those elements of the seed that have not perished, but which go on existing in the plant that grows up out of them. This tenet, then, of the emanation of the existent out of the non-existent is inadmissible; inasmuch as we see, on the one hand, that entity does not issue out of nonentity,—you cannot make a bow out of a pair of hare's horns, or a garland out of sky-flowers; and, on the other hand, that entity does issue out of entity, as golden trinkets are made out of existing gold, and other things out of things that are."

It is thus that Śankarāchārya refutes the *Asadvāda*, *Śūnyavāda*, or nihilism of the Buddhists. Elsewhere he points out that the last residuum of abstraction carried to its highest point is not nonentity, but entity. The entity thus reached is, of course, a pure indetermination of being; and the principle of movement to account for the existence of all the variety of life is found in Māyā. All differences are figments of illusion; the pure indifference of being, thought, and bliss alone is true.

Let us now see how the great Indian schoolman states and refutes the *Vijñānavāda* or sensationalism of the Buddhists. The statement and refutation of this theory also are taken from his gloss on the aphorisms of the Vedānta.[1]

[1] Śārīrakamīmānsābhāshya ii. 2, 28.

CHAP. VII.

S'ankarāchārya's statement of Buddhist sensationalism.

"The theory of the sensationalists proposes to account for the whole world of everyday life, with its cognitions and cognisable objects, as something internal, as only a form taken by the mind of the migrating sentiency. They say that even if there were things outside the mind, the distinction between the perceptions and the things perceived could only be furnished by the mind itself. If you ask, they say, how it can be known that all the things of daily life are internal to the mind, and that there are no outward things, it must be replied that external things are impossible. The external things you plead for, they continue, must be either atoms, or masses made up of atoms, such as posts and pillars and the like. Now, atoms cannot present themselves as posts and pillars, for there is no presentation of an atom; nor, again, can masses of atoms present themselves as posts and pillars, for you could not say whether these posts and pillars were the same or not the same as the atoms. In the same way it may be shown, they say, that the external things are not universals, or qualities, or actions."

We do not know that the post is a mass of atoms, because we do not know that the several atoms, each of which is beyond all perception, can come together in such a way as to form a mass that can be seen and handled. Again, if the posts and pillars and other outward things are not atoms, or made up of atoms, they cannot be placed under the category of substance. The sensationalist is represented as employing the language of the Naiyāyikas and Vaiśeshikas, and requiring to find some one or other of their categories under which to place the outward things which are under dispute. They cannot be placed under the head of substance, for substances are, in the Naiyāyika and Vaiśeshika philosophies, atomic aggregates. The sensationalist proceeds to try whether they can be placed under either of the three categories of universality, quality, or action, there being no other category under which they could possibly be ranked. He finds that they cannot, for every universal, every quality, and every action is either one with the thing to which it belongs or not one with it. If it is one with it, the thing is a thing no more; if it is not one with it, it cannot stand to it in any other relation than that of an independent thing outside it, and such an independent thing it cannot be. Such appears to be Ānandagiri's explanation of this obscure argument.

"Further, they say, the particularisation of the several cognitions as they succeed each other in the mind, in such a way that this is a cognition of a post, that of a wall, this of a water-pot, that of a piece of cloth, and so on,—this particularisation supposes some distinction in the cognitions themselves, and you must admit that the cognition has the same form as the object cognised. This once admitted, the hypothesis of the existence of external things is gratuitous; for the forms of the objects are not without but within the cognitions.

"Again, as the perceptions and the percepts are always presented simultaneously, and as if one be not presented the other is not presented, they are inseparable. They would not be inseparable if they were not really one in nature; for if they were two different things, there would be nothing to prevent the presentation of the one in the absence of the other. There is therefore no external world.

"The nature of external perception is similar to that of a dream. The presentments we call posts and pillars and so forth, appear to us in our waking experience in a relation of subject and object; precisely in the same way that the presentments of a dream, of an illusion, of a mirage, or of a reverie, appear to us in the relation of subject and object; and in each state equally in the absence of any things external to us. In each state the presentments are alike presentments.

CHAP. VII.

"If you ask us, they proceed, how to account for all the variety of the presentments of the senses, in the absence of external things to give rise to that variety; it may be replied that this variety proceeds from the variety of ideal residues of past sensations. There has been no beginning to the process of the æons; and thus there is no reason to deny that sensations give rise to ideas and ideas to fresh sensations, in the same way that the seed produces the plant and the plant the seed in endless progress, and thus give rise to all the variety that is around us. You, they say, no less than we ourselves, teach that in dreams and reveries the variety of the consciousness arises from the variety of residual ideas or mental images, and there is proof enough that variety of ideas is followed by variety of presentments, and want of variety in the ideas by want of variety in the presentments. We do not allow that the variety in perception is due to the action of external things. And thus again we assert that there is no external world."

Such is Śankarāchārya's statement of the Buddhist theory of sensationalism. His refutation of that theory proceeds upon an appeal to the primitive convictions of the human race. The reader will be interested in remarking to how great an extent the arguments of Reid and his successors are anticipated by the Indian schoolmen perhaps more than eleven hundred years ago. The refutation is as follows:—

S'ankarāchārya's refutation of sensationalism.

"To all this we reply that external things do exist. It is impossible to judge that external things have no existence, and why? because we are conscious of them. In every act of perception some one or other outward thing is presented to the consciousness, be it post or wall, or cloth or jar, or whatever else it may be; and that of which we are conscious cannot but exist. If a man, at the very moment he is conscious of outward things through his senses, tells us that he is not conscious of them, and that they have no existence, why should we listen to him, any more than we should listen to a man who, in the moment of eating and enjoying, told us that he was not eating and was not enjoying what he ate?

"Perhaps you will reply that you do not say you are not conscious of any object, but only that you are not conscious of an object external to the consciousness. Yes, it is true that you say this, but you say it in the plenitude of your self-conceit, and you say nothing that you can prove. The consciousness itself certifies to us that the thing is external to the consciousness. No one is conscious of the post and the wall as forms of perception, and every plain man knows that the post and the wall are the objects of perception. It is thus that all ordinary people perceive things. The sensationalists repudiate external things and at the same time talk about them freely, as when they say that the percept is internal and that it only appears to be external. They are all the while dealing with a perception that all the world knows to be external; and as they insist on refusing an external world, they say the external thing only seems to be external. If there be nothing external, how can anything seem external, that is, be like an external thing? No one says, Vishṇumitra looks like the son of a childless mother. If we are to accept the truth as it is given to us in our experience, we must affirm that the thing perceived is presented externally, not only that it is presented like an external thing.

"I suppose you will rejoin that you decide that the thing perceived is *like* an external thing, because it is impossible that anything should really be external. This is no fit decision, for the possibility and impossibility of things are to be learned in the exercise of the faculties; and the exercise of the faculties is not to follow any preconception about the possibility or im-

CHAP. VII. possibility of things. A thing is possible, if it is cognisable in perception or in the exercise of any other faculty. A thing is impossible, if it is incognisable to each and all the faculties. How can you say that an external world is impossible, on the strength of difficulties in the shape of the positive and negative inferences you adduce, if the existence of this external world is at the same time presupposed in the exercise of every faculty?

"Again, you cannot argue that there are no outward objects, on the ground that the perception takes the form of the outward object; for if there were no outward object in existence, the perception could not take the form of an outward object. You will have to admit then that the reason that the perception and the object perceived are always presented simultaneously, is not that the object is one and the same with the act of perception, but that the object is the occasion of the perception.

"Again there is the perception of a jar, and there is the perception of a piece of cloth. Here the difference lies not in the perception, but in the things perceived, the jar and the cloth; in the same way as there are white cows and black cows, and these differ, not in being cows, but in being the one white and the other black. So, further, there is the perception of a jar and the memory or representation of a jar, and in this case the difference lies in the acts of presentation and representation, not in the jar perceived and represented; in the same way as the smell of milk and the taste of milk differ as smell and taste, and not in respect to the milk smelt and tasted.

"If you say that the thing we are conscious of is the perception, you should more properly say that the external thing is that of which we are conscious. You will no doubt rejoin that the sensation, as you call the perception, shines in its own light like a lamp, and that we can be conscious of it, and that the supposed external thing does not shine in its own light, and that we cannot be conscious of it. The irradiation of the perception by itself, which you propose, is extremely absurd; it is as if you said that a fire burned itself. At the same time, you are such a great philosopher that you will not allow the clear and plain belief of plain people, that the external thing is presented to consciousness by a perceptive act that is not the thing itself. It is of no use to urge that a sensation, which is not an external thing, presents itself to the consciousness, for to say that a thing acts upon itself is an absurdity.

"I foresee that you will rejoin that if the sensation is to be apprehended by something not itself, that something must again be apprehended by something not itself, and so *ad infinitum.* You will also rejoin that if there is to be a fresh cognition to cognise the perception, the perception already shining of itself like a lamp, the cognition and the perception being both alike, the one cannot be supposed to shed its light upon the other; and thus it is an idle hypothesis that makes the sensation or perception one thing, and the consciousness of the sensation or perception another thing. Both your rejoinders are null, for there is no need to suppose a consciousness of that which is conscious, viz., of the Self that witnesses or irradiates the perception; and we only suppose a consciousness of the perception, not a consciousness of a consciousness of the perception. There is no fear of an infinite regression. And as regards your second rejoinder: the witness or Self that irradiates the perception and the perception that it irradiates are essentially different, and may thus be held to stand to one another in the relation of thing knowing and thing known. The witness or Self is self-posited, and cannot be repudiated.

"When you talk about a sensation, incognisable to any faculty, shining of itself with nothing ulterior to give the light of consciousness to it, a sensation that there is no sentient being to cognise, you might as well say that there are a thousand lamps shining inside such and such an impenetrable mass of rocks, but that there is no one to see them. You are talking nonsense.

"The philosopher who denies the existence of external things asserts that the presentments of posts and walls, and pots and pans, and so forth, in the waking experience, arise in the absence of all external things, like the things seen in a dream; the presentments being presentments alike, and nothing more, whether we wake or dream. This we deny. The perceptions of the waking state differ from the presentments of a dream; the perceptions are not negated, and the presentments of sleep are negated. On waking out of his sleep, a man denies the reality of what he saw in a dream. He says, for example, that he had a false presentation of an interview with a great man, but that no such interview took place, only his inward sense was dull and sleepy, and thus the illusion arose. Reveries, hallucinations, and the like states are all negatived, each in its proper mode of sublation; but the thing perceived in the waking state, be it post or pillar, or what it may, is never negatived in any later state of mind. The visions of a dream are representations, the visions of the waking experience are presentations; and the distinction between perception and memory, or presentation and representation, is self-evident. In perception the thing is present, in memory it is absent. When I recollect the son I am missing, I do not perceive him, but only want to perceive him. It is of no avail for you to assert that the presentations of the waking experience are as false as the presentments of a dream, in that both are alike presentments and nothing more; for you are all the time yourself conscious of the difference between presentations and representations."

Śankarāchārya's arguments will at first sight appear

CHAP. VII.

Is S'ankaráchārya self-consistent? The external world is only relatively and provisionally real.

inconsistent with his doctrine of the unreality of all things save the one and only Self. Has not he told us himself that the world is only a series of dreams, through which the soul is fated to wander until it recover its unity with the sole reality, the fontal spiritual essence? The inconsistency will be seen to be less than it appears, if we remember that the external things in his philosophy, the philosophy of the Upanishads, are as real as the minds that perceive them. This degree of reality they have, and the presentments of a dream have not. Individual souls and their environments are true for the many; they have an existence sufficient to account for all that goes on in daily life; they are real[1] from the standpoint of everyday experience. The visions of a dream are false from this standpoint. Individual souls and their environments are false for the reflective few; their existence disappears in the higher existence, to be won by abstraction and spiritual intuition; they are unreal[2] from the standpoint of metaphysical truth. So long as a man is engaged in the avocations of common life, the things he has to deal with are real enough for him. If neither he nor they have the true and real being[3] that belongs to Self alone, they have their own conventional existence,[4] an existence that is enough to account for all we are and do and suffer. If we use the language of metaphysical truth, we must say that the existence of the soul and its environment, apart from the Self, is only enough to account for all we *seem* to be and do and suffer; that it is spurious, fictitious, mere semblance; that it may be negatived by spiritual intuition or ecstasy. But such an existence is very different from the merely apparent existence[5] of the presentments of the dreaming phantasy, which are negatived by the ordinary experience of the unphilosophic man. This conven-

[1] *Laukikavyavahārataḥ.* [2] *Paramārthataḥ.* [3] *Pāramārthikī sattā.* [4] *Vyāvahārikī sattā.* [5] *Prātibhāsikī sattā.*

CHAP. VII. tional existence of souls and their environments is an apparent existence for the philosopher; not an apparent existence for the many; for them it is real enough. They at least find no lack of truth in the miseries they have to go through. Beyond the apparent existence of the images of a dream there is a lower depth of unreality, the unreality that belongs to such mere figments of the imagination as the horns of a hare, the flowers of the sky, the son of a childless mother. These things are the nonsensical pure and simple.[1] Now the world-fiction and its figments, souls, and the things they see and do and suffer, are not pure and simple nonsense; not things that have a merely apparent existence even for the many; but things that have a conventional existence for the many, and an apparent and fictitious existence only for the philosophic few, who have attained to an insight into the one high verity, the sole existence of the characterless Self.

The philosophy of the Sānkhyas. A real and independent principle of emanation, Pradhāna or Prakṛiti. A plurality of Purushas or Selves.

Judging the succession of Indian systems by the nature of the notions they exhibit, and there is no other way to judge it, the system that follows next will be the philosophy of the Sānkhyas. In this philosophy, with the purpose of presenting a firmer front against the Buddhists, a still higher degree of reality is assigned to the mind and its environments, to the world at large, than in the primitive Indian philosophy, the philosophy of the Upanishads. The world is said to have a separate and independent origin or principle of emanation; it comes out of Prakṛiti or Pradhāna. This Prakṛiti or principle of emanation is the equilibrium of the three *primordia rerum* of Indian philosophy, pleasure, pain, and indolence or indifference. These are the basal sensibility out of which, on an impulse[2] given by the law of nemesis that upsets their equilibrium, mind,[3] as yet unconscious, emanates; from mind personality[4] pro-

[1] *Tuchchhamātra.*
[2] *Guṇakshobha, Prakṛitikshobha.*
[3] *Buddhi.*
[4] *Ahankāra.*

ceeds, and from personality the as yet imperceptible rudiments of the world, and so on. The world is thus a reality, no illusion, not a figment-world even for the philosopher. It is real for him, as well as for the multitude. This is the first step the Sāṅkhyas, or enumerative philosophers, take in the direction of common sense. They take a second step in the same direction, at the expense, it must be expressly stated, of their ingenuousness, by pretending that the term Brahman in the Upanishads is only a collective term for a plurality of Selves or Purushas. They say that the texts of the Upanishads that teach that all souls are one in the unity of the one and only Self, merely assert a common nature in all souls. There are many Selves, they pretend, and their unity is generic, not numerical. This is a mere *tour de force* on the part of the Sāṅkhyas, as must be evident enough to any attentive reader of the preceding chapters of this work. They further say that when Brahman is said in the Upanishads to be the *principium*, the origin of the worlds, the term Brahman is only a synonym for Prakṛiti or Pradhāna: a perfectly monstrous assertion. They allow full reality to the Purushas or Selves, and a lower but still true and independent reality to the minds and bodies and environments of the Purushas. These minds, bodies, and environments are emanations out of Prakṛiti, and are said by the Sāṅkhyas to have a practical or conventional existence, inasmuch as they are in unceasing change, and never at a stand. The world is not negatived for them, not sublated, by a perfect knowledge, as it is in the primitive philosophy of the Upanishads, but the Purusha is detached from it. The mind ceases to mirror its ceaseless modes upon that Purusha or Self on which a perfect knowledge has been reflected. Mind is reflected or mirrored on the Purushas, and the Purushas give light to mind, the light of consciousness. A soul is extricated from

The Sāṅkhyas pervert the plain sense of the Upanishads.

metempsychosis as often as one of the Purushas is separated from the mind, so soon as the world ceases to cast its reflections upon it, and to shine in its light.

In support of their thesis that the world has an independent and real principle, Prakṛiti or Pradhāna, the Sānkhyas bring forward in particular two passages of the Upanishads, one from the Kaṭha and the other from the Śvetāśvatara. A translation of the Śvetāśvatara will be given in the next chapter. It is necessary, before giving it, to discuss the position of the Sānkhya philosophy, as the Śvetāśvatara Upanishad has been sometimes thought to lend countenance to Sānkhya teaching, or to be in fact a Sānkhya Upanishad.

In the Upanishads Prakṛiti is another name for Avidyā or Māyā.

Before looking at the passages the Sānkhyas insist upon as teaching their views, it must be noted that Prakṛiti is often used in the philosophy of the Upanishads and the Vedānta precisely as a synonym for Avidyā or Māyā, the self-feigning world-fiction, and that Purusha is also often used as a precise equivalent for Brahman the one and only Self. In fact, if we pay attention to the strictly Vedāntic teaching of the Śvetāśvatara Upanishad and the Bhagavadgītā, and to the Sānkhya language in which that teaching is couched, as also to the references they make to Kapila and Jaimini, the reputed authors of the Sānkhya and Yoga or demiurgic Sānkhya systems, the only conclusion that we can form is that the Sānkhya was originally nothing more than a nomenclature for the principles of the philosophy of the Upanishads; and that the distinctive tenets of the subsequent Sānkhya school, viz., the independence and reality of Prakṛiti and the plurality of Purushas, are later developments. In its origin the Sānkhya appears to have been nothing more than a series of terms to note the successive emanations from Prakṛiti or Māyā. It was only in later times that it became a separate philosophy. It is beyond all doubt that the teaching of the Śvetāśvatara Upanishad and of the Bhagavadgītā, notwithstanding their Sānkhya phrases and Sānkhya references, is as purely Vedāntic as that of any Vedāntic work whatever.

S'ankarāchārya disallows the Sānkhya appeal to the Katha Upanishad.

The passage of the Kaṭha Upanishad which the Sānkhyas produce in support of their peculiar tenets is as follows.:—

"For their objects are beyond and more subtile than the senses; the common sensory is beyond the objects, the mind is beyond the sensory, and the great soul is beyond the mind.

"The ultimate and undeveloped principle is beyond that great soul, and Purusha the Self is beyond the undeveloped principle. Beyond Purusha there is nothing; that is the goal, that is the final term."

The Sānkhyas hold that the undeveloped principle of this passage is their own Prakṛiti or Pradhāna, the independent principle out of which the world proceeds, and that the mind here mentioned is their own second principle, the first emanation out of Prakṛiti. Śankarāchārya examines this view in the beginning of the fourth section of the first book of his commentary on the aphorisms of the Vedānta, and undertakes to prove from the context that the undeveloped principle is not the Pradhāna of the Sānkhyas, but the world-fiction Māyā, which is the body of Īśvara,[1] the body out of which all things emanate. The great soul mentioned in this passage is, he says, either the migrating soul, or the divine emanation Hiraṇyagarbha. The text is the immediate sequel of the allegory of the chariot. "The text," he says, "does not indicate any such independent principle of emanation as the Pradhāna of the Sānkhya tradition. The word *undeveloped* is merely a negative term, the negative of the developed. It applies therefore to something imperceptible and inscrutable, but it is not to be taken as a special name of a special thing. It is not the current name of an entity. It is

[1] The cosmic body, the *kāraṇaśarīra*.

CHAP. VII. true that the term is one of the technicalities of the Sānkhyas, and with them a synonym of their Pradhāna, but in explaining the sense of the Vedic text it is not to be taken as the specific name of the principle of emanation. The order of enumeration is similar to the order in which the Sānkhyas enumerate their principles, but that is no proof that the things enumerated are the same. No one in his senses on finding an ox in a horse's stall would pronounce it to be a horse. We have only to look at the allegory of the chariot, which immediately precedes the words of the text, to find that the undeveloped principle is not the Pradhāna invented by the Sānkhyas, but the cosmic body, the body of Īśvara, out of which all things emanate. In this allegory the soul is seated in a chariot, and the body is the chariot.

The undeveloped principle of the Kaṭha Upanishad not Pradhāna but Māyā, the cosmic body, the body of Is'vara, the cosmic soul.

"Know that the soul is seated in a chariot, and that the body is that chariot. Know that the mind is the charioteer, and that the will is the reins.

"They say that the senses are the horses, and that the things of sense are the roads. The wise declare that the migrating soul is the Self fictitiously present in the body, senses, and common sensory."

If the senses are not held in check, the soul proceeds to further migrations. If they are held in check, it reaches the farther limit of its journey, the sphere of Vishṇu the supreme. The sphere of Vishṇu the supreme is shown to be the one and only Self, the farther limit of its journey, as being beyond the senses, and the other things enumerated in the text. Sounds, colours, and other sensible objects, the roads along which the horses run, are beyond the senses. The common sensory is said to lie beyond these sensible objects, because the operation of the senses upon their objects is determined by the common sensory. The mind is said to be beyond the common sensory, because every mode of pleasurable and painful experience accrues to the migrating soul only through the mind.

The great soul said to be beyond the mind is the migrating soul, the occupant of the chariot. It is said to be great because it is the possessor. Or the great soul may mean the soul of Hiraṇyagarbha, the first emanation out of Īśvara, great as being the sum of all individual minds. The body, then, is the only thing left to be accounted for in the allegory of the chariot, and it follows that the body is the undeveloped principle. It will be asked how the body, a visible and tangible thing, can be spoken of as the undeveloped. The undeveloped is surely something invisible and intangible. It must be replied that the body here spoken of is invisible and intangible, the cosmic body, the body of Īśvara, out of which all things emanate. This body is the world-fiction; and thus the undeveloped principle in the text is the potential world of name and colour, the world before it has come into being, as yet nameless and colourless, the power of the seed of the world-tree not yet passing into actuality."

The Sānkhya appeal to the S'vetās'vatara Upanishad disallowed.

The second of the texts of highest importance to the pretensions of the Sānkhyas, is a verse of the Śvetāśvatara Upanishad.

"There is one unborn being, red, white, and black, that gives birth to many offspring like herself. One unborn soul lingers in dalliance with her, another leaves her, his dalliance with her ended."

The Sānkhyas contend that the one birthless procreant, red, white, and black, here spoken of, is Prakṛiti or Pradhāna, the independent originative principle of the world, the equipoise of the three *primordia rerum*; pain being spoken of as red, pleasure as white, and indifference as black. One Purusha lingers with her, passing from body to body; another leaves her as soon as he has passed through the pains and pleasures of metempsychosis and attained to liberation. Śankarāchārya urges that this text by itself is insufficient to prove that the doctrine of Pradhāna has any Vedic war-

CHAP. VII. rant.[1] The text must be interpreted in accordance with the context, and in harmony with a similar passage in the Chhāndogya Upanishad: "The red colour of fire is the colour of heat, white is the colour of water, and black the colour of earth." The plain indication of the context is that the unborn one is Māyā or Śakti, the fiction of the Archimagus or power of the Demiurgus, or Īśvara, the universal soul or world-projecting deity. The Chhāndogya Upanishad teaches how this creative power, the potentiality of name and colour, is developed into heat, water, and earth, out of which the bodies of plants, and animals, and man are fashioned. The unborn souls in the text are not the Purushas of the Sānkhya philosophy, but the Jīvas or migrating souls of the Vedānta. The birthless procreant is explained also in Śankarāchārya's commentary[2] on the Śvetāśvatara Upanishad to be the Māyā or Śakti, the fiction or the power of the Demiurgus, that develops into heat, water, and earth. The Māyā or Prakṛiti of the Vedānta is often described in the same way as the Pradhāna or Prakṛiti of the Sānkhyas, as the union of the three *primordia rerum, triguṇātmikā māyā.* The Vedāntins have therefore no interested motive in identifying the red, white, and black with the colours of light, water, and earth, rather than with pain, pleasure, and indolence. Śankarāchārya's exposition is certainly the natural, no less than the traditional and authoritative, interpretation of the text. In fact, the teaching of the Śvetāśvatara is precisely the same as that of the other Upanishads.

The Sānkhyas deny the existence of Īs'vara, the cosmic soul, or world-evolving deity.

Another point at issue between the Sānkhyas and the Vedāntins, or followers of the philosophy of the Upanishads, should be noted. This is that the Sānkhyas deny the existence of the Īśvara, Demiurgus, or world-projecting deity, proclaimed in the Upanishads. The Sānkhya teaching in this matter may be given in the words of

[1] Śārīrakamīmānsābhāshya, I. 4, 8, and 9.

[2] Śvetāśvataropanishadbhāshya, iv. 5.

Vāchaspatimiśra in his Sānkhyatattvakaumudī, or elucidation of the Sānkhya principles. "The unconscious," he says, "is seen to operate towards an end; the unconscious milk of the cow, for example, operates towards the growth of the calf. It is in the same way that Prakṛiti, the principle of emanation, unconscious as it is, acts with a view to the liberation of Purushas or Selves. A Vedāntin may urge that the operation of the milk is not solely the work of an unconscious thing, the milk operating under the supervision of Īśvara. But this plea is useless, for every intelligent being acts either from self-interest or from beneficence, as we see in the life of the present day. Neither self-interest nor beneficence can have had any part to play in the evolution of the world, and therefore the world has not an intelligent author. A creator who has already all he can desire can have no interest in creating anything; nor can he be imagined to operate from a motive of beneficence. Prior to a fresh creation or palingenesia of the world there is no misery, as the migrating souls have neither bodies, senses, nor environments. What is there, then, that the tenderness of the Demiurgus could wish to extricate them from? If you say that the beneficence of the Demiurgus has reference to the misery of the souls to come as soon as he has made the world or projected the spheres of recompense, this plea implies a logical circle you will not be able to get out of; the act of creation will proceed from the beneficence of the world-projecting deity, and his beneficence will proceed from the act of creation. What is more, a Demiurgus actuated by beneficence would not create sentient beings under disparate conditions, but in a state of co-equal happiness. Disparity of conditions, you rejoin, proceeds from disparity of works in former lives. If so, away, say we, with this superintendence of works, and the recompense of works by a supreme intelligence. It is easier to suppose that the blind and

CHAP. VII.

fatal operation of the law of retribution sets Prakṛiti at work in evolving the spheres of recompense; for there would be no misery at all but for the evolution of bodies, senses, and environments out of Prakṛiti by the law of retribution."

S'ankarāchārya's defence of the teaching of the philosophy of the Upanishads in regard to Is'vara.

Śankarāchārya undertakes to refute this tenet of the Sānkhyas, and to maintain the existence of the Īśvara or Demiurgus proclaimed in the philosophy of the Upanishads. His refutation is as follows:[1]—

"It is argued that the Demiurgus cannot be the principle out of which the world emanates, and why? because he would be unjust and cruel. He makes some living beings extremely happy, as the gods; others extremely miserable, as the lower animals; to others, as to men, he assigns an intermediate position. If the Demiurgus creates so unequal a world, he must have the same preferences and aversions as one of ourselves, and there will be an end to the purity and other divine attributes given to him in revelation and tradition. Nay, he must be pitiless and cruel to a degree that even bad men would reprobate, as first involving his creatures in misery, and then retracting them all into himself, to be projected out of himself again. The Demiurgus, then, is not the principle of origination of the world. To this we reply, that injustice and cruelty do not attach to the Demiurgus, and why? because he acts with reference to something beyond himself. He would be indeed unjust and cruel, if he acted altogether of himself in evolving this unequal world; but it is not of himself but with reference to something farther that he projects the spheres of recompense. You ask in reference to what. In reference, we reply, to the good and evil that the migrating souls have done in their former lives. The world is a world of inequalities, because of the various works that have to be recompensed to the migrating souls that are projected anew

[1] Śārīrarakamīmānsābhāshya, ii. 1, 34-36.

The migrating souls, not Is'vara, are to blame for the inequality of their lots.

at the beginning of each æon, and the Demiurgus is not to blame. The Demiurgus may be likened to a rain-cloud. The cloud is the one cause alike of the growth of rice, barley, and other kinds of grain; and the peculiar possibilities of the various seeds are what make the one to grow up as rice, the other as barley, the others as other kinds of grain. The Demiurgus is in like manner the one common principle of the evolution of gods, men, animals, and other creatures; and the peculiar works, good and evil, of the several migrating souls give rise to their different embodiments, divine and human, and the rest. The Demiurgus is not guilty of injustice or cruelty, inasmuch as he operates in creation in conformity to the law of retribution. You ask how we know that he acts in conformity to this law in producing these higher, middle, and lower spheres of recompense. We know it because Vedic revelation teaches it in the texts,—If he wishes to raise up a soul into a higher embodiment, he makes it do good works, and if he wishes to lead a soul down into a lower embodiment, he makes it do evil works; and, A man becomes holy by holy works and unholy by unholy works in previous lives. Tradition also teaches that the favour and disfavour of the world-projecting deity are proportionate to the good and evil works of the migrating souls, in such words as,—I receive them just as they approach me.

"You will argue against all this that there is no distinction in things prior to creation, and that therefore prior to creation there is no law of retribution to account for the inequalities of the world that is to be, the Vedic text saying, Existent only, my son, was this in the beginning, one only, without duality. You will say that we involve ourselves in a logical circle, in saying that the law of retribution is a result of the variety of embodiments produced in the creation, and the variety of embodiments again is a result of the law

CHAP. VII. of retribution. You will further say that the Demiurgus operates in creation with reference to a law of nemesis that follows after the variety of embodiments, and that the first creation in the series of creations must have been one of pure equality, there not having yet arisen any such retributive fatality in consequence of a prior variety of embodiments. In all this, we reply, you produce nothing to disprove our theory of the Demiurgus. *The series of creations has had no beginning.* Your plea would be good if the series had a beginning, but it has none; and consequently there is nothing to gainsay the position that the law of retribution and the inequalities of life produce and reproduce each other, like seed and plant and plant and seed.

The world has had no beginning. Souls have been in migration from eternity.

"You will next ask us how we know that the series of creations has had no beginning. Our reply is this, —that if the series had a beginning, something must have come out of nothing; and if something can come out of nothing, even liberated souls may have hereafter to return to metempsychosis, and to suffer miseries that they have done nothing to deserve. There would no longer be anything to account for the inequalities of happiness and misery in the world. This consequence would be as repugnant to your principles as it is to ours. The Demiurgus then is not the author of the inequalities of life. The cosmical illusion in and by itself is not the source of these inequalities, being uniform. The world-fiction becomes the source of these inequalities only by reason of the law of retribution, latent in it owing to the residue of good and evil works as yet unrecompensed. There is no logical circle implied in the statement that retribution leads to bodily life, and bodily life to retribution, for the process of metempsychosis is one that has had no beginning, and that produces and reproduces itself like seed and plant, and plant and seed."

Another point of difference between the philosophy

CHAP. VII.

The Sānkhya doctrine of real modifications is antithetic to the Vedāntic tenet of fictitious emanations.

of the Upanishads and the philosophy of the Sānkhyas must be marked. In both philosophies alike things are said to pre-exist in the things they emanate out of. In the philosophy of the Upanishads the successive emanations are fictitious things[1] that present themselves in the place of the one and only Self as it is overspread with illusion. In the philosophy of the Sānkhyas the successive emanations[2] are real modifications of a real and modifiable principle, Prakṛiti. The doctrine of fictitious emanations is stated in the following passage of Nṛisiṃhasarasvatī's Subodhinī, a commentary on the Vedāntasāra or Essence of the Upanishads: "All the figments of the world-fiction may be made to disappear in such a way that pure thought or the Self shall alone remain, in the same manner as the fictitious serpent seen in a piece of rope may be made to disappear, and the rope that underlies it may be made to remain. The rope was only rope all the time it falsely seemed to be a snake. The fictitious world may be made to disappear as the fictitious snake is made to disappear, and this is its sublation.[3] Anything that exists in its own proper mode of existence, may pass into another form in either of two ways—the way of real emanation, and the way of fictitious emanation. Real emanation takes place when a thing really quits its present mode of being and assumes a new mode; as when milk ceases to be pure milk and emanates in the new form of curdled milk. Fictitious emanation takes place when a thing remains in its own mode of being, and at the same time fictitiously presents itself in another mode; as the piece of rope remains a piece of rope, but presents itself as a snake to the belated wayfarer. In the Vedānta the world of semblances that veils the Self, is not allowed to be a modification or real emana-

[1] *Vivarta.* This doctrine is called *Vivartavāda.*
[2] *Pariṇāma.* This doctrine is called *Pariṇāmavāda.*
[3] *Apavāda, bādha.*

tion of the Self; for if the Self were modifiable and mutable, it would not be, as it is, perduring and eternal. But in the true doctrine that the world is a false presentment or fictitious emanation that presents itself in the place of the Self, the Self remains unmodified and immutable."

In reference to this same Sānkhya tenet of real emanations Śankarāchārya says: "It is of no use to raise the question how the variety of creation can arise without the Self's forfeiting its pure and characterless being; for it is said in the sacred text that a varied creation arises in the one and only Self in the dreaming state of the soul. There are no chariots, no horses, no roads, but it presents to itself chariots, horses, and roads, and there is in this creation no suppression of the pure and characterless being of the Self."[1] And again: "The Self does not lose its pure and simple nature, for the variety of name and colour is only a figment of the world-fiction, a modification of speech only, a change, a name. Vedic revelation, in teaching that all things issue out of the Self, does not teach that things are real emanations or modifications of the Self; the very purpose of this revelation being to teach that the Self is the fontal spiritual essence, free from all that is, and all that is done and suffered, in the lives we live."[2]

[1] Śārīrakamīmānsābhāshya, ii. 1, 28.

[2] Śārīrakamīmānsābhāshya, ii. 1, 27.

CHAPTER VIII.

THE SVETASVATARA UPANISHAD.

"The fakirs of India and the monks of the Oriental church were alike persuaded, that in total abstraction of the faculties of the mind and body, the purer spirit may ascend to the enjoyment and vision of the Deity. The opinion and practice of the monasteries of Mount Athos will be best represented in the words of an abbot who flourished in the eleventh century. 'When thou art alone in thy cell,' says the ascetic teacher, 'shut thy door and seat thyself in a corner; raise thy mind above all things vain and transitory; recline thy beard and chin on thy breast; turn thy eyes and thy thoughts towards the middle of thy belly, the region of the navel, and search the place of the heart, the seat of the soul. At first all will be dark and comfortless; but if you persevere day and night, you will feel an ineffable joy; and no sooner has the soul discovered the place of the heart, than it is involved in a mystic and ethereal light.'"—GIBBON.

"Hypatia did not feel her own limbs, hear her own breath. A light bright mist, an endless network of glittering films, coming, going, uniting, resolving themselves, was above her and around her. Was she in the body or out of the body? The network faded into an abyss of still clear light. A still warm atmosphere was around her, thrilling through and through her. She breathed the light and floated in it, as a mote in the midday beam."—KINGSLEY.

CHAP. VIII.

The S'vetās'vatara Upanishad teaches the same doctrines as the other Upanishads.

THE perusal of the Śvetāśvatara Upanishad will satisfy the reader that its teaching is the same as that of the other Upanishads, the teaching that finds its full and legitimate expression in the system known as the Vedānta. Notwithstanding Sānkhya phrases, and references to the Sānkhya philosophy and its reputed founder, Kapila, this Upanishad, like the other Upanishads, teaches the unity of souls in the one and only Self; the unreality of the world as a series of figments of the self-feigning world-fiction; and as the first of the fictitious emanations, the existence of the Demi-

CHAP. VIII. urgus or universal soul present in every individual soul, the deity that projects the world out of himself, that the migrating souls may find the recompense of their works in former lives. The Śvetāśvatara Upanishad in Sānkhya terms propounds the very principles that the Sānkhya philosophers make it their business to subvert. The inference is that the Sānkhya was originally only an enumeration of the successive emanations out of Māyā or Prakṛiti, a precise series of terms to note the primitive philosophy of the Upanishads, and that the distinctive tenets of what is now known as the Sānkhya philosophy are later developments. The most important of these later tenets are, as has been seen, the reality and independence of Prakṛiti or Pradhāna, the reality of the emanations of Prakṛiti, the plurality of Purushas or Selves, and the negation of an Īśvara or world-projecting deity.

The Sānkhya originally a nomenclature for the principles of the philosophy of the Upanishads.

The Śvetāśvatara Upanishad is an Upanishad of the Taittirīya or Black Recension of the Yajurveda. This Upanishad is marked by several peculiarities. It employs Sānkhya terms, and refers to Kapila, the first teacher of the Sānkhya philosophy; a philosophy that seems to have been in its earliest form only a fresh, clear statement of the emanation of the world out of Māyā; Prakṛiti being a precise equivalent of Avidyā or Māyā, and Purusha of Brahman, the one and only Self. Its language is compressed and at times a little obscure, but its teaching is full and explicit, and it is very frequently referred to by the Indian schoolmen for the purpose of enforcing and illustrating their doctrines. It is particularly insistent on the practice of Yoga, or the fixation of the body and limbs in a rigid and insensible posture, and the crushing of every feeling, desire, and thought in order to rise to the ecstatic vision of and re-union with the Self. The Demiurgus or world-projecting deity is in this Upanishad identified with Rudra, Hara, or Śiva. It will be remembered that Śiva is the divine self-torturer, the typical Yogin, and that the worship of this deity is supposed to have been adopted from the indigenous tribes of the Himalaya.

CHAP. VIII.

The Śvetāśvatara Upanishad is as follows:—

S'vetās'vatara Upanishad. First Section.

I. "OM. The expositors of Brahman say, What is the origin of all things? Is it the Self? What do we come out of, what do we live by, and what do we pass back into? Tell us, you who know Brahman, what we are actuated by as we continue amidst the pleasures and pains of life.

"Is the source of things to be held to be time, or the nature of the things themselves, or the fatal retribution, or chance, or the elements, or the personal soul? The aggregate of these is not the origin of things; for that aggregate exists not for its own sake, but for the sake of the soul. The soul again is not competent to be the origin of the world, for there is some further cause of the pleasures and pains the soul goes through."

All things emanate out of the S'akti or Māyā of Is'vara, the power or fiction of the cosmic soul.

"Sages pursuing ecstatic union by fixing the thoughts upon a single point have come to see that the source of all things is the power of the divine spirit,[1] the power that is hidden beneath the things that emanate out of it. It is that one deity that actuates and controls all those proposed principles of emanation, including time and the personal soul."

It cannot be the migrating soul itself that makes the vision of the world, for this soul is subject to the law of retribution, and has no choice in regard to the spheres of recompense it is to pass through. It is not the Self as it is in and by itself that is the source of the world; Brahman *per se* is neither the origin nor not the origin of things. Brahman, as fictitiously overspread by the world-fiction, becomes the first of manifested and unreal beings, the Archimagus, the arch-illusionist, the world-evolving deity. All things

[1] The Śakti of Īśvara.

CHAP. VIII. originate out of his illusion, his creative power, Māyā, Śakti, Prakṛiti; and this power of the divine spirit or Demiurgus, is veiled from all eyes beneath the successive emanations that proceed out of it and make up the world of migrating souls and their environments.

Īs'vara is the cycle of the universe.

"We meditate upon that deity, the Demiurgus, as the wheel with one felly and three tires, with sixteen peripheries, with fifty spokes and twenty wedges to fix the spokes, a wheel that is multiform, with one cord, with three diverse paths, and with one illusion proceeding from two causes."

The creative spirit, Īśvara, is the Brahmachakra, the wheel of Brahman, or maze of metempsychosis. The one felly is the cosmical illusion. The three tires are the three *primordia rerum*, the three Guṇas, Sattva, Rajas, and Tamas, pleasure, pain, and indolence. The sixteen peripheries are the five elements, the five senses, the five organs of motion, and the common sensory. The fifty spokes are fifty varieties of mental creation enumerated by the Sānkhyas. The twenty wedges are the five senses, the five organs of motion, and the objects of each. The one cord is desire. The three several paths are the path of obedience to the prescriptive *sacra*, the path of neglect of these, and the path of gnosis.[1] The two causes of illusion are the good and evil works that prolong the migration of the soul through spheres of recompense, so long as it fails to find its real nature.

The river of metempsychosis.

"We meditate upon that deity as the river with five streams from five springs, the river swift and winding, with the organs of motion as its waves, with the five senses and the common sensory as its fountain-head, with five eddies, swollen and rapid with fivefold misery, with five infirmities as its five reaches."

The five streams are the five senses, and the five springs are the five elements. The five eddies are the five objects of sense. The five miseries are the misery

[1] *Dharma, adharma, jnāna.*

prior to birth, and the pains of birth, decay, sickness, and death. The five infirmities are those of the Sānkhya enumeration, illusion, mistake of the not-self for self, desire, aversion, and terror. These are the five reaches of the river of metempsychosis. The common sensory, *manas*, is said to be its fountain-head, because every phase of experience is a modification of this sensory.

"The migrating soul wanders in this wheel or maze of Brahman, in which all things live and into which they shall return, so long as it thinks itself separate from the deity that actuates it from within; but it goes to immortality as soon as it is favoured by that deity.

The triad—the world, the individual souls, and the cosmic soul—is based on Brahman.

"This Self is sung as the supreme Brahman. Upon it is the triad; it is the firm base of all things, and is imperishable. They who in this world know the Self, so soon as they know it and meditate on it alone, are merged in the Self, and freed from future births."

The triad that fictitiously overlies, or presents itself in the place of Brahman, is the migrating soul, their environments, and the universal soul or Demiurgus. These are alike unreal, mere figments of the world-fiction, and Brahman alone is, and is unchanging and imperishable.

"The powerful Demiurgus upholds the world, both its principle and its manifested forms, the imperishable principle and perishable forms, the undeveloped principle and the developed forms. The soul is powerless, and is in bondage that it may receive the recompense of its works; but when it comes to know the divine Self it is loosed from all its ties.

Maya or Prakriti a birthless being that gives birth to all things.

"There are two things unborn without beginning, the knowing deity and the unknowing soul, the powerful deity and the powerless soul. There is also the one unborn *genetrix* without beginning, energising that the migrating souls may have the recompense of their works. Further there is the infinite Self that is manifested under every form, and that does nothing and

CHAP. VIII. suffers nothing. As soon as he finds out the nature of these three, the sage is one with all things, one with Brahman."

The soul and the world-evolving deity are alike fictitious presentments, that take the place of Brahman, the underlying verity. In the vision of the perfect theosophist, both his own particular soul and the universal soul or deity within him fade and melt away into the unity of the characterless Self. The soul is individual, the deity within is universal, the soul within all souls. The soul is powerless, the deity all-powerful. The soul has little knowledge, the deity knows all things. The soul is unsatisfied in its desires, the deity is satisfied in every desire. The soul is in a single body, the deity is present in every soul and every body. The soul migrates and suffers misery, the deity is exempt from migration, and lives in the perfect bliss that the soul shares only at times in dreamless sleep. And yet the differences between soul and soul are fictitious; they are all one in the universal soul or deity; and the differences between the soul and the deity are also fictitious; they are both one in the unity of the impersonal Self. All things are one, and their variety in semblance is due to the operation of the inexplicable Prakṛiti or

Māyā the handmaid of the Demiurgus.

Māyā, the *genetrix ingenita*, the handmaid of the Archimagus. The sage finds out the nature of these three, the soul, the deity, and his illusive power; learns that they are alike fictitious semblances; and enters into the fulness of bliss beyond the veil of semblance. The cessation[1] for him of the operancy of the world-fiction is his liberation from metempsychosis.

"The perishable is Pradhāna, the principium. The immortal and imperishable is Hara. The one divine being rules the perishable principium and the perishable individual souls. There is often at last a cessation of the cosmical illusion through meditation upon the im-

[1] *Viśvamāyānivṛitti.*

perishable Self, through union with it and entrance into its being. CHAP. VIII.

"On knowing the divine being there is a falling away of all ties. As soon as the infirmities are put away there is an escape from births and deaths. A third state arises from meditation on the deity as soon as the body is left behind—the state of universal lordship. The sage that after this state reaches a state of isolation, has all that is to be desired."

Meditation leads to exaltation to the courts of Brahmā, and to extrication from metempsychosis.

The theosophist can, if he will, ascend after death to the paradise of the supreme divinity, the Brahmaloka. This paradise, in which he is to possess everything that he can desire, lasts only till the close of the æon in which he ascends into it. He must, therefore, when he is exalted there, complete the process of extricating himself from metempsychosis by the knowledge of Brahman. This is the only final rest and satisfaction of the soul.

"This Self is to be known as everlasting, as abiding in itself, for there is nothing beyond the Self that can be known. The migrating souls, their environment, and the deity that actuates them from within,—these three are revealed to be the Self.

"The Self is to be made to shine forth in the body by repetition of the mystic OM; in the same way as fire is unseen so long as it is latent in the fire-drills, and so long as its latency is not put an end to, and is seen as often as it is struck out of the fire-drills that it resides in.

The repetition of the mystic syllable Om reveals Brahman, as friction reveals the fire latent in the fire-drills.

"Let the sage make his body the nether, and the mystic syllable the upper fire-drill; and by the prolonged friction of meditation let him gaze upon the divine Self that is concealed within him.

"This Self is to be found within himself by the sage that seeks it with truthfulness and with self-coercion; like the oil that is in the oil-seeds, the butter within the cream, the water within the rivers.

CHAP. VIII.

"He finds the Self that permeates all things, the fount of spiritual insight and of self-coercion, within his body, as the curds are within the milk. That is the Self in which the fulness of bliss resides."

The next section opens with a prayer that Savitṛi, the sun-god, may irradiate the faculties of the aspirant.

Second Section. Invocation of the sun-god by the aspirant about to practise Yoga.

II. "May Savitṛi, fixing first my inward sense and then my senses, that I may attain to the truth, provide for me the light of Agni and lift me up above the earth.

"We strive with all our might, with concentrated mind, and by the grace of Savitṛi, to attain to blessedness.

"Fixing the senses with the inward sense, may Savitṛi produce in us senses by which there shall be bliss, and which shall reveal the divine being, the great light, by spiritual intuition.

"Let the sages that fix the inner sense and the senses, give great praise to the great, wise Savitṛi, who alone, knowing all knowledge, appointed sacrificial rites.

"I meditate with adorations on that primeval Self that ye reveal. My verses go along their course like suns; and all the sons of the immortal who dwell in celestial mansions hear them."

After this invocation to the sun-god and the other gods that preside over the various faculties of the mind and body, the sage is supposed to offer a libation of Soma to Savitṛi.

"The mind is fixed upon the rite, the fire is struck out, the air is stirred, and the Soma-juice flows over.

"Let the sage worship the primeval Self with a libation of Soma to Savitṛi, O thou that wilt perform ecstatic meditation upon the Self; for thy former rites no longer bind thee to metempsychosis."

His former works and sacrifices will no longer affect the aspirant to liberation; they will be burnt up like a bundle of reeds in the fire of spiritual knowledge. His libation to Savitṛi is a final rite for the purification of his mind before entering upon the practice of Yoga, the rules for which are next prescribed. The aspirant is to fix his body and limbs in a rigid and insensible posture, and to crush every thought and feeling, that he may rise to the ecstatic vision of the Self, the light within the heart.

Fixation of the body, and withdrawal of the senses from the things of sense.

"Fixing his body immovably with the three upper portions erect,[1] and fixing his senses with the inward sense upon the heart, let the sage cross over all the fear-bringing streams of metempsychosis in the spiritual boat, the mystic OM.

"He must check his breath, and stop every movement, and breathe only through the nose, with his inward sense repressed; he must with unfailing heed hold fast the inward sense, a chariot with vicious horses.

"Let him pursue the ecstatic vision in a level spot free from fire, from pebbles and from sand, amidst sweet sounds, and water, and leafy bowers, in a place that soothes the mind and does not pain the eyes.

Signs of the approach of the ecstatic vision.

"First a frost, then a smoke, then the sun, then a fire, then a hot wind, then a swarm of fireflies, then lightning, then a crystal moon,—such are the shapes that precede and usher in the manifestation of the Self in the ecstatic vision.

"When the fivefold nature of Yoga has been realised,[2] when the earth, water, light, fire, and ether have arisen, there is no further sickness, decay, or pain, for him that has won a body purified in the fire of ecstasy.

"Lightness, healthiness, freedom from desires, clearness of complexion, a pleasant accent in speaking, a

[1] The chest, the neck, and the head.

[2] Apparently this means, when the sage has passed through and beyond the consciousness of the properties of the five elements, in his process of abstraction.

CHAP. VIII. pure odour, and diminution in the excretions, announce the first success in Yoga.

"As an earth-stained disk of metal is bright and shines as soon as it is cleaned, the embodied soul that has gazed upon the spiritual reality has reached its end, and its miseries are left behind.

This vision unites the soul with the one and only Self that permeates and animates the world.

"As soon as the visionary sage has seen the spiritual reality with his own soul as a lamp to light him, he knows the divine Self that is not born and never fails, untouched by all the emanations; and he is loosed from every tie.

"For this divine Self is towards every quarter; it is the first that passes into being. This it is that is in the womb; this is that which is born and that which shall be born. It stands behind all living things; it has faces everywhere.

"The deity that is in fire and in the waters, that permeates all the worlds, that is in plants and trees,—to that deity be adoration, adoration."

The third section treats of the first emanation from Brahman, the Īśvara, Demiurgus, or world-evolving deity, in language similar to that of the Purushasūkta.

Third Section. The glories of Rudra or S'iva, identified with Īs'vara, the cosmic soul.

III. "There is one deity that holds the net,[1] who rules with his powers, who rules all the spheres with his powers, who is one and only one in the origination and manifestation of the world. They that know this become immortal.

"For there is only one Rudra, sages allow no second thing, who rules these spheres with his powers. He stands behind and within all living things; and after he has projected and sustained the spheres, he retracts them into himself at the close of the æon.

"He has eyes everywhere, faces everywhere, arms everywhere, feet everywhere. He incloses all things with his arms, his wings; he is the one deity that gives birth to sky and earth.

[1] The cosmical illusion in which migrating souls are ensnared.

"He is the origin of the gods, the divine power of the gods, the lord of all things, Rudra, the great seer, he that in the beginning begot Hiraṇyagarbha. May he endow us with a lucid mind.

"O Rudra, who dwellest in the mountains, look down upon us, not in thy fearful aspect, but with that form of thine that is auspicious, that reveals holiness, that is most blessed.

"Thou that dwellest in the mountains, protector of the mountains, make propitious that dart thou holdest in thy hand to throw. Hurt not man, nor hurt the world.

"There is an infinite Self that is beyond this world, the Self that is hidden in the several bodies of all things living, and that encompasses the world, the lord of all; and they that know this Self become immortal.

"I know this great Purusha, sun-bright, beyond the darkness. He that knows it passes beyond death. There is no other path to go by.

"Beyond this is nothing. There is nothing lesser, nothing greater, than this. It stands fast in the heavens like a tree, immovable. All the world is filled with that Self, that Purusha.

"That which is beyond this world is colourless, is painless. They that know this Self become immortal, and others go again to misery.

"All faces, all heads, all necks are its faces, heads, and necks. It abides in the heart of every living thing. That deity permeates all things, and is everywhere and in perfect bliss.

"Purusha, the deity that actuates the mind from within, is a great lord. He has in his power the recovery of the purity of the soul, he is luminous and imperishable.

"Purusha is of the size of a thumb. It is the Self within, ever lodged within the hearts of living things, ruling the thoughts in the heart, manifested in the inward sense. They that know this become immortal.

CHAP. VIII.

"Purusha has a thousand heads, a thousand eyes, a thousand feet. He compasses the earth on every side, and stands ten fingers' breadth beyond.

"Purusha is all this; he is that which has been and that which is to be, the lord of immortality, and the lord of that which grows up by food.

"He everywhere has hands and feet, everywhere eyes and heads and faces, everywhere he has ears. He dwells in the body and permeates it all."

It is not always easy to mark the transitions in this Upanishad from Brahman *per se* to Īśvara or Brahman as manifested in the world, from the impersonal Purusha to the divine Purusha or Archimagus. The translation here offered to the reader follows the intimations of the scholiast Śankarāchārya. Wherever Purusha is spoken of as a person we are to understand Īśvara.

Antithetic epithets of Purusha or Brahman.

"It has no organs, but manifests itself in every mode of every organ and faculty. It is the lord, the ruler of the world, the great refuge of the universe.

"The Self becoming the migrating soul moves outwards to the perception of external things. It is the actuator of all the world, of things that move, and things that move not.

"It has neither hands nor feet, but moves rapidly and handles all things. It sees without eyes, and hears without ears. It knows all that is to be known, and there is none that knows it. This, they say, is the great primeval Purusha.

"The Self seated in the hearts of living things, is lesser than the least and greater than the greatest. He that by the favour of the creating deity[1] sees this undesiring Self, this mightiness, this lord, has left all miseries behind.

"I know this Self of all souls, unchanging, from

[1] *Dhātuḥ prasādāt* may be translated either as in the text, "by the favour of the creating deity," that is, by the favour of the Demiurgus; or "by the purity of his senses," the senses of the visionary sage being pure as withdrawn from external things.

before all time, present everywhere, and everywhere diffused, which the expositors of Brahman declare to have had no genesis, and which they say shall have no end.

CHAP. VIII.

Fourth Section.

"IV. That divine being, one only, of no race or colour, feigns a purpose and evolves a variety of races in virtue of the variety of his powers, and withdraws them into himself at the end of the æon. The world is in him in the beginning. May he endow us with a lucid mind.

The universe is a varied manifestation of Brahman.

"That Self only is fire; it is the sun, it is the wind, it is the moon, it is the stars, it is Hiraṇyagarbha, it is the waters, it is Prajāpati.

"Thou art male and thou art female; thou art youth and thou art maiden; thou art decrepit and totterest along with a staff; thou comest to the birth; thou hast faces everywhere.

"Thou art the dark bee, thou the red-eyed parrot; thou art the thunder-cloud, thou the seasons, thou the seas. Thou art without beginning, thou pervadest all things; from thee proceed all the worlds.

"There is one unborn being,[1] red, white, and black, that gives birth to many offspring like herself. One unborn soul lingers in dalliance with her, another leaves her, his dalliance with her ended.

Allegory of the two birds on one tree.

Two birds,[2] always together and united, nestle upon the same tree;[3] one of them eats the sweet fruit of the holy fig-tree, and the other looks on without eating.

"In the same tree the migrating soul is immersed, and sorrows in its helpless plight, and knows not what to do; but its sorrow passes as soon as it sees the adored lord, and that this world is only his glory.

"That Self is the supreme expanse that passes not away; in it are the Ṛichas, the hymns of praise; in it

[1] The world-fiction, Māyā or Prakṛiti. See above, p. 203.

[2] The migrating soul or Jīva, and the universal soul, Demiurgus or Īśvara. See above, p. 108.

[3] The body.

CHAP. VIII.

dwell all the gods. What shall he that knows not this do with hymns of praise? They that know it, they are sped.

"That Self is proclaimed by the hymns, the sacrifices, rites, and ordinances, by the past and by the future, and by the Vedas. It is out of this Self that the arch-illusionist projects this world, and it is in that Self that the migrating soul remains entangled in the illusion."

The Self is veiled beneath illusion, and with illusion as a fictitious counterpart or body,[1] manifests itself in its first emanation as Īśvara, the Archimagus, or world-projecting deity. The Self is in and by itself the unconditioned, but in virtue of the self-feigning world-fiction, the principle of unreality that has co-existed with it from everlasting, it presents itself as the fictitious creator of a fictitious world.

Prakṛiti is Māyā, and Is'vara is the arch-illusionist.

"Let the sage know that Prakṛiti is Māyā, and that Maheśvara[2] is the Māyin or arch-illusionist. All this shifting world is filled with portions of him.

"He alone presides over emanation after emanation: the world is in him, and he withdraws the world into himself. He that knows that adorable deity, the giver of the good gift of liberation, passes into this peace for ever.

"He is the origin and the exaltation of the gods, the ruler over all, the great seer Rudra. See how he passes into fresh manifestation as Hiraṇyagarbha. May he endow us with a lucid mind.

"He is lord over all the gods; upon him the worlds are founded; he rules all living things, two-footed or four-footed. Let us offer an oblation to the divine Ka.[3]

"He is more supersensible than the supersensible; he dwells in the midst of the chaos of illusion, the multiform creator of the universe, the one soul that

[1] Upādhi. [2] Īśvara, Rudra, Hara, or Śiva. [3] Prajāpati.

encircles all things. He that knows this Śiva passes into peace for ever. CHAP. VIII.

"He is the upholder of the world throughout the æon, the lord of all, hidden within all living things. Holy sages and gods have risen to union with him. They that know him cut the cords of death.

"He is hidden in all living things, like the filmy scum upon ghee, the one divine soul that encompasses the world. He that knows this Śiva is extricated from all bonds.

"This divine being, the maker of the world, the universal soul, is ever seated in the hearts of living things, and is revealed by the heart, the intellect, the thought. They that know this become immortal."

Is'vara, the cosmic soul, is present in every heart.

The universal soul, or maker of the world, is present in the ether in the heart of every living creature, mirrored upon its mind, as the sun is reflected upon an infinite variety of watery surfaces. He is revealed in the thought that all things are one; in the vision in which all things lose their differences and melt away into their original unity. The semblances of duality and of plurality in the waking and the dreaming states are illusory. The soul rises above them into the pure bliss of dreamless sleep and of meditative union with Īśvara. He is to rise above this union with Īśvara to the vision of the characterless Self. The three states of the soul are the darkness of the world, through which the theosophist is to rise into the light of spiritual intuition.

"When there is no darkness, there is neither night nor day. There is neither existence nor non-existence, but pure and blissful being only. That is imperishable, that is adorable even to the sun-god himself, and from it proceeds the eternal wisdom.

In the divine Self there is neither night nor day, but only an unspeakable blessedness.

"No man has grasped this, above, below, or in the midst. There is no image of this, and its name is the infinite glory.

CHAP. VIII.

"His form is present in no visible spot, and no man sees him with the eye. They that know him thus with heart and mind become immortal.

Invocation of Rudra for aid in meditation.

"Now and then a sage, in fear of the miseries of metempsychosis, turns towards him because he is without beginning. O Rudra, save me for ever with thy right, thy gracious, countenance.

"Harm us not in child or grandchild, or in cattle or in horses, nor slay our servants in thy anger. We have the sacrificial butter, and invoke thee at our holy assembly.

Fifth Section. Knowledge and illusion.

"V. Knowledge and illusion, these two, are laid up and hidden in the imperishable and infinite Self above, and in it are as yet unmanifested. Illusion passes, but knowledge is undying. He that dispenses knowledge and illusion is other than they.

"There is one being who actuates phase after phase of being from within, all colours, and all emanations. He fosters with knowledge the Ṛishi Kapila, that arose in the beginning, and beheld him coming into being."

Kapila, the founder of the Sānkhya philosophy, is lauded in the S'vetās'vatara Upanishad and the Bhagavadgītā, purely Vedāntic works.

This being is the immortal internal ruler, the universal soul, or Īśvara. The colours referred to are the red colour of fire, the white colour of water, and the black colour of earth, as in the fourth Khaṇḍa of the sixth Prapāṭhaka of the Chhāndogya. Śankarāchārya explains that Kapila is either a metonym for the golden-hued Hiraṇyagarbha, the divine being that emanates out of Īśvara, or the Ṛishi Kapila, the founder of the Sānkhya philosophy. In the Bhagavadgītā (x. 26), Kṛishṇa, in that poem identified with the Demiurgus, says, "Among perfect sages I am the Muni Kapila." Kapila is not in this place identified with Hiraṇyagarbha by either Śankarāchārya or by Śrīdharasvāmin, the chief scholiasts of the Bhagavadgītā; nor do they attempt to explain the eulogy of the founder of the Sānkhya philosophy in this purely Vedāntic work. In the second chapter of the Bhagavadgītā (ii. 39) we read: "This view has been proclaimed to thee according to the Sānkhya doctrine." Here Śankarāchārya and Śrīdharasvāmin interpret Sānkhya by "spiritual reality," the object of Sānkhya, *i.e.*, the spiritual intuition or ecstatic vision of the fontal essence. They would therefore construe the text: "This view as regards the Self or spiritual reality has been explained to thee." In the third verse of the third chapter Kṛishṇa says, "I revealed in the beginning of the world that there are two modes of life, that of the Sānkhyas in the pursuit of knowledge, and that of the Yogins in the observance of sacred rites." Śankarāchārya and Śrīdharasvāmin say that the Sānkhyas of this passage are the theosophists versed in the teaching of the Upanishads and intent upon the ecstatic vision of the Self; and that the Yogins are those that follow the immemorial ordinances with a view to the preliminary purification to the mind. Again in the fourth verse of the fifth chapter Kṛishṇa says, "It is the foolish, not the wise, that say the Sānkhya and the Yoga differ." Here again Śankarāchārya and Śrīdharasvāmin explain the Sānkhyas to be the sages that have renounced all things in quest of the knowledge that leads to extrication, and the Yogins to be those that follow the prescriptive *sacra* in order to purify their minds for that quest. In the twenty-fourth verse of the thirteenth chapter Kṛishṇa says, "Some gaze upon the Self by meditative ecstasy, some see the Self by the mind purified with meditation, others by Sānkhya meditation, and others by Karmayoga." Śankarāchārya and Śrīdharasvāmin in this place take the term Sānkhya to mean the philosophy of the Sānkhyas, the recognition of the differences between Prakṛiti, or the three *primordia rerum,* and Purusha; but they certainly intend Prakṛiti and Purusha to be taken in the Vedāntic sense, as precise equivalents of Māyā and

CHAP. VIII. Brahman. Karmayoga they explain, as before, to be the following of the prescriptive pieties. The teaching of the Bhagavadgītā is throughout the same as that of the Upanishads; and the only explanation of the references to Kapila and the Sānkhya philosophy in this poem, as also in the Śvetāśvatara Upanishad, would seem to be that the Sānkhya was originally a more precise set of terms for the enumeration of the emanations out of Prakṛiti or Māyā, and of the differences between Māyā and Purusha or Brahman. The divergence of phraseology must subsequently have led to a divergence of views; and thus the Sānkhya philosophy formulised itself, with its repudiation of Īśvara, and its position of the reality and independence of Prakṛiti, of the reality of the duality and plurality of the world of experience, and of the plurality of Purushas or Selves.

To return to the text of the Śvetāśvatara Upanishad.

Is'vara spreads the net of metempsychosis in the fields of illusion.

"This one deity spreads out his net in many modes for every one in this field of illusion, and draws it in again. Thus the great lord again and again evolves the Prajāpatis, and exercises dominion over all things.

"He shines like the sun, irradiating all spaces above, below, between. Thus this potent and adorable deity alone presides over the various origins of things.

"He is the origin of the world; he ripens the nature of each thing, and develops all things that can be developed. He alone presides over this universe, and variously disposes the *primordia*.

"That Self is hidden in the Upanishads, which are hidden in the Vedas. That Brahmā (Hiraṇyagarbha) knows to be the source of the Veda. The gods and Ṛishis that of old have known that Self, have become one with it, have become immortal."

The text now proceeds to speak of the various forms of life in which the one and only Self illusively presents itself.

"This is followed from life to life by the influence of

former works; this is the doer of works that shall be recompensed; and this is the soul that has the recompense of that which it has done. This in all the variety of its forms migrates from body to body according to its works, associated with the three *primordia*, travelling along three paths,[1] the ruler of the vital airs.

"It is of the size of a thumb, yet splendid as the sun. It takes to itself volition and personality, together with the mental modes and the functions of the body. In its individual manifestation it is seen to be of the size of the point of a goad.

"The living soul is to be known as the fraction of the point of a hair a hundred times divided, and at the same time it is of infinite extension.

"It is neither male, nor female, nor sexless. It is preserved in every various body that it assumes.

"The embodied soul, desiring, touching, seeing, illuded, passes into form after form, in sphere after sphere of recompense, in accordance with its works; even as the body has a continuous growth by the assimilation of food and drink.

"The embodied soul invests a variety of bodies supersensible and sensible with the lasting influence of its works in earlier embodiments; and, according to the nature of its works and the nature of its bodies, is united with some fresh body, and seems to be another.

"The deity is without beginning and without end; in the midst of the illusion; the creator of the world, manifold in its manifestations; the only spirit that encompasses the universe. He that knows him is loosed from every tie.

"They free themselves from the body who know the divine being that is cognisable to the purified mind; that has no body, that makes things to be and not to

[1] The path of *dharma* or religion, the path of *adharma* or irreligion, and the path of *jñâna* or spiritual knowledge.

CHAP. VIII. be; free from the cosmical illusion; the maker of the elements of the organism.

Sixth Section. The world is an exhibition of the glory of the Demiurgus.

"VI. Some sages say that the nature of things is the originating principle, others that it is time. This they say in their confusion, but it is the glory of the deity that keeps the wheel of Brahman, the cosmic cycle, still revolving.

"It is the all-knowing author of time, all-perfect, by whom this world is eternally pervaded. The retributive fatality is set in motion by him to produce form after form of spurious being, to be viewed as earth, water, fire, air, and ether.

"He makes that work and pauses; and again and again brings the underlying spiritual reality into union with some emanation, with one, or two, or three, or eight emanations, and into union with time and with the invisible functions of the mind."

The eight emanations of Prakṛiti or Māyā here referred to are earth, water, fire, air, ether, the common sensory, personality, and mind.

"If the sage resolves all these emanations, together with the three *primordia* and also all his mental modes, into Īśvara the creative deity, these things cease to exist for him, and he puts away his good and evil works. As soon as his works are annulled, he passes forward, separate from those emanations.

"But before this he must have meditated upon the adorable deity that is present in his mind, and manifests itself in every various form, the essence of all that is. This deity is the origin of all things, the source of the illusions that give rise to the successive embodiments of the soul; beyond the present, past, and future, unlimited by time.

"That deity is beyond the appearances of the world-tree and the presentments of time; and this manifested world proceeds out of him in its revolutions. He that knows this lord of glory, that brings righteousness and puts away all imperfections, within his mind, immortal, the substance of the universe,—passes beyond metempsychosis.

"We know that deity to be the god above all gods, the lord above all lords, beyond the world-fiction, the adorable ruler of the spheres of recompense.

"He has no body and no organs, and none is equal to him or greater than he. His various power is revealed to be above all things, and this power is his essence, an energy of knowledge and of action.

"There is no lord or ruler over him in this world, no mark of his existence. He is the origin of all things. He is the lord above the deities that preside over the organs of sense and motion. There is none that begets him, and none that is lord above him.

Is'vara the divine spider.

"This deity, essentially one, is like a spider, and covers himself with threads drawn from Pradhāna. May he grant us a passage back into the Self.

"He is the one deity veiled in every living thing, the soul that is in every soul. He permeates every form of life, recompensing the works of every creature, and making his habitation in them, as the witness within, the light within, isolated, apart from the *primordia*.

"He is the one being that energises freely in the many migrating souls that energise not at all. It is he that develops the germ of things into its variety of forms. Everlasting bliss is for those sages that see this deity in their own minds, within themselves, and for none besides."

The migrating souls are themselves inert. Their bodies and their senses act, but they do not act, and the actions of their bodies and their senses are produced by the Demiurgus. There is no individual liberty of action. Their bodies are mere puppets, and the Demiurgus pulls the strings. It is he that produces in them their good and evil works, and it is he that rewards and punishes the works that he has wrought in them. All that they seem to see and do and suffer, is the jugglery of this arch-illusionist.

"He is eternal in the eternal souls, conscious in the conscious souls; he is the one soul that metes out weal and woe to many souls. He that knows this deity, the principle of emanation to be learned in the Sānkhya and the Yoga, is loosed from every tie.

The Self is the light of the world.

"The sun gives no light to that, nor the moon and stars, neither do these lightnings light it up; how then should this fire of ours? All things shine after it as it shines; all this world is radiant with its light.

"This is the one soul in the midst of this world. This is the fire that is seated in the midst of the water. He that knows this Self passes beyond death, and there is no other path to go by."

The Self is a fire, for it burns up the world-fiction and its figments in the purified mind of the theosophist in ecstatic union with it. It is seated in the midst of the water, in the bodies of all living things, which emanate out of the world-fiction, one of the names of which is water, the "undifferenced water" of the Nāsadīyasūkta.

"He is the maker of all things, and he knows all things. He is the soul of all and the source of all, the perfect and omniscient author of time. He is the sustainer of Pradhāna, the principium, and of the migrating souls; the disposer of the *primordia*, and the origin of metempsychosis and of liberation, of the preservation of the world and the implication of the soul.

"Such is the immortal Demiurgus, residing in the soul, knowing all things, and present everywhere; the sustainer of the world, who rules over the world for ever. There is no other principle that is able to rule over it.

"Aspiring to extrication, I fly for refuge to that divine soul that is the light within the mind; who at the beginning of an æon evolves Hiraṇyagarbha out of himself, and evolves the Vedas.

"The Self is without parts, without action, and without change; blameless and unsullied; the bridge that leads to immortality; a fiercely burning fire. CHAP. VIII.

Only knowledge saves us from the miseries of repeated lives.

"When men shall roll up the sky like a hide, then and not till then shall there be an end to misery without knowing the divine Self.

"Śvetāśvatara, the sage, through the efficacy of his austerities and through grace to know the Vedas, revealed to the recluses the high, pure Brahman that has been rightly meditated upon by many Ṛishis.

"This highest mystery of the Upanishads, revealed in a former age, is not to be imparted to any man who is not a quietist, a son, or a disciple.

"If he has unfeigned devotion to the deity, and to his spiritual teacher as to the deity, these truths thus proclaimed reveal themselves to the excellent aspirant. They reveal themselves to that excellent aspirant."

Such is the Śvetāśvatara Upanishad. The reader will have seen that it teaches the same doctrine as the other Upanishads. Archer Butler is an admirable interpreter of the imperfect materials before him when he writes: "The cultivators of practical wisdom incessantly labour for the possession of a supernatural elevation. Prolonged attitudes, endurance of suffering, unbroken meditations upon the divine nature, accompanied and animated by the frequent and solemn repetition of the mystical name Om, are the means by which the Yogin, for perhaps three thousand years, has sought the attainment of an ecstatic participation of God;[1] and, half-deceiver, half-deceived, affects to have already soared beyond earthly limitations, and achieved hyperphysical power. Towards the complete consummation of this final liberation, the Vedas[2] proclaim that there are three degrees, two preliminary,—the possession of transcendent power in this life, that is, of magical endowments, and the passage after death into the courts of Brahmā,—which are only precursory to that last and

[1] Rather of the divine Self. [2] The Upanishads.

CHAP. VIII. glorious reunion with the First Cause himself,[1] which terminates all the changes of life in an identification with the very principle of eternity and of repose. Upon the mild sages of the Ganges these views probably produce little result beyond the occasional suggestion of elevated ideas, perhaps more than counterbalanced by the associations of a minute and profitless superstition. But upon the enormous mass of the nation these baseless dreams can only result in the perpetuation of ignorance and the encouragement of imposture: to both of which they manifestly and directly tend,—to the former, by being unfitted for the vulgar mind; to the latter, by countenancing pretences to supernatural power."

[1] Rather the first cause itself.

CHAPTER IX.

THE PRIMITIVE ANTIQUITY OF THE DOCTRINE OF MAYA.

"And, like the baseless fabric of a vision,
The cloud-capp'd towers, the gorgeous palaces,
The solemn temples, the great globe itself,
Yea, all which it inherit, shall dissolve;
And, like an insubstantial pageant faded,
Leave not a wrack behind. We are such stuff
As dreams are made of, and our little life
Is rounded with a sleep."—SHAKESPEARE.

"The sensible world must be called, as we have properly called it, and as Plato certainly meant to call, and sometimes did call it, the nonsensical world, the world of pure infatuation, of downright contradiction, of unalloyed absurdity; and this the whole material universe is, when divorced from the element which makes it a knowable and cogitable thing. Take away from the intelligible world,—that is, from the system of things by which we are surrounded,—the essential element which enables us, and all intelligence, to know and apprehend it, and it must lapse into utter and inutterable absurdity. It becomes more than nothing, yet less than anything."—FERRIER.

CHAP. IX.

The world dissolves itself in the view of the meditating Yogin.

LET us recall to our mind the Yogin as the Upanishads have pictured him to us, seated in a posture of body rigid and insensible, with his feelings crushed and his thoughts suppressed. His senses are withdrawn from the sensible things around him; his inward sense is fixed upon a single point; and he is intent upon reaching the pure indetermination of thought, the characterless being, that is the last residue of abstraction pushed to its furthest limit. In the progress of his ecstatic meditation, first his body and his visible and palpable environment fade away, recede, and disappear; he passes into the vesture of the airs of life; he is conscious no longer of his surroundings and of his organism, but only of the vital functions. He has passed beyond the body into the tenuous *involucrum* of his soul. His vesture of the airs of life fades away, recedes, and disappears into his vesture of inward sense; he is no longer conscious of the vital functions, but only of the imagery within that simulates the things of sense. His vesture of inward sense fades away, recedes, and disappears into his mental vesture; he is no longer conscious of the simulative imagery, but only of his mental life. And now his tenuous *involucrum* begins to melt away. His mental vesture fades away, recedes, and vanishes into the vesture of characterless bliss; he is no longer conscious of his mental life, but only of the surcease of every fear and care and sorrow, for his individuality is fast dissolving. Last of all, his vesture of characterless bliss fades away, recedes, and vanishes, and the light of fontal being, thought, and bliss alone remains. This light is unwavering and unfailing. The whole world is a dissolving view that fines into paler and paler aspects, and finally disappears; the light it shone in is still there, the light of the underlying Self, in the absence of which the world would lapse into blindness, darkness, nothingness. The ecstatic vision is the dawn before which the darkness of the figments of the world-fiction rolls away, and the Self rises more bright and glorious than the sun. The sage leaves the sorrows of his heart behind him, reaches the point where fear is no more, and is one with the light of lights beyond the darkness of the world-fiction. He is in the body, but is no longer touched by the good and evil that he does, but "free as the casing air." At last his body falls away from him, the feverish dream of life after life is over, and he is extricated from metempsychosis. His soul has returned into the Self, as water into water, light into light, ether into the ether that is everywhere.

CHAP. IX.

The current opinion that the doctrine of Māyā is an innovation upon the primitive Vedānta is untenable.

It has been often said that the doctrine that the individual soul and the world have only a dream-like and illusive existence, is no part of the primitive philosophy of the Upanishads, but a later addition of the Vedāntins, the modern representatives of that philosophy. This is a statement that has been iterated by Orientalist after Orientalist from the time of Colebrooke to the present day. The doctrine of Māyā, or the unreality of the duality of subject and object, and the unreality of the plurality of souls and their environments, is the very life of the primitive Indian philosophy; and it is necessary to prove that Colebrooke was mistaken in denying its primitive antiquity, and to point out the source of his error. It is the purpose of this chapter, therefore, to prove that the unreality of the world, as an emanation of the self-feigning world-fiction, is part and parcel of the philosophy of the Upanishads. The great Vedāntic doctor, Śankarāchārya, was right in holding it for such, and his philosophy is the philosophy of the Upanishads themselves, only in sharper outlines and in fresher colours. The Vedānta has a just title to be styled, as it is styled, the Aupanishadī Mīmānsā.

Colebrooke the author of this opinion.

In his essay on the Vedānta, read before a meeting of the Royal Asiatic Society in 1827, Colebrooke said: "The notion that the versatile world is an illusion (Māyā), and that all that passes to the apprehension of the waking individual is but a phantasy presented to his imagination, and every seeming thing is unreal and all is visionary, does not appear to be the doctrine of the text of the Vedānta. I have remarked nothing which countenances it in the Sūtras of Vyāsa or in the gloss of Śankara, but much concerning it in the minor commentaries and elementary treatises. I take it to be no tenet of the original Vedāntin philosophy, but of another branch, from which later writers have borrowed it, and have intermixed and confounded the two systems. The doctrine of the early Vedānta is complete and consis-

CHAP. IX.

tent without this graft of a later growth." A statement false from first to last.

Māyā is a vital element of the primitive Indian cosmical conception.

It must be already clear enough to an attentive reader of the foregoing chapters of this work, that the unreality of migrating souls and the spheres they migrate through, and the sole reality of the impersonal Self, is the very cosmic conception of the Upanishads. Any assertion, however, of Colebrooke carries with it so much weight, and his present assertion has been so often repeated by later Orientalists, that this denial of the primitive antiquity of the tenet of Māyā must be refuted *in extenso.* The denial throws darkness over the whole progressive series of Indian cosmologies, and must be put aside in order to secure the first step of the historical exposition. The picture of things presented in the Upanishads is the primitive Indian philosophy, the starting-point for any critical treatment of the successive systems. It is the basis on which any future historian of Indian philosophy will have to build.

Part of Colebrooke's statement is a glaring error.

Part of Colebrooke's assertion is untrue on the face of it. He says that he finds nothing in the gloss of Śankara to countenance the doctrine that the world is an illusion. This part of his statement has already received its correction at the hands of Professor Cowell.[1] "This is hardly correct as regards Śankara, since in his commentary on the Vedānta aphorisms (ii. 1. 9), he expressly mentions the doctrine of Māyā as held by the teachers of the Vedānta, and he quotes a śloka to that effect from Gauḍapāda's Kārikās. Compare also his language in the opening of his commentary on the second book. There is also a remarkable passage in his commentary on the Aitareya Upanishad, i. 2. It may be remarked (this passage says) that a carpenter can make a house as he is possessed of material, but how can the soul, being without material, create the world?

[1] In a note in his edition of Colebrooke's Essays, vol. i. p. 400.

But there is nothing objectionable in this. The world can exist in its material cause, that is, in the formless, undeveloped subject which is called soul (or Self), just as the subsequently developed foam exists in water. There is therefore nothing contradictory in supposing that the omniscient Demiurgus, who is himself the material cause of names and forms, creates the world. Or better still, we may say that as a material juggler without material creates himself as it were another self going in the air, so the omniscient deity, being omniscient and mighty in Māyā, creates himself as it were another self in the form of the world." It is hard to understand how Colebrooke could have made such a mistake as regards the gloss of Śankara, Śankarāchārya's commentary on the aphorisms of the Vedānta. A cursory inspection of the gloss is enough to find the tenet of illusion stated or supposed on every page. It is often expressly taught, as shall be proved by copious extracts.

The Sūtras or aphorisms of the Vedānta are in themselves obscure.

The mistake is excusable enough as far as regards the text of the Vedānta or Sūtras of Vyāsa. In themselves, and apart from the traditionary interpretation, the Sūtras or aphorisms are a minimum of *memoria technica*, and nearly unintelligible. Nevertheless it shall be shown that the doctrine denoted by the term Māyā, if not the term itself, is to be found in the Sūtras. Colebrooke himself cannot have attached much importance to what he supposed to be the negative testimony of these aphorisms. He himself says: "The Śārīrakasūtras[1] are in the highest degree obscure, and could never have been intelligible without an ample interpretation. Hinting the question or its solution, rather than proposing the one or briefly delivering the other, they but allude to the subject. Like the aphorisms of other Indian sciences, they must from the first have been accompanied by the author's

[1] That is, the aphorisms of the Vedānta.

CHAP. IX. exposition of the meaning, whether orally taught by him or communicated in writing." This is most true, and let it be noted that Śankarāchārya is the greatest of the prescriptive expositors of the Sūtras of the Vedānta. The Indian systems were handed down in a regular line of succession,[1] an unbroken series of exponents. They were to be learned only from an authorised expositor, a recognised successor of the primitive teachers. Śankarāchārya is in possession, with his doctrine of illusion. The burden of proof lies with those who assert that the tenet of Māyā is an innovation on the primitive philosophy of the Upanishads.

Texts of the Upanishads teach the unreality of the world.

Before proving the presence of the doctrine of Māyā in the Sūtras of Vyāsa and the gloss of Śankarāchārya, it will be well to point out again some of the primitive texts in which that doctrine is enounced. The Vedānta is only a systematic exposition of the philosophy of the Upanishads. Śankarāchārya says that the Sūtras of the Vedānta are a string on which the gems of the Upanishads are strung. The word Vedānta is itself a synonym of the word Upanishad, and the Vedānta system is itself often styled the Aupanishadī Mīmānsā, or philosophy of the Upanishads.

This doctrine present in a Vedic hymn.

Ascending perhaps higher than the Upanishads, we find this doctrine present in the celebrated Nāsadīyasūkta, Rigveda x. 129. "It was not entity," says the Rishi, "nor was it nonentity." Putting aside the assertion of Colebrooke, which shall be shown to rest only on the statement of an antagonist of the Vedānta, there is no reason to question Sāyaṇa's interpretation of this hymn. Sāyaṇa's interpretation is the traditionary exposition, and is found in other Indian philosophical books, as, for example, in Rāmatīrtha's Padayojanikā or commentary on the Upadeśasahasrī of Śankarāchārya, and in the Ātmapurāṇa. Sāyaṇa tells us that the Nāsadīyasūkta describes the state of things

[1] *Āmnāyaparamparā, āchāryaparamparā.*

between two æons, the state technically known as the *pralayāvasthā*. An earlier world has been withdrawn into the world-fiction Māyā, out of which it sprang, and the later world is not yet proceeding into being. In this state of dissolution, says Sāyaṇa, the world-fiction, the principium of the versatile world is not a nonentity; it is not a piece of nonsense, a purely chimerical thing, like the horns of a hare, for the world cannot emanate out of any such sheer absurdity. On the other hand, it is not an entity, it is not a reality like the one and only Self. Māyā, the principle here spoken of, is neither nonentity nor entity, but something inexplicable, a thing of which nothing can be intelligibly predicated. No nihilistic teaching is intended, for it is said further on in the same hymn, "That one breathed without afflation." This one and only reality is the characterless Self. Real existence is denied not of the impersonal Self, but of Māyā. Such is the traditional interpretation of the first verse of the Nāsadīyasūkta. It is a natural interpretation, and if we, with our thoughts fashioned for us by purely irrelevant antecedents, try to find another for ourselves, we are pretty sure to invent a fiction. The Nāsadīyasūkta seems then to be the earliest enouncement of the eternal coexistence of a spiritual principle of reality and an unspiritual principle of unreality.

It is presumably already plain enough that the Upanishads teach the fictitious and unreal nature of the world. The fictitious character of the world of semblances is everywhere implied in the doctrine of the sole existence of the impersonal Self. It is not only implied, but stated, in the following passages. In the Bṛihadāraṇyaka Upanishad we read:—

Present in the Bṛihadāraṇyaka Upanishad.

"Indra (the Demiurgus) appears multiform by his illusions (or fictions, or powers), for his horses are yoked, hundreds and ten. This Self is the horses (the senses), this is the ten (organs of sense and motion), this is the

CHAP. IX. many thousands, the innumerable (migrating souls). This same Self has nothing before it or after it, nothing inside it or outside it."

In another text of the same Upanishad very frequently cited by the Indian schoolmen :—

"What Self is that? asked the prince. The Rishi said, It is this conscious soul amidst the vital airs, the light within the heart. This Self, one and the same in every mind and every body, passes through this life and the next life in the body, and seems to think, and seems to move."[1]

In another important passage of the same Upanishad the eternal objectless thought of the Self[2] is contrasted with the fleeting and evanescent cognitions of the soul; and the real existence of the Self with the quasi-existence of everything else than Self. This passage is :—

"This same imperishable Self is that which sees unseen, hears unheard, thinks unthought-upon, knows unknown. There is no other than this that sees, no other than this that hears, no other than this that thinks, no other than this that knows. Over this imperishable principle the expanse is woven warp and woof.

"As in dreamless sleep the soul sees, but sees not this or that, so the Self in seeing sees not; for there is no intermission in the sight of the Self that sees, its vision is one that passes not away: and there is nothing second to that, other than that, apart from that, that it should see.

"As in dreamless sleep the soul hears, but hears not this or that, so the Self in hearing hears not; for there is no intermission in the hearing of the Self that hears, its audition is one that passes not away: and there is nothing second to that, other than that, apart from that, that it should hear.

"As in dreamless sleep the soul thinks, but thinks

[1] *Dhyāyatīva lelāyatīva.*

[2] *Nityaṃ nirvishayaṃ jñānam.*

not this or that, so the Self in thinking thinks not; for there is no intermission in the thought of the Self that thinks, its cogitation is one that passes not away: and there is nothing second to that, other than that, apart from that, that it should think.

"As in dreamless sleep the soul knows, but knows not this or that, so the Self in knowing knows not; for there is no intermission in the knowing of the Self that knows, its knowledge is one that passes not away: and there is nothing second to that, other than that, apart from that, that it should know.

Only a quasi-existence allowed to everything else than the Self.

"Where in waking or in dreaming there is, as it were, something else, there one sees something else than oneself, smells something else, tastes something else, speaks to something else, hears something else, thinks upon something else, touches something else, knows something else."

Mark the qualification "as it were," *yatra vā 'nyad iva syāt.* We might also translate, "Where in waking or in dreaming there seems to be something else." This allows only a quasi-existence, a fictitious presentation, to all that is other than the Self.

In another passage of the same Upanishad we read: "This same world was then undifferenced.[1] It differenced itself under names and colours (that is, under visible and nameable aspects); such a thing having such a name, and such a thing having such a colour. Therefore this world even now differences itself as to name and colour; such a one having such a name, and such a thing having such a colour. This same Self entered into it, into the body, to the very finger-nails, as a razor into a razor-case, or as fire resides within the fire-drills. Men see not that Self. That whole Self breathing is called the breath, speaking it is called the voice, seeing it is called the eye, hearing it is called the ear, thinking it is called the thought. These are

[1] Prior to its evolution at the beginning of an æon.

CHAP. IX.

only names of its activity. If then a man thinks any one of these to be the Self, he knows not; for the Self is not wholly represented in any one of these. Let him know that the Self is the Self, for all things become one in the Self."

Many names are given in the Upanishads to the principle of unreality.

All things quit their name and colour, lose their visible and nameable aspects, and pass away into the characterless unity of the Self. The principle of unreality that co-exists from all eternity with the principle of reality, is most frequently named in the Upanishads *avyākṛita,* the undifferenced, uncharactered, or unevolved; and the process of the evolution, emanation, or manifestation of things is generally styled their differentiation under name and colour, or presentation in various visible and nameable aspects, *nāmarūpavyākaraṇa.* The principle of unreality has many other names in the Upanishads. It is the expanse, Māyā, Prakṛiti, Śakti, darkness, illusion, the shadow, nescience, falsity, the indeterminate.[1]

In another passage of the Bṛihadāraṇyaka Upanishad we read:—

"They that know the breath of the breath, the eye of the eye, the ear of the ear, the thought of the thought,—they have seen the primeval Self that has been from before all time.

"It is to be seen only with the mind: there is nothing in it that is manifold.

"From death to death he goes, who looks on this as manifold.

"It is to be seen in one way only, it is indemonstrable, immutable. The Self is unsullied, beyond the expanse, unborn, infinite, imperishable."

The expanse is the cosmical illusion. In another passage of the Bṛihadāraṇyaka Upanishad the seeming

[1] *Avyākṛitam, ākāśam, paramavyoma, māyā, prakṛitiḥ, śaktis, tamo, 'vidyā, chhāyā, 'jñānam, anṛitam, avyaktam,* Śankarāchārya on Śvetāśvatara Upanishad i. 3.

duality of subject and object is spoken of as disappearing in the all-embracing unity of the Self.

The duality of subject and object has only a quasi-existence.

"Where there is as it were a duality (or, where there seems to be a duality), one sees another, one smells another, one speaks to another, one thinks about another, one knows another; but where all this world is Self alone, what should one smell another with, see another with, hear another with, speak to another with, think about another with, know another with? How should a man know that which he knows all this world with? Wherewithal should a man know the knower?"

Mark again the qualification "as it were," *yatra dvaitam iva bhavati.* The duality of subject and object is only quasi-existent, a fictitious presentment.

The unreality of the world is taught in the Chhāndogya Upanishad. Things many are only "a modification of speech, a change, a name."

The unreality of the world is taught with no less plainness in the following passage of the Chhāndogya Upanishad:—

"As everything made of clay is known by a single lump of clay; being nothing more than a modification of speech, a change, a name, while the clay is the only truth:

"As everything made of gold is known by a single lump of gold; being nothing more than a modification of speech, a change, a name, while the gold is the only truth:

"As everything made of steel is known by a single pair of nail-scissors; being nothing more than a modification of speech, a change, a name, while the steel is the only truth:

"Such, my son, is that instruction, by which the unheard becomes heard, the unthought thought, the unknown known. Existent only, my son, was this in the beginning, one only, without duality."

The Indian schoolmen are never tired of quoting this text, and proclaiming that the visible and nameable aspects of the world, as they fictitiously present themselves in place of, and veil, the one and only Self, are nothing more than "a modification of speech, a change, a name." The reader may be reminded in the next place of the following verses of the Muṇḍaka Upanishad:—

The Muṇḍaka Upanishad speaks of the order of daily life and Vedic worship as an illusion.

"They that are infatuated, dwelling in the midst of the illusion, wise in their own eyes, and learned in their own conceit, are stricken with repeated plagues, and go round and round, like blind men led by the blind.

"As its kindred sparks fly out in thousands from a blazing fire, so do the various living souls proceed out of that imperishable principle, and return into it again.

"That infinite spirit is self-luminous, without and within, without origin, without vital breath or thinking faculty, stainless, beyond the imperishable ultimate."

The ultimate here spoken of is the undeveloped principle that develops itself into all the variety of the visible and nameable, the primitive world-fiction. In the following verses of the same Upanishad the same principle is spoken of under the name of darkness. The Self is the light of lights beyond the darkness:—

"It is over this Self that sky and earth and air are woven, and the sensory with all the organs of sense and motion. Know that this is the one and only Self. Renounce all other words, for this is the bridge to immortality.

"This Self dwells in the heart where the arteries are concentred, variously manifesting itself. OM: thus meditate upon the Self. May it be well with you, that you may cross beyond the darkness.

"The sage, quitting name and colour, enters into the self-luminous spirit, beyond the last principle, in like manner as the rivers flow on until they quit their name and colour, and lose themselves in the sea."

The Kaṭha Upanishad contrasts the life of illusion with the life of knowledge.

In the Kaṭha Upanishad we read:—

"Far apart are these diverse and diverging paths, the path of illusion and the path of knowledge. I know thee, Nachiketas, that thou art a seeker of knowledge, for all these pleasures that I have proposed have not distracted thee.

"For their objects are beyond and more subtile than the senses, the common sensory is beyond the objects, the mind is beyond the sensory, and the great soul Hiraṇyagarbha is beyond the mind.

"The ultimate and undeveloped principle is beyond that great soul, and Purusha the Self is beyond the undeveloped principle. Beyond Purusha there is nothing; that is the goal, that is the final term."

Here that out of which all things emanate is the undeveloped principle, *avyakta*. *Avyakta* is also called *avyākṛita*, that which has not yet passed over into name and colour. This principle is the same as the expanse which is said in the Bṛihadāraṇyaka Upanishad to be woven across and across the Self. It is also the same, Śankarāchārya says, as the sum of the powers of every organism and every organ that shall be, the germ of the spheres of recompense.

The unreality of the world is implied in the sole reality of the Self everywhere taught in the Upanishads.

Thus, then, we see that the Upanishads teach that there is only one thing that exists, the impersonal Self. They teach also that there is a quasi-duality, a differentiation of something previously undifferenced into visible and nameable aspects. They teach that the things of the world of experience are a modification of speech only, a change, a name; that is, that apart from the underlying Self these things have only a nominal existence. The undifferenced, the source of name and colour, is called the expanse, and is said to be woven across and across the impersonal Self. It is the darkness, the darkness that must be passed beyond in order to reach the light. The order of things in which the follower of the prescriptive *sacra* lives, the sacrificers, the sacrifices, the works, and the recompenses of works, are all illusion, *avidyā*. They that live according to the immemorial usages, putting their trust in them, "dwelling in the midst of the illusion, wise in their own eyes,

CHAP. IX. and learned in their own conceit, are stricken with repeated plagues, and go round and round, like blind men led by the blind." The Upanishads teach plainly that this order of things is unreal. "There is nothing second to that Self, other than that, apart from that, that it should know."

The tenet of Māyā is thus no modern invention. The thought, if not the word, is everywhere present in the Upanishads, as an inseparable element of the philosophy, and the word itself is of no infrequent occurrence. The doctrine is more than implicit in the Upanishads, and explicit in the systematised Vedānta. No earlier Vedānta, such as Colebrooke supposes, could have been complete and consistent without this element, and it is no graft of a later growth. In fact the distinction between an earlier and a later Vedānta is nugatory. There has been no addition to the system from without, but only a development from within; no graft, but only growth.

Thus far it has been shown that the unreality of the world is a datum of Indian thought earlier than the Śārīrakaṣūtra or aphorisms of the Vedānta. The next task is to prove that the same doctrine is taught in the text of the Vedānta, these aphorisms themselves, and also in the fullest and plainest manner in the gloss of Śankara.

The unreality of the world is taught in the aphorisms of the Vedānta.

It has been already said that perspicuous statements are not to be looked for in the Sūtras or aphorisms. As Colebrooke says, they are in the highest degree obscure, and they could never have been intelligible without an ample interpretation. The aphorisms nevertheless do testify to the unreality of the world. In the fourth section of the first Pāda of the second Adhyāya of the Śārīrakasūtra, we read about the various objections raised against the doctrine that Brahman is at once the real basis underlying the world,[1] and the

[1] *Upādāna.*

principle that occasions it to come into being.[1] The reader will remember that Brahman is the reality in place of which the figments of the world-fiction present themselves; as the sand of the desert is the relative reality in place of which the waters of the mirage present themselves; and also, though unaffected by it, the principle that sets the world-fiction Māyā in motion, as a loadstone itself unmoved sets any adjacent pieces of steel in motion. Brahman acts, or is said to act, in virtue of its presence at and its illuminancy of the cosmical illusion; as a Raja acts, or is said to act, by being present at and witnessing the exertions of his people. In reference to one of the objections to this doctrine it is said in the thirteenth aphorism, "If any one object that on our doctrine there will be no distinction of subject and object, as the soul will be one with its environment, we reply that the distinction will still exist just as we see it in every-day life." The opponent is supposed to argue that if the soul and its environment are alike unreal, and resolvable into fictitious emanations out of the one and only Self, the distinction of subject and object will altogether disappear, and that this is a distinction that refuses to be done away with, a distinction that persists in spite of every effort to negate it. The author of the aphorisms replies that the distinction will remain as it is, a distinction of every-day experience. Śankarāchārya in his comments on this aphorism remarks, "The distinction will hold good in our teaching, as it is seen in common life. The ocean is so much water, and the foam, the ripples, the waves, and the bubbles that arise out of that water are alike one with it, and yet they differ among themselves. The foam is not the ripple, the ripple is not the wave, the wave is not the bubble; and yet the foam is water, the ripple is water, the wave is water, the bubble is water. The distinction

Duality is a distinction of every-day experience.

[1] *Nimitta.*

CHAP. IX.

The manifold is only "a modification of speech, a change, a name."

of subject and object is of a similar nature. The soul is not the environment, the environment is not the soul; the soul is Self, the environment is Self." The aphorism that immediately follows is, "That they are nothing else than that appears from the terms modification," &c. This refers to the text of the Chhāndogya Upanishad: "As everything made of clay is known by a single lump of clay; being nothing more than a modification of speech, a change, a name, while the clay is the only truth," &c. This text means nothing else than that the many as many has only a nominal existence, reality residing in the one. True being is characterless and uniform. Śankarāchārya says in the course of his remarks upon this aphorism: "The whole order of subject and object, of migrating souls and of their fruition of recompenses, is, apart from the Self, unreal; in like manner as the ether in this and that pot or jar is nothing else than the ether at large that permeates all things, itself one and undivided; and in like manner as the waters of a mirage are nothing else than the sands of the desert, seen for a while and vanishing, and having no real existence." The twenty-eighth aphorism of the first Pāda of the second Adhyāya is: "And likewise in the Self there are diversified objects." On this Śankarāchārya remarks: "It is of no use to object, How can there be a various creation in the one and only Self, unless it abolish its own unity in order to pass into plurality? For there is a multiform creation in the one and only Self, in the dreaming state of the soul, without any suppression of its unitary nature. We read in the Bṛihadāraṇyaka Upanishad, There are no chariots, no horses, no roads, but it presents to itself chariots, horses, and roads. In the world of daily life gods and thaumaturgists are seen to create multiform creations, elephants, horses, and the like, themselves meanwhile remaining what they are. In the same way a

The variety of the world is like the variety of a dream.

manifold creation is competent to the Self, one though it be, without any forfeiture of its simple essence." Another aphorism to the point is the fiftieth Sūtra of the third Pāda of the third Adhyāya,—"And it is a mere semblance." This aphorism occurs in the course of an exposition of the relation of the migrating soul to Īśvara, the world-evolving deity or Demiurgus. The forty-ninth aphorism has already stated that there is no confusion in the retributive awards; each migrating soul being linked to its own series of bodies, and thus taking no part in the individual experiences of other souls. The aphorism now before us goes on to say that the individual soul is, as individual, a mere appearance. "The individual soul," such is Śankarāchārya's interpretation, "is only a semblance of the one and only Self, as the sun imaged upon a watery surface is only a semblance of the one and only sun in the heavens. The individual soul is not another and independent entity. The sun mirrored upon one pool may tremble with the rippling of the surface, and the sun reflected upon another may be motionless. In the same way one soul may have experience of such and such retributions, and another soul may remain unaffected by them."

The migrating soul is as such a mere semblance.

Surely in all this we have the tenet of the unreality of the world in the text of the Vedānta, and the full-blown dogma of illusion in the gloss of Śankara. Whatever may be our respect for the authority of Colebrooke, it is time to see things with our own eyes, and to cease to let him see them for us.

So much for the text of the Vedānta. We come now to the gloss of Śankara, and there can be no mistake as regards the character of his teaching. Here are some specimens of it.[1] "If we allowed any independent pre-existence as the principle out of which the world emanates, we should be open to the charge of teaching

Śankarāchārya emphatically proclaims the unreality of the world in his commentary on the aphorisms of the Vedānta.

[1] Śārīrakamīmānsābhāshya i. 4, 3.

Pradhāna as the Sānkhyas do. But the pre-existence or potentiality of the world which we maintain, is not independent like that asserted by the Sānkhyas, but dependent on the Demiurgus. The potentiality we contend for must be conceded to us. It is indispensable, for without it no account could be given of the creative operancy of the Demiurgus; for if he had no power, no Śakti, he could not proceed to his creative energy. If there were no such potentiality the liberated souls themselves would return to metempsychosis; for they escape out of metempsychosis only by burning away that germinating power in the fire of spiritual intuition. This power of the seed of the world-tree is illusion, Avidyā, also called the undeveloped or unexplicated principle, the world-fiction, the great sleep of the Demiurgus, in which all migrating souls must continue to sleep so long as they wake not to their proper nature. This same undeveloped principle is sometimes spoken of as the expanse, as in the text of the Bṛihadāraṇyaka Upanishad,—The ethereal expanse is woven warp and woof across the imperishable Self. At other times it is spoken of as the imperishable, as in the text of the Muṇḍaka Upanishad,—Beyond the imperishable ultimate. At other times as Māyā, as in the text of the Śvetāśvatara Upanishad,—Let the sage know that Prakṛiti is Māyā, and that Maheśvara is the Māyin or arch-illusionist. This same Māyā is unexplicated or undeveloped in that it cannot be described either as existent or as non-existent. Hence it is said in the Kaṭha Upanishad,—The undeveloped principle is beyond that great soul. If we take the great soul to be Hiraṇyagarbha, the great soul emanates out of the undeveloped, out of the world-fiction. If we take the great soul to be the migrating spirit, it may still be said that the undeveloped is beyond the great soul, for the migrating soul owes its individual life to the undeveloped principle. The undeveloped is Avidyā, illusion, and all that the soul does and suffers, it does and suffers because it is illuded."

A little further on Śankarāchārya says,[1] "Until this illusion ceases the migrating soul is implicated in good and evil works, and its individuality cannot pass away from it. As soon as the illusion passes away, the pure and characterless nature of the soul is recognised in virtue of the text, That art thou. The accession and departure of this illusion makes no difference to the sole reality, the impersonal Self. A man may see a piece of rope lying in a dark place, may mistake it for a snake, may be frightened, shudder, and run away. Another person may tell him not to be afraid, for this is not a snake, but only a piece of rope. As soon as he hears this he lays aside his fear of the snake, ceases to tremble, and no more thinks of flight. And all the time there has been no difference in the real thing. That was a piece of rope, both when it was taken for a snake, and when the misconception passed away."

The world is a fictitious presentment, unreal as an optical illusion.

In another place the same schoolman writes,[2] "The one and only Self is untouched by the cosmic fiction,[3] in the same way that a thaumaturgist is untouched at any moment, present, past, or future, by the optical illusion he projects, the illusion being unreal. A dreamer is unaffected by the fictitious presentments of his dream, these not prolonging themselves into his waking hours, or into his peaceful sleep. In a like way the one abiding spectator of the three states of waking, dreaming, and pure sleep, is unaffected by those successive states. For this manifestation of the impersonal Self in the three states is a mere illusion,[4] as much so as the fictitious snake that presents itself in the place of the rope. Accordingly a teacher of authority has said, When the soul wakes up out of its

1 Śārīrakamīmānsābhāshya, i. 4, 6.
2 Śārīrakamīmānsābhāshya ii. 1, 9.
3 *Sansāramāyā.*
4 *Māyāmātra.*

CHAP. IX. sleep in the primeval illusion, it wakes up without beginning, sleepless, dreamless, without duality."

Falsity of the many, truth only of the one.

In another passage Śankarāchārya writes: "In the text of the Chhāndogya Upanishad, A modification of speech only, it is stated that every emanation is fictitious; and truth or reality is astricted to the one and only highest principle[1] in the text, All the world is animated by that, that is real. The words which follow, That is Self, that art thou, Śvetaketu, teach that the individual, migrating soul is the Self. The oneness of the soul with the Self is already a fact, and not a thing that requires a further effort to bring about; and therefore the recognition of the truth of the text is sufficient to put an end to the personality of the soul; in the same way as the recognition of the piece of rope is sufficient to abolish the snake that fictitiously presents itself in place of the piece of rope. No sooner is the personality of the soul negated than the whole spontaneous and conventional order of life is sublated along with it, to make up which the lower and plural manifestation of the Self fictitiously presents itself. As soon as a man sees that his soul is the Self, the whole succession of everyday life, with its agents, its actions, and its recompenses, ceases to have any further existence for him. This is indicated in the text of the Bṛihadāraṇyaka Upanishad, Where the whole world is Self alone, what should one see another with? It is not correct to assert that this non-existence of the world of daily life is true only in a particular state of the soul, viz., in its state of extrication from metempsychosis, for the words That art thou do not limit the oneness of the soul and the Self to any such special condition of the soul."

The soul is never anything else than the one and only Self; and all that it is, and sees, and does, and suffers, is never anything else than a figment of the

[1] *Ekam eva paramakāraṇam.*

world-fiction. Śankarāchārya proceeds to enforce this teaching by a reference to the allegory of the highwayman in the Sixth Prapāṭhaka of the Chhāndogya Upanishad, which he has just quoted. This allegory is, the reader will remember, as follows: "A highway man leaves a wayfarer from Kandahar blindfold in a desolate waste he has brought him to. The wayfarer left blindfold in the waste, does not know what is east or north or south, and cries out for guidance. A passer-by unties his hands, and unbinds his eyes, and points out the way towards Kandahar. The man goes on, asking for village after village, and finally arrives at Kandahar. In a like way a man is guided by a spiritual teacher in his progress towards the final goal, the one and only Self." Supposing the reader to be familiar with this allegory, he goes on to say, "The parable of the highwayman teaches that a man who lives for the fictions of everyday life is implicated in metempsychosis, and that a man who lives for the truth is extricated from it. In teaching this it teaches that unity alone is real, and that plurality is a figment of fictitious vision or illusion.[1] The phases of everyday life have a kind of truth prior to the knowledge that the soul is the Self, as the phases of a dream are true till the sleeper wakes up out of his dream. No one becomes aware of the unreality of all that goes on in daily life, the fictitious nature of the soul, of the things around it, and of the recompenses of its actions, until he learns that his soul is one with the solely real Self. Until he learns this every one loses sight of his essential oneness with the Self, and supposes that the modes of manifested being are he and his. In this way the procedure of daily life and the religion of the Vedas are valid, until we wake to the truth that the soul is one with the characterless Self. It is as with a man in his dreams. He sees a variety of scenes and situations, and this is, until he

The world is a dream from which the soul of the sage awakes to the vision of the truth.

[1] *Mithyājñāna.*

CHAP. IX. wakes up, an assured perceptional experience, and not a mere semblance of perception.

"Perhaps some one will say, If the world is a figment, the teaching of the Upanishads is a part of the world, and therefore itself a figment. How can any one learn from this teaching the truth that the soul is the Self? A man does not die of the bite of the snake he sees in a piece of rope, nor is he any the better for drinking the water of a mirage or bathing in it. This objection is null. Men have been known to die of drinking a beverage merely imagined to be poison. When they sleep and dream they are bitten by unreal snakes, and bathe in unreal water. The objector will say that the snake-bite and the bath are unreal also. We reply that the snake-bite and the bathing of the dream are unreal, but the vision of them by the dreamer is a fact, for this apprehension is not negatived on waking up. As soon as the sleeper wakes he knows that the snake-bite and the bath were figments, but he does not judge his vision of them to have been a figment."

The self-feigning fiction is the body of the cosmic soul or Demiurgus. The cosmic soul and cosmic body, apart from the Self, are alike unreal.

A little further on he writes: [1]"The omniscience of the Demiurgus is relative to the evolution of Avidyā, the germ of name and colour, of the visible and nameable aspects of things. In such texts as, From this same Self the ether emanated, it appears that the world comes out of, is sustained by, and passes back into the Demiurgus ever pure, intelligent, and free, all-knowing and all-powerful; not out of, by, and into Pradhāna or any other unconscious principle. Name and colour, the figments of illusion, the body as it were of the omniscient Demiurgus, not explicable as existent or as non-existent, the germs of the world of metempsychosis, are called in Śruti and in Smṛiti the Māyā, Śakti, or Prakṛiti of the world-evolving deity. The omniscient Demiurgus is other than these, as is said in the text, It is the expanse which unfolds itself into name and

[1] Śārīrakamīmānsābhāshya, ii. 1, 14.

colour, and these are in the Self. The Demiurgus then manifests himself in the fictitious forms of the names and colours presented by the cosmical illusion; as the all-pervading ether manifests itself in fictitious limitation as in this and that pot or jar. In the domain of the ordinary, unphilosophic life, the Demiurgus presides over all the innumerable migrating spirits or conscious souls. These souls are identical with himself, in the same way as the ether localised in this or that jar is identical with the ubiquitous ether one and undivided; and they are individualised by attachment to the various bodies and organs fashioned out of the names and colours presented by the world-fiction. Thus, then, the Demiurgus is a Demiurgus, is all-knowing and all-powerful, only in relation to the limitations of his fictitious body, the cosmical illusion. In real truth this conventional order of things, with its presiding deity and the souls presided over, has no existence in the Self; for the Self is a pure essence apart from all the fictitious limits of individual life. And therefore it is said, That is the infinite in which one sees nothing else, hears nothing else, and knows nothing else; and again, When all this world is Self and Self alone, what should one see any one with? In such passages as these the Upanishads teach that, in the state of pure reality, every form of conventional existence, all that we are and do and suffer in this daily life, ceases to have any being."[1] Īśvara, Śankarāchārya means, is the first figment of the world-fiction. Suppress the world-fiction, and Īśvara is no longer Īśvara but Brahman, for Īśvara belongs to the world of every-day, conventional existence, not to the real world, the spiritual unity, into which the theosophist aspires to rise.

CHAP. IX.

It would be easy to multiply proofs that the tenet of illusion is taught in the gloss of Śankara. But this is

[1] *Paramārthāvasthā = mokshāvasthā.*

CHAP. IX.

needless: the passages already presented to the reader prove that this tenet is taught as directly and unmistakably in Śankarāchārya's commentary on the aphorisms of the Vedānta as in any of his other works. There is as much to countenance it in the sūtras of Vyāsa and the gloss of Śankara, as in the minor commentaries and elementary treatises. It is no graft of a later growth, but a vital element of the primitive philosophy of the Upanishads. Śankara found this tenet in the Upanishads, and there we cannot fail to find it also. It is everywhere implied in the idea of the sole reality of the Self; and not only so, but the reality of duality is expressly denied, and a principle of unreality is expressly announced, the undeveloped germ of the visible and nameable aspects of the world, the expanse that is woven warp and woof across the Self. That the world is a series of shows and semblances that come and go and have no stay, is part and parcel of the earliest type of Indian philosophy. This philosophy has had its growth and development, but each later has had its virtual pre-existence in each earlier stage. What has been more implicit has become more explicit, but there has been no addition from without, no interpolation of foreign elements. The assertion of the Orientalists that the doctrine of Māyā is a comparatively modern importation into the Vedāntic system is groundless, and the hypothesis of a primitive Vedānta in harmony with the system known as the Yogadarśana or demiurgic Sānkhya is untenable.

The source of Colebrooke's error was his acceptance of the assertion of Vijnānabhikshu, an opponent of the philosophy of the Upanishads.

This brings us to the source of Colebrooke's error. His mistake arose from the acceptance of the polemical statement of an opponent of the Vedāntins, Vijñānabhikshu, the celebrated exponent of the aphorisms of the Sānkhya, the author of the Sānkhyapravachanabhāshya. According to Dr. Fitz-Edward Hall, Vijnānabhikshu in all probability lived in the sixteenth or seventeenth century of the Christian era. In his commentary on the Sānkhya aphorisms, Vijñānabhikshu propounds a theory that the several Darśanas or systems of Indian philosophy, are successive steps of ascent to the full truth of the demiurgic Sānkhya or Yoga philosophy. This demiurgic Sānkhya he holds to be identical with the primitive form of the Brahmamīmānsā or Vedānta. Each system, he says, is valid for the instalment of truth which it conveys. Where any system negatives part of the truth, it does so because the portion of truth negatived is no part of the instalment of truth propounded in that particular system. Thus, for example, he would treat the Sānkhya denial of Īśvara, the Demiurgus or world-evolving deity. Otherwise such a negation, he says, may be regarded as an audacious averment of private judgment.[1] Or again, he says, we may regard the untrue portions of any of the earlier systems as a test of faith designed to exclude from the full truth those that are unprepared to receive it; a test to shut out the unworthy aspirant from a release from metempsychosis. As a part of this attempt, his own personal effort, to treat the systems as successively complementary revelations, he tries to force the Vedānta, or philosophy of the Upanishads, into accord with the demiurgic Sānkhya. Now to this there are two great obstacles, the Vedāntic tenet of the unreality of the world, and the Vedāntic tenet of the unity of souls in the Self. Vijñānabhikshu accordingly pronounces that the doctrine of Māyā is a modern invention of persons falsely styling themselves Vedāntins, but really crypto-Buddhists,[2] scions of the Vijñānavādins or Buddhist sensational nihilists. He appeals to a primitive Vedānta that teaches the two ruling tenets of the Sānkhya, the reality of the world, and the plurality of Purushas or Selves. It has been proved in this chapter that such a primitive Vedānta never existed. Vijñānabhikshu's

[1] *Ekadeśiyānām prauḍhavādaḥ.*

[2] *Prachchhannabauddha.*

Vijñānabhikshu's statement is altogether baseless.

assertion that the primitive Vedānta taught the plurality of Purushas or Selves has not deceived anybody: why should we admit the deception of his concomitant assertion that the primitive Vedānta taught the reality of the world? The two statements are alike put forth in the teeth of all the facts, and are equally false; though possibly his statement that the primitive Vedānta taught the plurality of Purushas is the more glaring falsity. It is true that Vijñānabhikshu cites a passage of the Padmapurāṇa in which the tenet of Māyā is said to be crypto-Buddhistic, and to have been proclaimed in the Kali age of the world, by Śiva in the person of a Brāhman, for the ruin of mankind. In the face of the plain teaching of the Upanishads this citation fails to move us. At the most it can only prove that Vijñānabhikshu was not the first to stigmatise the doctrine of Māyā as a piece of crypto-Buddhism. We have nothing to do but to look at the Upanishads and at the aphorisms of the Vedānta, to weigh the traditionary and authoritative expositions of the Vedāntic doctors, and to judge for ourselves. The Vedāntic schoolmen, Śankarāchārya and the rest, speak to us *ex cathedrâ*, and we have seen how natural and effortless their exposition is. We may set aside the mere assertions of their adversaries. Be it remembered, too, that Vijñānabhikshu's proposal to treat the several systems as progressive instalments of the truth, has no countenance in the works of Indian scholasticism. The systems are in those works exhibited on every page as in open hostility against each other. Vijñānabhikshu's treatment of the philosophy of the Upanishads is false from first to last; and Colebrooke's assertion falls with the fall of the assertion of Vijñānabhikshu.

The ocean of metempsychosis is unreal, the Self, the sun that shines upon its waves, alone is real.

In the very beginning of Indian philosophy, in the teaching of the Upanishads no less than in the teaching of the Vedantic schoolmen, the world is an illusion. The migrating souls, their environments, their places of reward and punishment, the gods, the world-evolving deity himself, are figments of a fiction that has feigned itself from all eternity. The one Self in all souls is the only true being. This Self shines in every mind, as one sun shines reflected upon innumerable waters. It shines on the ocean of metempsychosis, lighting up all its waves. "It seems to think, it seems to move," in the migrating souls that are its fictitious presentments in this fictitious world; as the sun seems to move with the motion of the waves that reflect it. These waves are the migrating souls. The Self seems to act and to suffer, to be soiled with all the stains of earthly life; and is all the time inert and impassive, a pure, unsullied brightness; a sun that looks down upon the imperfections of the world and is untainted by them. The reader may be reminded of the simile with which Ferrier illustrates the teaching of Xenophanes. The sensible world is for Xenophanes "a mere phenomenon, and possesses no such truth as that which reason compels us to attribute to the permanent one, which according to Xenophanes is God. His tenets on this point may be illustrated as follows: Suppose that the sun is shining on the sea, and that his light is broken by the waves into a multitude of lesser lights, of all colours and of all forms; and suppose that the sea is conscious, conscious of this multitude of lights, this diversity of shifting colours, this plurality of dancing forms, would this consciousness contain or represent the truth, the real? Certainly it would not. The objectively true, the real in itself, is in this case the sun in the heavens, the one permanent, the persistent in colour and form. Its diversified appearance in the sea, the dispersion of its light in myriad colours and in myriad forms, is nothing and represents nothing which substantially exists; but is only something which exists phenomenally, that is, unsubstantially and unreally, in the sea."

CHAP. IX.

With this proof of the primitive antiquity of the doctrine of Māyā, we may close this survey of the philosophy of the Upanishads.

Recapitulation. The philosophy of the Upanishads a new religion, a more perfect way for the recluses of the jungle.

This philosophy was a new religion with a new promise, a religion not of the many but of the few. The promise is no longer a promise of felicity in this life or in a higher life, but a promise of release from the sorrows of the heart, of a repose unbroken by a dream, of everlasting peace, in which the soul shall cease to be a soul, and shall be merged in the one and only Self, the characterless being, characterless thought, and characterless beatitude.

It took the place of the earlier Vedic religion, as this lost its vitality, and as the beliefs in μετενσωμάτωσις and the miseries of every form of life prevailed.

The primitive Vedic religion had already become a half-living form of words. The hymns of the Ṛishis, the daily observances, the lustrations and sacrifices were still handed down and repeated from age to age, as revered elements of the common life; and the repetition of these, and the hope of rising in this life or in an after-life, still made up the religion of the multitude. This religion was not moral and emotional, but mechanical; each item of conformity carrying with it its promised item of reward. Wealth was to be accumulated for the winning of merit; for the wealthy sacrificer might aspire to a place in a paradise, or the position of a deity. The gods were to be praised and fed with sacrifices, that they might send rain and feed their worshippers; and the praises, prayers, and sacrifices were to be offered up in proper form by professional liturgists.

Upon this religion supervened the beliefs in the migration of the soul, and in the misery of every form of life, beliefs accruing from contact and intermixture with the melanous indigenes. A new estimate presented itself of the value of the rewards of conformity with prescriptive usages, and of costly rites. The whole earth replete with riches will not make a man immortal. Death is still before the eyes of the rewarded worshipper, and death is to bring no peaceful sleep; the dream of life will be followed by an after-dream, and this by another, in endless succession. The worshipper is deluded, and his reward is a delusion. The pleasures the gods have, and may give him, are tainted and fugitive, as all pleasures are: they are things that may or may not be to-morrow. Care follows the recompensed conformist into the very paradise his merits win for him: he cannot stay there for ever, and he will see many there in higher places than himself. The whole order of the popular religion, with its rites and their rewards, is a darkness, an illusion, and light and verity must be looked for somewhere else. The thirst for pleasure, and the craving for religious recompenses, are the springs of the actions of the soul, which implicate it in metempsychosis. This thirst and craving lie at the root of the world-tree. Volition [1] is the origin of evil. The aspirant to release from metempsychosis must refrain from every desire and every act of will. Good works, no less than evil works, are imperfections that must be put away. They lead only to higher embodiments, to higher spheres indeed, but still to spheres tainted with misery; for the pleasures even of a paradise are fleeting and unequally allotted. So long as the living being acts, so long must he suffer the retribution of his good and evil acts in body after body, in æon after æon. The religion of immemorial usages and of liturgic rites belongs to the people of the world, and, like every other form of activity, tends only to prolong the miseries of metempsychosis. From the true point of view taught to the initiated, in the philosophy of the Upanishads, action and passion, works and the recompenses of works, the religion of ancestral rites and usages, the sacrifices, and the gods sacrificed to, are alike unreal. They are

[1] *Sankalpaṃ varjayet tasmāt sarvānarthasya kāraṇam*, Viveka-chūḍāmaṇi, v. 330.

CHAP. IX.

figments of the world-fiction, and for the finished theosophist they have no existence. They belong to the world of semblances, the dream of souls as yet unawakened. Nevertheless these things have their fruits in the phantasmagory of metempsychosis, and to taste these fruits the unawakened soul must pass from body to body, from sphere to sphere, as through dream after dream. They that live in the world and neglect the prescriptive pieties, pass along the evil path,[1] again and again to ephemeral insect lives. They that live in the village in obedience to the religion of rites and usages, ascend after death along the path of the progenitors[2] to the lunar world. There they sojourn for a while till their reward is over, and return to fresh embodiments. They that add a knowledge of the significance of these rites, and of the nature of the gods, to their conformity, ascend after death along the path of the gods[3] to the solar world. There they proceed to the courts of Brahmā, the supreme divinity; to abide there till the close of the æon, and to be sent back into the world at the next palingenesia. These have followed the way of works,[4] the religion of usages and rites, a religion which has its higher use in purifying the mind of the votary, it may be in the course of many successive lives, until he is ready to enter the way of knowledge,[5] to be initiated into the religion of renunciation and ecstatic vision, the theosophy of the anchorites of the forest. Moral and religious excellence has its only true value in the preliminary purification of the soul, in so far as it tends to fit the mind for the pursuit of liberating light and intuition. This kind of excellence lies chiefly in conformity to the traditionary routine of life and Vedic ritual. The Brāhman has come into the world with three debts to pay,—his debt to the Rishis to repeat and transmit their hymns and the exposition of

The old religion left as valid for the many, with three paths for the passing soul,—the evil path, the path of the progenitors, and the path of the gods.

The old religion has its highest use in purifying the mind of the aspirant to liberation.

[1] *Kashṭhā gatiḥ.* [2] *Pitṛiyāṇa.* [3] *Devayāna.*
[4] *Karmamārga.* [5] *Jnānamārga, brahmavidyā.*

their hymns; his debt to the Pitṛis or ancestral spirits, to beget children to offer cakes and water for them to live upon in the next generation; and his debt to the gods, to make oblations to them for their sustenance, that they may be able to send the fertilising rain upon the fields. These debts belong, it is true, to the world of semblances: the Brāhman may proceed straight from his sacred studentship to the forest, if he will; and yet, in general, it is not till he has paid these debts that he is to retire to the jungle, to meditate at leisure on the vanities of life and the miseries of the procession of lives to come, and to strive to win release from further life in the body by self-torture, by the crushing of every thought and feeling, by rising to vacuity, apathy, and isolation, that he may refund his personality into the impersonality of the one and only Self. This is the new religion, a religion of cataleptic insensibility and ecstatic vision for the purified and initiated few, that seek for final liberation. Not exertion, but inertion, is the path to liberation. There is no truth and no peace in the plurality of experience; truth and peace are to be found only in the one beneath it and beyond it. This one existent is the Self, the spiritual essence that gives life and light to all things living,[1] permeating them all from a tuft of grass up to the highest deity of the Indian worshipper. This Self, this highest Self, Ātman, Brahman, Paramātman, is being, thought, and bliss, undifferenced; other than which nothing is, and other than which all things only seem to be. This one and only Self is near to all, dwelling in the heart of every living thing, present in the mind within the heart. The light within the ether of the heart is the light that lightens all the world. Withdraw it, and all things will lapse into blindness, darkness, nothingness.[2] To see it, to become one with it, to pass away into that light of lights beyond the darkness of the world-fiction,

The old religion became one of conformity to immemorial pieties. The new religion is an attempt to rise above bodily and mental conditions to ecstasy and re-union.

[1] *Sattāsphūrtiprada.*

[2] *Tadabhāve jagadāndhyam prasajyeta.*

CHAP. IX.

is the only aspiration of the wise. This light is hidden from the unwise, who dwell in the midst of the illusions of the world; they can no more see it than a blind man can see the sun. The wise man sees it as the cloud of illusion disperses, and the ecstatic vision dawns upon his mind. In order to see it the personality must be put away; and it is only when this light within shall reveal itself to the pure intelligence, only when every thought and feeling and volition shall have melted away in the rigorous contemplation of it, that the personality of the aspirant shall pass away into impersonality and everlasting peace. The darkness of the cosmical illusion passes, and the light remains for ever, a pure, undifferenced light, a characterless being, thought, and blessedness. If a man will see this light, he must first loose himself from every tie, put away all the desires of his heart, part from his wife and children, and from all that he has, and retire into the solitude of the forest; there to engage in a long course of self-torture, and of that suppression of every feeling, desire, and thought that is to end in catalepsy and ecstatic vision.

The new theosophy no more spiritual than the old observance of prescriptive *sacra*.

There is little that is spiritual in all this. The primitive Indian philosophers teach that the individual self is to be annulled by being merged in the highest Self. Their teaching in this regard has been so often mistaken and misstated, that it is important to insist upon the difference between the ancient Indian mystic and the modern idealist. The difference must have made itself plain enough to the reader of these pages. He will have seen for himself how the Indian sages, as the Upanishads picture them, seek for participation in the divine life, not by pure feeling, high thought, and strenuous endeavour,—not by an unceasing effort to learn the true and do the right,—but by the crushing out of every feeling and every thought, by vacuity, apathy, inertion, and ecstasy. They do not for a moment mean that the purely individual feelings and volitions are to be suppressed in order that the philosopher may live in free obedience to the monitions of a higher common nature. Their highest Self is little more than an empty name, a *caput mortuum* of the abstract understanding. Their pursuit is not a pursuit of perfect character, but of perfect characterlessness. They place perfection in the pure indetermination of thought, the final residue of prolonged abstraction; not in the higher and higher types of life and thought successively intimated in the idealising tendencies of the mind, as among the progressive portions of the human race. The epithets of the sole reality, the highest Self, are negative, or if positive they are unintelligible. It is a uniformity of indifferent being, thought, and bliss. It is a mass of thought and bliss, as fire is a mass of heat and light. It is thought always the same and ever objectless, thought without a thinker or things to think of. It is a bliss in which there is no soul to be glad, and no sense of gladness. It is a light which lightens itself, for there is nothing else for it to lighten. This is the gain above all gains, a bliss above all other bliss, a knowledge above all other knowledge. It is no part of the spirit of the Indian sages to seek to see things as they are, and to help to fashion them, as they ought to be, to let the power at work in the world work freely through them; to become "docile echoes of the eternal voice, and pliant organs of the infinite will." This neither was nor could be the spirit of men of their race, their age, and their environment. The time, and the men for these things had not yet appeared. This is the spirit in which many a man now works, to whom philosophy is a name, and who would smile to hear himself called an idealist. It is not the spirit of the ancient Indian sage, Brahmanical or Buddhist. For these there is no quest of verity and of an active law of righteousness, but only a yearning after resolution into the

It is no aspiration and energy towards the true and the good, but only a yearning for repose from the miseries of life. Yet it is the highest product of the Indian mind.

CHAP. IX. fontal unity of undifferenced being; or, in the case of the Buddhist, a yearning after a lapse into the void, a return to the primeval nothingness of things. The effort is to shake off every mode of personal existence, and to be out of the world for ever, in the unbroken repose of absorption or annihilation.

Such as they are, and have been shown to be, the Upanishads are the loftiest utterances of Indian intelligence. They are the work of a rude age, a deteriorated race, and a barbarous and unprogressive community. Whatever value the reader may assign to the ideas they present, they are the highest produce of the ancient Indian mind, and almost the only elements of interest in Indian literature, which is at every stage replete with them to saturation.

THE END.